The Learning Edge

How Smart Managers and Smart Companies Stay Ahead

Calhoun W. Wick

Lu Stanton León

McGraw-Hill, Inc.

New York   San Francisco   Washington, D.C.   Auckland   Bogotá
Caracas   Lisbon   London   Madrid   Mexico City   Milan
Montreal   New Delhi   San Juan   Singapore
Sydney   Tokyo   Toronto

Library of Congress Cataloging-in-Publication Data

Wick, Calhoun W.
    The learning edge : how smart managers and smart companies stay
ahead / Calhoun W. Wick, Lu Stanton León.
        p.   cm.
    Includes bibliographical references and index.
    ISBN 0-07-070082-6 (acid-free paper)
    1. Management—Study and teaching (Continuing education)
2. Executives—Training of.   3. Strategic planning.   4. Competition.
I. León, Lu Stanton.   II. Title.
HD30.4.W53   1993
658.4'0071'5—dc20   92-35218
                                                                  CIP

1 2 3 4 5 6 7 8 9 0   DOC/DOC   9 8 7 6 5 4 3

ISBN   0-07-070082-6

*The sponsoring editor for this book was Betsy N. Brown, the editing supervisor
was Frances Koblin, and the production supervisor was Donald Schmidt. It was
set in Palatino by McGraw-Hill's Professional Book Group composition unit.*

Printed and bound by R. R. Donnelley & Sons Company.

This book is printed on recycled, acid-free paper containing a
minimum of 50% recycled de-inked fiber.

To Ann,
The love of my life,
whose idea this book first was

Contents

Preface

What propels one executive to success while another, equally capable, is left behind? When I was in the executive search business in New York City, that question drove me to distraction. Time after time while interviewing candidates, I found that two managers with equal experience and academic success had developed disparate levels of ability. The discrepancy resulted from more than hard work or luck. Everyone I interviewed put in long hours and their luck seemed equally distributed.

Since leaving the headhunting business and starting my own research and consulting firm, I have recognized that the same performance gap develops between companies that face seemingly equal opportunities. For example, Wal-Mart has outperformed both Kmart and Sears, although it started as a small regional player when the others were industry leaders. How does one company gain such an advantage over the other?

It all boils down to the ability and passion to learn. Smart managers and smart companies learn better and faster than their competitors. They discover ways to create the capabilities they need for success and then put them into action before their rivals, resulting in increased value to their customers.

The ability to learn is not an amorphous quality. When interviewing leaders of companies like Boeing and Motorola, I asked if they recognize different rates of learning among their managers. They all do. And further, they said that the best learners are the most valuable managers in their companies. The manager who demonstrates both stronger skills and the ability to learn at an accelerated rate is the person most often selected for promotion. Meanwhile, their slower-footed counterparts miss the cut. What better endorsement for the value of learning than from those selecting the future leaders in the business world?

The dozens of executives and CEOs interviewed for this book bolstered my observations and conclusions from 12 years of studying managers and their on-the-job growth. Little of lasting value comes from professional training that is confined to a classroom with no connection to—or reinforcement from—the real working world. Learning cannot survive in a bell jar. It needs the support and immediacy of everyday application or it quickly suffocates.

In an environment where learning thrives, the process as well as the end product tell the tale: people are happier, production runs more smoothly, errors and defects decrease, customers are pleased, and profits are up. When leaders view organizational learning and professional growth as valuable commodities, a company is well on its way to gaining a competitive advantage. A *learning organization*—that is, a company that continually improves by rapidly creating and refining the capabilities needed for future success—breeds success. By paying attention to learning on individual and organizational levels, business leaders are more apt to find ways to provide better quality and better service at a lower price.

Becoming a Smart Manager

This book is divided into four parts. The first part details the importance of intentional learning at work and shares our research findings based on interviews and questionnaires completed by hundreds of managers.

The second part presents a detailed, five-step process for learning through work and is applicable to everyone, regardless of company rank or title. In it we explain clearly and concisely how to identify a learning goal, develop an action plan, and then carry it through to completion. Powerful learning tools, such as benchmarking, visualization, and learning from mistakes, are described, coupled with examples of how they have been used successfully throughout the business world. You'll also be forewarned of problems you may encounter, and you'll discover how to solve them.

Becoming a Smart Company

The third part presents a formula that identifies the elements crucial for creating a learning organization. By measuring your company against the formula, you can identify your company's strengths as well as its learning weaknesses. Additionally, through interviews with prominent CEOs as well as managers of smaller, growing companies, you'll read about real-life business problems and how intentional learning provided the solutions. Among others, this section includes interviews with Kay Whitmore at Eastman Kodak, Phil Condit at Boeing, Ray Stata at Analog Devices, Nev Curtis at Delmarva Power & Light, and Jamie Houghton at Corning Inc. These senior executives describe how they approach learning and make it catch fire in an organization.

The fourth and final part provides an in-depth look at five learning organizations and offers some unique ways to foster learning, ranging from cattle drives to a search for the world's most demanding customers.

This book is written to give you a learning edge. In it, we present managers and companies that have used intentional learning to achieve measurable career and business success. Their strategies can be adapted to work for you and your company. The lesson from smart managers and smart companies is clear: you're never too smart to learn.

Calhoun W. Wick
Lu Stanton León

Acknowledgments

We began this book with the seed of an idea that was planted firmly in research and observation. That seed blossomed and grew with each company we visited and every person we interviewed. We are deeply indebted to the scores of managers who so willingly shared their insights and hard-won learnings. For every story we used, dozens were left out. For every person acknowledged in the text, scores of others go unmentioned. We are grateful to them all for their time, their energy, and their wisdom.

There are a few people we must single out:

Nev Curtis, for his willingness to share the key learning experiences he gained during a distinguished career, and for the constant value he places on people.

George Clement and Bud Kissel, for their early support and continuing interest.

Tony Cardinal, for his counsel and encouragement. His clear thinking and inquiring mind were an inspiration.

Gail Robinson, who taught us the power of learning. She generously shared her thinking and helped sharpen ours.

Members of the Learning From Experience Network, for their willingness to push boundaries and to learn from one another.

Betsy Brown, our editor at McGraw-Hill, for her enthusiasm and valuable suggestions.

A special thanks goes to Gayle McGrath, who put extraordinary hours into transcribing taped interviews and was masterful in handling all the mind-boggling details involved in writing a book. At the same time she provided a much-needed reality check when we enthusiastically tried to bite off more than we could chew.

And finally, thanks to Ann, Peg, Alletta, Tish, Irene, and Warren, and to Luis, Sofia, and Emilia, for there is nothing better than a supportive family.

PART 1

The Power of Learning

1
Mastering the Learning Labyrinth

We understand that the only competitive advantage the company of the future will have is its managers' ability to learn faster than their competitors.   ARIE P. DE GEUS
Former Planning Director for the Royal Dutch/Shell Group[1]

While I was trout fishing in the Poconos recently, I watched as a mallard moved smoothly across the narrow stream, leaving barely a ripple in its wake. The elegant motion was effortless, almost nonchalant. Then I recalled, how during an interview 2 weeks earlier, Marion Gislason of J. P. Morgan had compared a learning organization to a paddling duck. This was my opportunity to see exactly what she meant. So I watched very carefully as the mallard came closer to shore and my perception changed: Below the surface that duck was paddling like mad to get where it wanted to go!

That same combination of apparent ease coupled with a determined, driving effort characterizes managers and organizations committed to an objective. To the casual observer, these managers and organizations don't seem to expend much energy or effort. Success appears to come naturally to them. The hard work, the determination, and the motivation are hidden from view.

In this book we want to take you below the surface to give you an accurate, compelling picture of what makes managers and companies successful. You'll find that the activator, the accelerator, and the quiet, unassuming source of all significant business breakthroughs is learning.

To be successful, a manager must be adept at learning from work experience. No one enters management's ranks with all the skills and knowledge needed to succeed. Competence must be cultivated from experiences throughout the course of a career. Learning from experience may occur intuitively over time as you learn what works and doesn't work in certain situations. Intentional learning, however, puts you a step ahead.

This book tells you how to make experiential learning intentional and deliberate. Intentional learning from experience can make average performers better, and it can help top performers achieve their maximum. It is for managers up and down the organizational chart. With intentional learning, managers at any level can take charge of their own progress and top executives can become leaders who not only accelerate their own learning but focus on creating a learning organization.

In companies across the country, the ability to learn is becoming a condition for employment, one that requires every successful manager's deliberate attention and commitment. As shown in Figure 1-1, work and learning are interlocking components that drive managers and companies to success. Companies must learn better than their best competitor, or their business is doomed to fall behind. Learning has become the key to organizational survival. Becoming a learning organization isn't a panacea for all business frailties. It doesn't mean a company can avoid every pitfall, but it does guarantee that the company will make a quicker comeback.

Although learning occurs from cradle to grave, we don't give the learning process much thought, particularly as it relates to work. The importance of the ability to learn at work has never been adequately pursued in any premeditated or informed way.

We often recognize *what* we have learned, but we have no concept of *how* we learned, or even more importantly, how much *more* we could have learned if we had given some thought to the process.

For those of us who want to capitalize on who we are and what we do, intentional learning from on-the-job experience may be our greatest investment opportunity. Whatever time and effort we devote to learning is an investment in ourselves and our future. Learning from experience should be pursued and nurtured with the same enthusiasm and deliberation we devote to planning our financial future or preparing the annual operating budget.

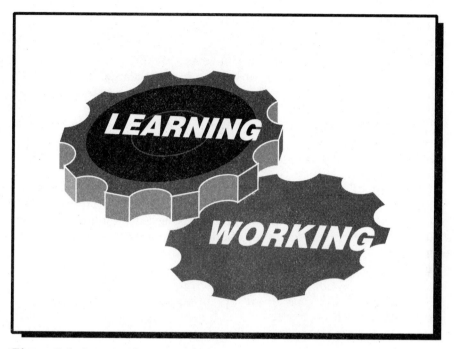

Figure 1-1 Learning from experience.

At first glance, the need to explain the importance of learning from experience seems absurd. Isn't such learning intuitive? Doesn't everyone do it? As columnist Russell Baker noted in a tongue-in-cheek diatribe about a particular covey of politicians: "They don't seem to learn from experience, which is also one way to define an idiot."[2]

That's a harsh definition rooted in truth. We all learn from experience, but the rate at which we learn is what separates the high achievers from those struggling in the rear. We may learn intuitively from experience, and we may know instinctively that learning is a desirable goal, but few of us realize our learning potential.

Why? Because we take learning for granted, almost as if what we learn is divined by providence, or at the very least, determined by our boss. It isn't. We can help determine what we learn, how much we learn, and how fast we do it; all of which shape our careers. When every learning opportunity is intentionally seized, quantum leaps in development can result. Work becomes less of a chore and more of a challenge.

Taking Charge of Your Own Learning

The notion of simultaneously working and learning within a current assignment seems foreign to most people and organizations. When I was in the executive search business, I found that most senior managers I interviewed were hungry for more responsibility and more opportunity to grow. It wasn't just the money that made people uproot their families and move halfway across the country for a new position. It was the compelling need to learn and grow, a need that wasn't being met at their current job.

Sadly, few of these candidates who were willing to risk a new assignment had aggressively sought learning opportunities within the job they were leaving behind. The option of taking learning into their own hands in their current company had not occurred to many of these managers.

On the other side of the coin, companies didn't know how to enable people to learn while they work. I was hired to look for executive talent because my clients had done a poor job developing their own people. As Gerald Roche, headhunter extraordinaire and CEO of the executive search firm Heidrick and Struggles, once said, "I often live off the carnage of failed management development programs."[3]

Those whose learning is primarily accidental and intuitive may have some success, but they'll never reach the outer limits of their potential. They learn just enough to get by, focusing on short-term goals. The manager may reason: If I bring this project in on time and under cost, it could mean a bonus.

The project may very well be on time and under cost and the manager may get his or her reward, but if there is no intentional learning along the way, the manager failed to get the most out of the assignment. The manager took one step forward when he or she could have taken two.

If you're going to have your eyes on a prize, it needs to be something truly worthwhile—such as learning for life or work enhancement. Learning at work could be defined as growth in knowledge, skill, or experience that improves your current job performance, leads to greater future responsibility, and provides greater satisfaction in work.

Some people like to learn simply for the sake of learning. They continually ask questions, search out new challenges, seek new experiences, and devour books. They do this not because of any preconceived end result but because they enjoy learning.

We all possess at least a smattering of that passion for learning. As Peter Senge says in *The Fifth Discipline: The Art & Practice of the Learning Organization*, "Real learning gets to the heart of what it means to be human. Through learning we re-create ourselves. Through learning we become able to do something we never were able to do. Through learning we re-perceive the world and our relationship to it. Through learning we extend our capacity to create, to be part of the generative process of life."[4]

The Benefits of Intentional Learning

Because most people are not only physically but fiscally grounded in the working world, learning isn't just a lofty endeavor. They learn because it produces measurable results, both financially and psychologically. How well you learn at work is important because:

- Learning can mean the difference between getting promoted, shuffled aside, or fired.

- The manager who intentionally learns at work will be equipped to face his next task with increased skills, greater personal awareness, and a broader perspective.

- Learning leads to a sense of control, a sense of purpose, and a greater sense of work satisfaction.

You can't fold these attributes and put them in your wallet, but they last far longer than any bonus and, over time, generate far greater financial rewards. From working with CEOs and other top managers, we've compiled the list of 16 specific benefits from intentional learning at work shown in Exhibit 1-1.

How well a business as a whole learns is similarly important because:

- Learning can mean the difference between accepting mediocre improvement or rapidly gaining market share.

- It enables a business to meet market changes and competitive threats and to take advantage of new technology.

- It can lead to business growth when combined with the right strategic direction and human resources.

The importance of intentional learning from experience was clearly demonstrated to me one winter morning as I sat in a CEO's top floor corner office, talking about whom he would promote to a key position. He went down the list of candidates, weighing their strengths, experience, and limitations. Then circling the name of his candidate of choice, he said with finality: "This is the one. He has the will to learn."

Learning Benefits

1. Increased self-confidence when approaching new tasks or presenting new ideas
2. Persistence and toughness in pursuing goals
3. Improved stress management and problem solving
4. Refined decision-making ability
5. Enhanced work-specific capabilities
6. Openness to creative approaches and unorthodox solutions to problems
7. More in-depth product knowledge
8. Sensitivity to the needs and viewpoints of others
9. Deeper understanding of organizational politics
10. Greater confidence in career planning
11. Better understanding of yourself
12. Improved goal-setting and time management skills
13. Enhanced team-building and negotiating skills
14. Better leadership qualities
15. Increased motivation to work
16. Greater personal satisfaction

Exhibit 1-1. Benefits linked to key learning experiences and achieving learning goals.[10]

The CEO described the variety of jobs the manager had experienced during the course of his career and how in each job he had to undertake significant learning to be successful. In many assignments this person was not initially the most qualified for the job but in a short period of time achieved an impressive level of mastery.

The CEO said the new job would be a huge promotion and a stretch; but he added: "I know this person has the ability to learn how to do it. That's why I'm going to give it to him."

Making Your Learning Continuous

Learning isn't something you can switch on and off during your working life. If you look closely at careers, you can see when people are learning and when their learning has shut down—or has been shut down by outside circumstances.

Like bottle rockets, some people burst on the scene with dazzling energy only to fizzle quickly into obscurity. Others spit and sputter through their work, unsure of their goal or how to reach it. But those who continuously and intentionally learn are like heat-seeking missiles whose target is challenge and growth. Their accelerated learning creates a positive career cycle with multifaceted rewards. Managers who learn rapidly are given more opportunities and are then ready for increased responsibility.

The best leadership positions, compensation, and benefits go to the managers who have learned most effectively, thereby increasing their skills and capabilities. Those with a learning lag are left behind.

For example, let's say you're running in a half-marathon. You've settled into a quick pace with a handful of other runners. For a while, the group seems content to run as a unit, matching stride for stride. But suddenly, on a steep incline, one person pulls away from the crowd, setting off a mental dilemma in the other runners: should they go with him and risk burning out before reaching the finish line, or maintain their comfortable pace, knowing they will complete the race in a respectable, albeit unheralded, position?

Usually, those with the strength to follow pick up their pace and stick with the leader. Some burn out. Some don't. Those left behind either maintain their slower pace or, demoralized, slow down even more.

Just as a runner must understand his pace and ability in relationship to others, it is important for managers to understand their learning rate and its consequences. If they are learning at a slower rate than a coworker, it is likely that the faster learner will be recognized more and given more opportunities.

Early Career Learning.   Kevin Walsh is a manager on the move with General Electric. In his first 10 years at GE he has worked in its international financial arm, helped negotiate jet engine contracts, headed a training program for the brightest financial people in the company, and most recently moved to a unit of GE Capital that finances multimillion dollar independent energy projects.

During each assignment, Walsh has asked himself what things are most important for him to learn and how he can most efficiently learn them. At the end of each assignment he reflects on what he has learned and how he can improve his learning process for his next assignment.

Over time, he has developed a checklist for approaching a new job, thus accelerating his rate of learning. His checklist includes these questions:

- What are the most critical success factors in this job?
- Who are the people I can most quickly learn from?
- How will I be measured? How will my boss be measured? How will the company be measured?
- What elements of my job will require the most time?

After Walsh moved into his current job, he talked about how he went about learning it, giving examples from his checklist.

- Who are the people I can most quickly learn from?

Here I was starting in a new job, and there was a lot for me to learn. I wanted to get up to speed quickly and to contribute as rapidly as I could. One way was to find the key resources, or pockets of resources, in the company.

And those resources are people. They are people who don't necessarily jump out at you from the organizational chart. They may have been with the company a while or have worked on some critical transactions, or they may be key lieutenants to top-level people.

The top people are, number one, difficult to gain access to, and, number two, not necessarily the ones you need to talk to right away.

For example, in this business we finance the big ticket items. In my case it involves energy projects such as cogeneration facilities. There are some people who have been here a while and they understand the industry and what the market is all about.

We also have a syndications group that will distribute pieces of our deals if we don't want to retain the entire investment. They are constantly talking to other lenders, so they have a good view of our competition.

I found it to be very useful to sit down and talk to the syndications group to find out what is happening in the market. For a lender, that means learning what rates and terms are appropriate for different types of deals, the degree to which they'll finance certain types of deals, or how much equity needs to be in a deal. So the people in the syndications group were a valuable resource.

- How will I be measured? How will my boss be measured? How will the company be measured?

It's been important to know how I'll be measured, how my boss will be measured, and how the business will be measured so I can structure my deals or look for deals that can deliver on all three scores.

How do you find out those things? I was told how I would be measured. For my boss, I found out by sitting down and talking to him about it. I'm measured on deal flow—volume basically. He's measured the same way, but he's also measured on the degree to which I'm successful in growing and doing what I'm supposed to do on my own.

And then there's a bit of a disconnect. At one time the business was primarily volume-driven, but now it is also heavily focused on net income. I learned that initially by getting my hands on a copy of a presentation used in a recent operating review.

And that's really an invaluable resource, to get your hands on the operating plans of the business to determine what the business leaders feel are the critical measurements of success.

Midcareer Learning. Another learner, John Hardinger, vice president and general manager of acrylics and consumer products at Du Pont, who had a background limited to technology and marketing, found himself running a $500 million manufacturing business about to embark on the construction of two new plants. Because Hardinger knew little about manufacturing, he set out to learn.

To find out how the company managed its plant-site work force, he went to the employee relations department. His visit sent shock waves through a department that had never been visited by someone at his level who was interested only in learning. Next he visited the engineering department to learn how new plants are planned and built.

In each plant under his management, he talked with the shop floor workers to understand their issues. In just 6 months, Hardinger could see the results of his commitment to learning.

"Now I'm more thoroughly prepared for this year's capital budgeting meeting," he said, "and I can hold my own against my peers who came up the manufacturing route. My new knowledge also will have an impact on the way we design our two new plants and how we expect people on the line to work in these plants. In fact, our business will be changing from top to bottom."

Hardinger was an intentional learner who, in the midst of downsizing, a major reorganization, and a changing marketplace, took the time to decide what he needed to learn and how to go about acquiring the knowledge.

He knew his strengths and successfully focused on diminishing his weaknesses. He exemplifies the kind of aggressive learning that produces distinctive careers.

Managers who are excellent learners know how to continually add greater value to an organization. They learn how to handle not only difficult situations but new situations. They learn how to achieve results while effectively interacting with people.

Never Too Late to Learn. Don Follett, chairman of a business he started 25 years ago, undertook a 3-year process to prepare his company for a management transition. First he learned how to conduct his own executive searches by selecting future members of his senior management team. These were the younger people who would ultimately replace him and his cofounder and lead the company in the decades ahead.

Then he learned how to test his new managers by giving them enough freedom so he could determine if they had the capabilities to be successful in the future; and if he realized they could not succeed, he replaced them with a manager who could. The result has been a crop of younger managers who have demonstrated their abilities and are continuing to master new skills.

Now in his late fifties, Follett has focused his learning on how to do business in the international arena, where his company has formed the first joint venture in its history.

During the last 5 years of his career, Follett's learning curve has been straight up.

Taking Responsibility and Being Curious

Contrast the learners just mentioned to people who passively wait for opportunities to fall in their laps. Without active learning, all they can expect is a commodity career where they are treated like replaceable merchandise. They offer little to their business that can't be supplied by someone else, a condition generally reflected in their paychecks. And they never make the cut when the boss is looking to fill a top position.

Although these people may be creative, they are often caught in a career quagmire and can't see learning as their way out. They publicly complain or privately despair about the lack of challenge in their job and lack of direction from the top. The longer they thrash about waiting for someone else to rescue them, the more frustrated they become, the deeper they sink into inertia, and the more vehemently they deny responsibility.

These nonlearners are casualties of the deadly DINMJ (development is not my job!) syndrome. They wait, and they wait, and they wait for higher management to come up with a development plan. Instead of being told how to grow, they're often told where to go. It never occurs to them that they have the ability to set their own learning agenda, that part of the responsibility rests heavily on their own shoulders.

For other nonlearners, the problem isn't so much a lack of initiative as it is a lack of curiosity. Curiosity is at the heart of the learning process. It leads us to delve deeper and longer, and to ponder possibilities. Ultimately, it leads us to knowledge.

Thom Harvey, CEO of Harvey & Harvey, Inc., a waste management company, is perpetually curious. One day we toured a recycling plant to decide whether he wanted to buy its equipment at auction. Another manager who accompanied us took one look at the condition of the equipment and said the plant was not for them.

But Harvey approached the task from another perspective. He kept asking questions and taking notes. Time after time he climbed up huge conveyor belts to look at the electric motors that ran the plant. At each motor he wiped off the grease and looked at the metal plate that told its size. I asked him why he was checking the motors. He said: "By knowing their size and the number of hours the plant runs a day, I can get a fair estimate of the electrical costs of running a facility like this. By combining capital cost, labor costs, electrical cost, and maintenance, which I was estimating as I went along, I have a good idea of what it will cost us to run a plant like this."

Think of the difference between how Harvey and his assisting manager viewed the plant. By not being curious, the manager had only learned about the most superficial features of the plant. In one hour Harvey had learned the economics of an entire business and the factors for its operational success.

When I talked to Harvey's manager about what Harvey had learned versus what he had learned, the manager said he recognized the need to intentionally become more curious, particularly about machinery. He decided to make increased curiosity an integral part of his development plan.

Learning Despite Dismal Conditions

We want to make the point early and often that a serious learner can continue to develop even under trying circumstances.

Three of the most dramatic examples are people who were held prisoners of war. During World War I, Charles de Gaulle was a prisoner of war for 3 years. Toward the end of his captivity he wrote a book on the strategies used by Germany and by the Allies. After the war many who read it said it was the best strategic treatise written, a remarkable feat for someone incarcerated.

While in a death camp during World War II, Victor Frankel developed his thesis on how some prisoners can survive and others cannot. He discovered that those prisoners who had meaning in their lives were most able to withstand debilitating and degrading conditions. He found that even in the midst of captivity, human beings have an unconquerable freedom if they use their will to learn as an aid to survival. After the war, Frankel published his inspiring insights in *Man's Search for Meaning*.

Admiral William Stockdale was the highest ranking prisoner during the Vietnam war. Surviving 5 years in the Hanoi Hilton and other equally degrading prisons, he learned how to achieve two-way communication with his wife in which he was able to pass on the names of Americans who were held in captivity. He learned how not to be broken by his tormenters and thus became a role model to hundreds of other American fliers.

If, in such limiting conditions as these, the doors to learning are not locked shut, imagine how much more open they are in the comparative freedom of your organization.

Responding to a Recession.   In business, even horrible conditions can make a company ripe for learning. James R. Houghton, CEO and chairman of the board at Corning Inc., said that during the recession in 1983, Corning was "mired deep in the mud and we had to do something different." The company needed to change its strategic direction. Houghton recognized that Corning had to learn to make quantum leaps in quality, but convincing the rest of management to jump on the total quality bandwagon wasn't easy.

"In the fall of 1983 we had a pretty grim meeting where we were looking up from the bottom," Houghton recalled. "I said, `We are going to spend a lot of money on quality. We are going to set up a quality institute, and we are going to pursue this thing with vigor throughout the company.'

"It fell on very deaf ears," Houghton said. "Ninety-five percent of the people at the meeting were totally cynical. They believed absolutely that the only reason I was doing this was that all new chairmen—I'd been chairman about 6 months—have to have new programs. Therefore, quality is Jamie's and don't worry: It will go away because all new programs tend to go away."

Houghton's commitment to learning to run a quality operation didn't go away. It got stronger.

"If anything it has intensified. It hasn't run out of steam at all," he said. "We had some businesses that came back from the brink. It's pretty easy to get people to change if you are convinced that unless you change in a big way, you're not going to make it."

When Your Boss Tries to Hold You Down.   Exercising control over your career isn't always easy. For reasons sometimes obvious, sometimes not, many executives have no interest in developing their employees. Others actually try to stunt their employees' growth. A friend of mine offers a perfect example of why you can't give in to a boss who wants to hold you down. After being aggressively recruited by a large chemical company, she was given a challenging management position that provided opportunities for growth and creativity.

She thrived in that position until her boss left and was replaced by someone who didn't value her or her work. While her peers were promoted, she was shuffled aside and given work of little importance. The management ploy was a familiar one: Don't fire them; make them quit.

She was hurt. She was angry. But she didn't give in. Instead of taking long lunch hours and reading newspapers in her office, she made sure she did the most with what she had been assigned. To avoid a learning lapse, she signed up for courses and workshops to further her development. After evaluating her situation, she began investigating other career avenues, both inside and outside the company.

"I didn't come here to be devalued," she said. And money says she won't be, even if it means sharp turns in her career. Her goal is learning and meaningful contribution. She's a heat-seeking missile. She may change directions, but she won't stop moving forward.

While recognizing the power of her boss's position, she accepts responsibility for her own career. She has since been promoted within the company to a job that she helped create. It is one full of challenges and possibilities.

Individuals cannot expect management to learn for them. Most managers are either too busy or unskilled, or they do not recognize your need to grow. Your white collar is not attached to a leash, so don't wait for your boss to throw you a bone. Take charge.

Learning for Life

Lifelong learning creates lifelong opportunities. Learners do not "retire." Their pilgrimage never ends.

In a 1991 article, *Sports Illustrated* noted that Billie Jean King, one of only four athletes to make *Life* magazine's list of the 100 most important Americans of the twentieth century, continues to passionately combine work—in her case tennis—and learning.

The author described being around King "like standing next to a warm motor. She gives off an electric hum of knowledge." She "continues to learn at an alarming rate." And she continues to share that knowledge with others.

In her symbiotic, ordered view of the world, tennis is about fortitude—facing up to things—and the value of a good effort for its own sake. To her mind, the sport should be properly executed, pleasing to the eye and emotionally and intellectually gratifying.

"It's about learning your craft," she says. "That's a wonderful thing—especially with today's consumerism and instant gratification. You can't buy that. It's about making decisions, corrections, choices. I don't think it's so much about becoming a tennis player. It's about becoming a person."[5]

Learning at work, whether it is tennis or business, is about "becoming a person." It deserves immediate attention. It requires lifelong commitment.

Learning Leaders and Learning Organizations

The second half of this book deals with learning leaders and creating learning organizations. The two go hand in hand. If you are a member of top management, you have the unique opportunity to inspire corporate learning. The role of the senior executive cannot be overstated.

As Peter F. Drucker says in his book *Management*, "A superior who works on his own development sets an almost irresistible example."[6] An active commitment to your own learning is your greatest leverage in getting your people to grow and develop.

When Houghton wanted Corning to become committed to total quality, he knew the learning had to begin with himself. "You start the fire at the top," Houghton said. "If you really start beaming it down, the employees down below believe you mean it. Then the fire starts to pop."

Once you've decided to become a learner, you're only a step away from becoming a learning expeditor. While you can't do other people's learning for them, you can certainly encourage them to learn for themselves. In *Management* Drucker states:

> Development is always self-development. For the enterprise to assume responsibility for the development of a man is idle boast. The responsibility rests with the individual, his abilities, his efforts.
>
> No business enterprise is competent, let alone obligated, to substitute its efforts for the self-development efforts of the individual. To do this would not only be unwarranted paternalism, it would be foolish pretension.
>
> But every manager in a business has the opportunity to encourage individual self-development or to stifle it, to direct it or misdirect it.
>
> He should be specifically assigned the responsibility for helping all men working with him to focus, direct, and apply self-develop-

ment efforts. And every company can make available to its managers development challenges and development experiences....

It is a necessity for the spirit, the vision, and the performance of today's managers that they be expected to develop those who will manage tomorrow. Just as no one learns as much about a subject as the man who is forced to teach it, no one develops as much as the man who is trying to help others to develop themselves.

Indeed, no one can develop himself unless he works on the development of others.[7]

Unlike cosmetic changes, such as adopting a new management style or changing a title, how we learn cuts to the core of who we are and colors everything we do.

Learning starts with individual managers being committed to their own discovery and growth. They need to have the curiosity and drive to make it happen. Managers who are successful learners are like powerboat drivers pulling a team of water skiers. By converting their energy for learning into action, those in their wake are pulled to explore new territory, to see their work in new ways, and to get increased results they never thought possible.

Stretch Assignments

If the first step in getting others to learn is to be a role model, the second is to recognize where the best learning takes place. From hundreds of interviews with CEOs and other managers, we've found that the best way to learn is by giving people challenging jobs that stretch their abilities.

At Lear Seating Corporation, a high-growth supplier to the automotive industry, the company relies on stretch assignments, not classroom training, to help its employees grow.

"We are not afraid to give people responsibility," said Robert Rossiter, president at Lear Seating. "People may not necessarily have had all the experience, but we put them in a challenging job and they are in a position where they know they are accountable and responsible. Then they make it their business to learn."

As an example, Rossiter said the company recently promoted three young managers to business unit managers. Two were engineers and the third a salesman.

"We've taken these three men and we are asking them to head their divisions and they will be running businesses with minimal experience," Rossiter said. "If you walk into a job where you don't have much experience, you really have to draw from every resource you can to gain knowledge."

"That's where we will find out if these men are true leaders and if they've really got the ability to do the job," he continued. "They cannot try to go in and say, `Here's how we should do it' because they don't have the experience. They'll have to say, `Ok guys, how do we get this done?' They will have to work together as a team."

Learning in the Showroom

On a recent winter evening I was looking for a new car and visited several dealerships. At the first dealership, I went directly to a model in the center of a large showroom devoid of other customers. Two salespeople were chatting off to one side. After 10 minutes of climbing in and out of the car, I was about to leave when a third salesperson approached me. He never questioned me about what I was looking for, but proceeded to tell me he didn't care for the model I was looking at because he preferred "big, comfortable cars." The sales manager, who I had met that morning in the service department, stood leaning against another car. Without a glimmer of recognition, he watched the whole proceeding and my hasty departure.

At the next dealership a salesperson approached me immediately. While he was off getting information and keys for a test drive, four other salespeople offered assistance. This was a dealership committed to teaching its salespeople the art of selling. Their CEO had set a goal to sell one out of every two cars sold in the state and had created a learning organization in order to achieve that goal.

At the first dealership, the sales manager and salespeople never realized they had missed a learning opportunity. They never asked why I walked out or how they could have improved their performance. The second dealership, however, is aggressive in continually auditing each salesperson's performance to learn why a sale is made or lost. The people there have developed a way to identify important areas needing work and a plan by which they learn more effectively and are held accountable.

The Learning Organization

The new role of leaders is not just to focus on results but to create a learning organization. As stated in a *Fortune* article entitled "What the Leaders of Tomorrow See":

> The most successful corporation of the 1990s will be something called a learning organization, a consummately adaptive enterprise

with workers freed to think for themselves, to identify problems and opportunities, and to go after them.

In such an organization, the leader will ensure that everyone has the resources and power to make swift day-to-day decisions. Faced with challenges we can only guess at now, he or she will set the overall direction for the enterprise, after listening to a thousand voices from within the company and without.

In this sense, the leader will have to be the best learner of them all.[8]

Although employees may not label it as such, they *know* when they work for a learning organization. It provides equal doses of authority, responsibility, and respect in a work environment where people share a passion for personal and corporate improvement.

People in a learning organization feel a deep sense of accomplishment for what their whole organization has been able to achieve and for the contribution their learning has made to the total effort. They feel a sense of responsibility to learn how to do things better and are proactive in seeking ways to improve what they do.

When they look up the line, they see a senior manager who is often a zealot about personal learning and a vocal champion for others to learn as well. Most often their organization has a clear vision and goals that stretch its staff. In fact, new knowledge or action is necessary for these goals to be reached; incremental improvement is not enough.

In describing learning organizations in *The Fifth Discipline*, Senge says:

> At its heart, the traditional view of leadership is based on assumptions of people's powerlessness, their lack of personal vision and inability to master the forces of change, deficits which can be remedied only be a few great leaders.
>
> The new view of leadership in learning organizations centers on subtler and more important tasks. In a learning organization, leaders are designers, stewards, and teachers.
>
> They are responsible for building organizations where people continually expand their capabilities to understand complexity, clarify vision, and improve shared mental models—that is, they are responsible for learning.[9]

When asked why their businesses must learn, managers say the issue is simple: Learn or die. They relate examples of losing business to a competitor who outlearned them.

Managers talk about how difficult it is to keep up, and about the problems their salespeople face when they can only offer their customers longer delivery times, products of lesser quality, or products at higher cost.

While they talk discouragingly of a competitor whose products reflect active learning, their faces brighten when describing competitors who once were great but whose products or services stagnated. Because these companies failed to improve, they are out of the competition.

Learning is no longer a luxury: it is at the heart of careers and companies determined to flourish in the future.

Servolift Eastern: Learning to Compete

Servolift Eastern, a Boston manufacturer of food handling equipment, is a good example of a company that used learning to its advantage. Walking through their factory 3 years ago was like negotiating a maze.

The production flow was choked by work-in-progress inventory that had been piled in aisles to be picked up later. More importantly, the lead time from order to shipment date was often 8 weeks or longer, causing many customers to place their orders elsewhere.

Today the same factory is a different world. Work-in-progress is no longer stored between stations. The brightly lit factory floor has an open feeling, workers communicate, and there is a sense of flow. Lead times are now down to less than 2 weeks. Effective use of time has become a competitive advantage, a phenomena the company's CEO credits to the company's new learning agenda.

Nath Srivastava, vice president of manufacturing and engineering for Servolift, said that the company's biggest weakness had been its confidence in what it was doing. It couldn't see that there might be a better way.

For example, Srivastava dismantled the company's functional-based layout and reintegrated those functions into a group-technology, product-based layout. That one change produced several advantages. It helped reduce the product lead time, and it made a dramatic improvement in quality.

"It was a kind of unlearning," said Srivastava, who was the primary instigator of the changes. "The biggest learning for them was unlearning what they had done for such a long time. When they saw the dramatic results, then they became the preachers."

Avery Dennison: Learning On and Off the Job

A similar story is told by Ron Buehner, a vice president of manufacturing for Avery Dennison, a label company. Concerned about the high cost of new plants, the manufacturing organization committed itself to finding ways to make better use of its existing 64 plants.

They discovered it took up to 8 hours to change the manufacturing process from making one kind of label to another. Recognizing that many people learn visually, they made a videotape of the changeover process.

The workers responsible for the changeover watched the videotape for the entire 8 hours it took. All were struck by how little happened. A worker would wander into the picture, make an adjustment and then leave to get a particular wrench.

It became evident that many delays were caused by not having the right parts or tools at hand. By visualizing what was causing the delays, individuals learned how to increase their efficiency. As a result, some plants have reduced the changeover time from 8 hours to 10 minutes!

The relationship between work and learning is further demonstrated by a mechanic at Avery Dennison who used his learning from experience outside of work to suggest an important change. Concerned with the length of time it took to connect high-pressure hoses, he suggested connecting them with the same kind of couplings he used on his farm tractor.

His idea was immediately shot down by numerous people, particularly highly educated engineers who said it couldn't work. Such resistance is often encountered by individuals who have decided to learn.

He refused to abandon the idea and finally asked his boss if he could get some couplings made by his farm implements dealer. The mechanic was concerned about the cost of $500 per coupling, but to his boss this seemed a small price to pay when each minute the machine was down cost Avery Dennison $800. The new couplings worked, saving the company precious minutes on each changeover.

Some of the better companies and managers intuitively recognize the workplace as the most fertile ground for growth and development. More and more organizations are searching for ways to enhance growth and to incorporate learning into every workday. When a firm becomes excellent at developing its people, it achieves a critical advantage. Accelerated executive development and the resulting immediate business payoffs are just two of the benefits. In a vibrant developmental culture, the norm is constant learning leading to continuous improvement.

In Part 4 of this book, you'll hear from top executives at five learning organizations. They relate why learning is important to them, some unique ways they encourage their managers to learn, and how they see themselves learning in the future.

Leaping Up the Learning Curve

Your growth and development at work may be sluggish, or it may already be on an upward curve, but by accelerating your learning, you'll see an immediate increase in your business abilities. Jumping onto the steeper, accelerated line will give you a competitive advantage over everyone who hasn't discovered the power of intentional learning at work.

You can accelerate your learning to get where you want to go faster and with greater satisfaction. To be successful, your rate of growth must be better than your peers. Intentional learning at work will provide the takeoff point for your career, increasing your ability to contribute, produce results, and lead.

Conversely, if your peers effectively accelerate their learning and you don't, you'll be the one left behind. You'll receive less challenging work and become the less attractive candidate for future promotions. For people who haven't achieved a differentiated contribution, the best they can hope for is a flat or modestly satisfying career. The worst they can expect is that their career becomes a negative spiral that sucks them to the bottom of the employment pile.

The same is true for companies. An organization that relies on learning to enhance its workers' abilities to contribute, produce results, and lead will create a competitive advantage for itself. A company's rate of growth has to be better than its best competitor or it will fall behind.

For businesses as well as individuals, the best learners will be awarded the most opportunities. But one thing is clear: The responsibility for learning begins and ends with the individual.

This book will give you the process, the tools, and the models to improve the way you learn and the rate at which you learn. But only you can determine how fast you move through the learning labyrinth.

Whether you're interested in becoming a better learner or creating a learning organization, you need to understand where learning occurs. If your first priority is to take charge of your own learning, continue on to Chapter 2, where you'll discover you don't have to go off in search of learning: your current business environment can provide unparalleled opportunities. If your first priority is to improve your organization's ability to learn, jump ahead to Chapter 5. Then return to Chapter 2 to discover how to take charge of your own learning.

2

When Work and Learning Converge: Mapping the New Frontier

We have to ask ourselves this question: Will the bombing attacks of last autumn and winter come back again...We are proceeding on the assumption that they will...Many new arrangements are being contrived as a result of the hard experience through which we have passed, and the many mistakes no doubt we have made. For success is the result of making many mistakes and learning from experience. If the lull is to end, if the storm is to renew itself, London will be ready.
                    WINSTON CHURCHILL
          July 14, 1941, Addressing the London County Council

If you were handed a sheet of paper and asked to draw a picture of managers learning at work, what would you draw? It would probably look something like this: a roomful of people in business suits, all seated and armed with pencils and paper as they watch a lecturer pace behind a podium in a classroom. Or maybe your sketch would show a manager sitting across the desk from his or her boss, having a one-on-one discussion on career development.

Both pictures accurately reflect most managers' mental prototype of learning, and in essence, they are the same. One is of passive classroom learning that occurs away from the workplace. Just as all eyes are on the lecturer, the focus is on the teacher and the teaching. The managers are given the questions and the answers. They receive but do not initiate. Everyone is offered the same lessons, but an observer can't tell who is learning and who isn't.

The other picture, of the manager having a sit-down discussion with a boss, also puts the onus on someone other than the manager. It is the boss who is dispensing knowledge and controlling the situation. It is the superior who is responsible for supplying the answers. The manager seeks and gets advice, but only his future actions will tell what he learned.

These two pictures capture our mental images, or "mental models," of learning at work. In *The Fifth Discipline*, Senge defines *mental models* as "deeply held internal images of how the world works, images that limit us to familiar ways of thinking and acting."[11] The danger, Senge says, is not in whether mental models are right or wrong, but in whether we are aware of their existence. By scrutinizing our mental models of learning we can measure their strengths and weaknesses. We then can determine if they accurately reflect current reality and can move us toward our learning goals.

Old Habits Carry a High Price

In *Discovering The Future: The Business of Paradigms*, clinging to outdated mental models can be costly. Joel Barker gives a good example of what happens when a mental model, or paradigm, no longer holds true. In 1968 the Swiss, long renowned for their watchmaking expertise, dominated the field with 65 percent of the world market and more than 80 percent of the profits. Yet 10 years later their market share had plummeted to below 10 percent, and in the following 3 years they had to release 50,000 of 65,000 watchmakers.

What happened? The introduction of the quartz movement watch, a watch that created a new paradigm for watches. As Barker points out, it was the Swiss themselves who invented the quartz watch but failed to recognize its value. In 1967 Swiss researchers presented it to watchmakers in Switzerland; they were not impressed with the totally electronic watch. It had no bearings, no gears, no mainspring, and they rejected it out of hand. The watch manufacturers were so confident that it was not the watch of the future that they didn't even protect the idea!

Later that year, when the Swiss researchers displayed the watch at the Annual Watch Congress, Texas Instruments of America and Seiko of Japan leaped on the idea and subsequently took control of watchmaking's future.

"The Swiss were blinded by their old paradigm," Barker says. "They assumed what had been successful in the past would be successful in the future."[12] They were disastrously wrong.

Because classroom training and mentor-based development dominate managers' vision of learning, they form the learning paradigm of corporate America. A growing body of research, however, supports what we somehow knew intuitively, that the most effective development for managers and white-collar professionals occurs not in the classroom but through the experience of the job itself. Because of serious flaws in both their conception and their implementation, classroom training and mentor-based development account for a surprisingly small share of the learning that actually takes place at work. But it isn't easy to disengage ourselves from our mental models of learning.

Why We Cling to Conventional Training

What precipitated the models for classroom training used so frequently in the workplace? All those years we spent in school. Since childhood we have identified the classroom as learning's habitat. We spent so many years facing a blackboard that it frames and ultimately limits our mental picture of learning.

We envision a teacher standing in front of rows of attentive students as he or she explains, coaxes, guides, and goads. The educational experience focuses on the teacher, who is responsible for the learning process. While the teacher may be excellent and the students eager, such a classroom setting rarely equips students to become expert learners. Instead they become dependent on remembering predigested learning—that is, learning what someone else extracted from experience.

In order to become expert learners, students must be able to wrest knowledge from their own experiences rather than to merely recite what they have been taught. This was driven home to me during a workshop at a conference of the National Association for Independent Schools. The project involved videotaping excellent teachers at work to create a video catalog of effective teachers and how they conducted their classes.

One video showed a high school social studies class of 20 students learning the cause and cure for stagflation during the 1970s, when

Gerald Ford was president. The class had been divided into teams of five, and team members were sharing with each other the research they had completed in the library. Their discussions were full of energy. While watching the videotape, I was struck by what happened when one student happened to overhear what another team was saying. She immediately engaged her team with the other team to wrestle through a point. After about 20 minutes, the camera turned toward the teacher who was sitting in the corner of the classroom listening to the students. After watching the tape, a member of the audience, who was a teacher, said, "That wasn't very good teaching because all the teacher did was sit there." Another member of the audience countered, "It may not have been what we most often think of as teaching, but it sure was excellent learning."

In that social studies class, the focus had shifted from the teacher as expert to the students, who had discovered a zest for learning. But even more telling was the comment of the member of the audience who did not recognize how well the teacher in the videotape had prepared his students to become active learners, responsible for using multiple resources to gather the information they needed to answer life's questions.

As life goes beyond formal education and we enter the business world, we, much like the critic in the audience, continue to carry a mental picture of passive classroom learning: teachers teaching, students listening and taking notes. When words such as *learning, development,* or *growth* pop up in the workplace, we pull out the old learning picture and try to apply the same model of education to our work. In order to learn, we assume we have to physically remove ourselves from our jobs, grab a pencil and paper, and sit in a classroom. The focus of much of the training in the business world, just as it is in earlier schooling, is on teaching and what is being taught as opposed to learning and how learning takes place.

That the model of education focused on teaching rather than learning was brought home to Dr. Gail Robinson, director of human resource development at Lever Brothers. She became interested in the learning processes of managers—how they learned to learn—in 1989. She was working at PepsiCo at that time, where the main method of executive development was learning from on-the-job stretch assignments; Robinson wanted to read everything she could about what makes experience such a great teacher.

She turned to the library at Columbia University's Teachers College, where her search for literature on learning from experience uncovered a minute number of references. The library had a roomful of books on teaching but only 4 feet of books on the subject of learning. "I was shocked," she said, "to realize that the whole focus of our educational system has been on teaching, not on learning."

This focus is now changing at Teachers College, where faculty and students have been exploring new approaches that concentrate on learning, not instruction.

The Trouble with Traditional Training

On-the-job learning isn't as easy to visualize as classroom teaching, even though its lessons are more varied and substantial. As noted in *The Lessons of Experience: How Successful Executives Develop on the Job*, "Knowledge of how the business works, ability to work with senior executives, learning to manage people who were once peers, negotiating with hostile foreign governments, handling tense political situations, firing people—these and many others are the lessons of experience. They are taught on the firing line, by demanding assignments, by good or bad bosses, and by mistakes and setbacks and misfortune."[13]

Training is not without merit. It can be a valuable tool in filling gaps in a manager's education. Formal training is excellent, for example:

- When a manager needs to learn a specific subject in a hurry
- When a company wants to supply a common perspective or baseline knowledge across the organizational spectrum
- As a way to introduce managers to new paradigms or tools, such as total quality management
- As a way to learn interpersonal skills that are not easily learned on the job, such as selling skills

Dave Wakefield, retired chairman and president of J. P. Morgan Delaware, tells of the time he became the chief administrator of Morgan's brand-new, rapidly growing mergers and acquisitions area.

"I could have used more formal training in the mergers and acquisitions when I went into it," Wakefield says. "You really do learn the M&A business by doing it. You know ten times as much after you've done a deal as you get from formal classroom training, but nevertheless you need some training to get you started."

Training works best when an individual has the commitment to learn what is being taught and the drive to implement what is learned. When the course also provides information needed for survival at work, the training can be even more valuable.

Several years ago Eastman Kodak CEO Kay Whitmore and I attended the same seminar at a Sloan Fellows Convocation at MIT. The seminar was about doing business in China. I have never seen a student question a professor as energetically and tenaciously as did Whitmore. He opened my eyes as to how serious some senior managers take their learning. When I asked him about it, he said that the training came at a particularly pertinent time.

"We as a company were actively wrestling with what was going to be our position and posture in China," Whitmore recalled. "So it was a very timely subject for us and I was looking for every vehicle I could find to enhance my learning about China. We had put in a big capital investment and the question was how to learn to make it pay off."

So my argument is not that there should be less training. In fact, I'd argue the opposite: We need more training, but it needs to be done effectively and with an understanding of its limitations. Companies in the United States spend about $40 billion a year trying to develop their employees, through formal training. That sounds like an impressive commitment to learning until you look at the breakdown. According to *Worker Training, Competing in the New International Economy* (a 1990 report of the Office of Technology Assessment, U.S. Congress, Government Printing Office, Washington, D.C.), most of that money, some $27 billion, is spent by 15,000 companies, or only 0.5 percent of all U.S. employers.

So the problem is twofold: Short shrift is given to any kind of intentional learning at work. And the training that does exist may not accomplish what most top executives expect because it has limited goals. Reflecting on the growth of his company's employees, the training and development director at a major New York bank said, "I often wonder how much impact our training has in terms of the results we seek. There seems to be a disconnection between what one learns in the classroom and its actual application."

Training can be a subset of learning, but it is an inadequate substitute. Training alone isn't powerful enough to develop key people in the organization because it rarely leads to broad leaps in learning or to creative and inventive ways of working. Yet those responsible for training and development focus on classroom training as an employee's primary education opportunity.

It is rare that companies provide individuals with learning tools to help them extract the maximum learning from their experiences, and therein lies the problem.

In businesses' misdirected search for the best learning at work, they've relied heavily on ineffective mental models. By focusing on classroom training and supervisor-as-teacher rather than real-life learning, companies have not held managers accountable for their own growth and development. The most promising learning, that from on-the-job experience, has been left to chance.

Why doesn't traditional company training produce the desired results? There are a number of reasons.

1. *Training doesn't tie in with the strategic business needs of the company.* Companies initiate new training programs the way some people try new diets, never leaving one in place long enough to produce measurable results. The multitude of training programs and the lack of follow-through imply that the results aren't taken seriously. When companies use this scatter-shot approach to employee training, they accomplish very little. It becomes more like a "program of the month" club. If this month's program doesn't motivate you, maybe next month's will.

In the meantime, managers can develop training burnout. As one frustrated engineer said when asked about his company's development opportunities, "This company gives a lot of lip service to development, but that is about all it is, lip service. These training programs come and go. There is no continuity. The problem is compounded by the rapid turnover in management. You don't even get to recognize your new boss before he or she is gone. At our company, the employees are jacks of all trades and masters of none."

2. *In training, one size doesn't fit all.*   Most training is not flexible enough to meet the unique needs of each individual. Vast amounts of money and time are spent yearly to teach people what they don't really need to know. One of our clients, despite having a master's degree in finance from the Stanford University Business School, was not exempt from a basic accounting course required of every new employee. That time would have been better spent on developing other proficiencies. Too much generic training is given across the board, whether everyone needs it or not.

3. *Managers often resist training and then sabotage its implementation.* They see training as an expensive waste of time that results in their own work backing up. If people don't have a compelling reason to learn, their cynical attitude often precludes their ability to hear. You can make them sit in a classroom but you can't make them learn.

I remember one seminar I taught on career planning that included managers, supervisors, and professionals. The focus of our work was helping the organization become more effective in getting the right person into the right job. To do this, individuals were equipped with tools and a process to identify their strengths, skills, and interests, and a way to communicate to their manager what was important to them.

Attending this particular seminar was a senior manager who didn't think individuals should have any input into their job assignments. In fact, we had a battle royal in the early afternoon. It was clear from his comments and behavior—he came in late and carried on side conversations—that this course was not one he wanted to attend.

Several weeks later a lower-level employee was walking across a plant site on his way to have a career discussion with his supervisor, as we had recommended in the seminar. This same senior manager saw him and asked where he was going. The employee explained he was on his way to his career discussion, to which the senior manager responded, "I'll tell you what your career discussion is. It's to go back and get your goddamned work done."

It was clear that the training that the senior manager had been forced to attend had actually increased his hostility and resentment of new possibilities rather than providing him with an opportunity. Surprisingly, the organization promoted this manager to an even more senior position several months later. Not surprisingly, in less than 6 months he was fired from this new job for inadequate interpersonal ability.

4. *For those who want to apply their classroom learning, stepping back into the workplace can be a dispiriting experience.* Managers excited about implementing what they have just learned return to mountains of mail, overdue reports, more meetings, and the crisis of the moment. The learning gets put aside, and often stays there. Much like New Year's resolutions, the intentions may be good but the follow-through is weak.

Although learning that occurs away from regular work may be difficult to transfer to ongoing tasks, as noted in *Managing for Excellence:* "Learning that occurs on the job, in ongoing interactions, is likely to be the most relevant to department members. Tasks can be assigned that broaden the subordinate's knowledge and skills, coaching can occur that builds competencies (as well as increases the probability of successful task accomplishment), and feedback can be given on an ongoing basis."[14]

5. *If there isn't any follow-through on what was learned in the classroom, who's to know the difference?* In most training there is no accountability for what was learned, and the implementation phase is the weakest link. Training programs that offer personal, expert follow-up are rare, and any measurements, if they exist, usually come at the end of the training session itself. Most often what is actually measured is the entertainment value of the process, not the learning component. Seldom is there a follow-up measurement at 3 months, 6 months, or a year to determine the business and personal impact of the training.

I remember going back to a plant site of a Fortune 100 company at the end of 6 months to conduct an audit on the implementation of development plans people had created during the seminar. We also wanted to discover what participants had learned through on-the-job application of what was taught in the seminar.

One participant remarked at the end of the audit: "This is the first time in 23 years with this company that someone has come back to see how we actually implemented what we learned in a course. Not only is it refreshing, but it says that the company is committed to what you taught us."

He continued: "I had another discovery as well. Knowing you were coming back and that we were going to be held accountable, I took much more seriously my responsibility to implement what we had learned rather than what usually happens when I know no one will ever question how well I put to use what I learned."

A company president tells of sending two people to the Harvard Advanced Management Program. When they returned, it appeared that their experience had little impact on their performance. The president said he wasn't sure he wanted to spend the time and money to have people go away if there wasn't any real improvement when they returned home.

In another case, a board member of a company reported: "Our company sent three people to a multiweek advanced management program. One returned home and left the company. The second returned home and the program seemed to have made no difference. The third returned home and was excited for a time, but I'm not sure that it made a real business difference. This is pretty thin gruel for losing manpower for nearly half a year at a cost of over $250,000 in salaries and other expenses."

6. *Managers who try to get the most out of their off-site training usually lack support for implementation once they return to the job.* Because their training generally occurs in a vacuum without the involvement of their immediate boss or coworkers, they come back to an office resentful of the extra work delegated during their absence. Coworkers are less than eager to hear about any new ideas that may have come out of the training. Many times bosses resent training for subordinates, viewing it not only as a waste of time but as a criticism of their leadership and mentoring abilities.

One client told us of going to an off-site course on how to be more in touch with his feelings and more open to those around him. Upon returning to his job, he candidly shared with his boss some of the insights he had while away and his expectations of how he wanted their organization to change. Five weeks later he was fired because he had raised issues his boss did not want to address.

Not having alignment and agreement with more senior managers can completely negate the positive effects of any kind of learning. Without organizational support, the odds are too great against the manager's new development taking root and producing results.

7. *A crush of time often means training is done in a pressed fashion that precludes real learning.* Because every training director understands the time crunch faced by line organizations, a 3-day training course often will be compressed into one, and its content finally becomes a minilecture with handouts. This is particularly true of programs for senior managers. The length of the courses these managers receive is inversely proportional to the position of these managers in the organization (the higher their level, the shorter the course given to them).

As we will see in the closeup look at Corning Inc., in Part 4, not all senior managers avoid taking their own medicine. Corning CEO Jamie Houghton takes his full strength. He was a member of Corning's first quality class and received the same course given to everyone else.

The Shift in Focus to Learning in the Workplace

In the business world today, the focus is shifting from classroom teaching to on-the-job learning. Companies are discovering that the best learning occurs in problem-solving situations at work.

At General Electric, senior managers with officer potential literally use the world as their classroom. A group of 40 participants is broken down into teams of 5. After a week of team building they spend the next 2 weeks developing solutions to an important business problem submitted by top management. The problems are real, and the solutions are difficult and complex, with very real consequences.

For example, two competing teams might go to India to critique GE Medical Systems' strategy for entering that country's market. Meanwhile, another two teams might go to Russia to make a recommendation on how GE might reenter that market in the power systems business. Or, two teams might go to China to explore opportunities for GE in that country. After 2 weeks the teams then reconvene in a central location, such as London, where they prepare a report that is then given to corporate officers.

The teams are judged on what they learned and on the quality of the recommendations they make to GE's senior management. At the end of the session the teams get together as a group to give each other feedback on what they learned, how they functioned as a team, and how to apply their new knowledge in the workplace.

Motorola has taken the learning from experience process a step further by making their learning teams responsible not only for recommending solutions but for implementing them as well. Selected vice presidents join 25-member teams that are responsible for solving important problems during a period of 2 to 3 years. The teams include both experts on the problem under consideration and managers unfamiliar with the problem. The teams report directly to the office of the CEO, and real and measurable results are expected.

For example, one problem addressed was how to accelerate the rate at which Motorola develops software for its products, an issue critical to Motorola's future. Deborah King, director of executive development, says, "We have developed a process in which learning and doing take place simultaneously."

J. P. Morgan, the most profitable money center bank in New York, has long used on-the-job experiences as a primary development tool. At Morgan, top managers say that by seeking the best employees and rewarding them with challenging responsibilities, the company inspires a fierce loyalty among managers attuned to the needs of the company and its customers.

"I would argue that after being with Morgan for 22 years, the area where I learned the most was by facing and taking new challenges," said Peter Woicke, a managing director. "On several occasions, I was literally thrown into the water with no major support from the bank. You could argue that the bank took certain risks by putting me in those positions. The challenge of doing and completing new things was the biggest learning for me."

And Morgan expects people to share what they know. Dave Wakefield, retired chairman and president of J. P. Morgan Delaware, says: "People are very open with the information that they have. It is expected when one person learns something, that they then will share it with another person."

Unfortunately companies that focus on learning from experience are still the exception rather than the rule. The ability to learn is the critical skill needed if businesses and individuals are to be successful. In his article in *Sloan Management Review*, Ray Stata of Analog Devices states, "In fact, I would argue that the rate at which individuals and organizations learn may become the only sustainable competitive advantage, especially in knowledge-intensive industries."[15]

Discoveries about Development at Work

When traditional training doesn't work, what does? We first began asking the question when we looked at personnel forms of some of our Fortune 500 client companies. Under the question of development for the upcoming year, the response usually was an upcoming training program or an unspecified "on-going activity" with no target completion date.

When we asked the managers how their development plans were progressing, we found that many times the managers never attended the stipulated training program because of the press of business. Although the boss endorsed the training, daily business demands took precedence and training was shelved. As for the "ongoing activity" listed on their development plans the managers would laugh and say that meant "never to be gotten to."

These interviews made us realize that the formal development systems of many excellent companies were having relatively little impact on how managers actually developed and increased their contribution. We also realized that managers were not getting accurate feedback on their performance. Yet we could see that individual contributions significantly increased over time. We asked managers whether the contribution they were making today was greater than their contribution 10 years ago. The answer was always yes.

We were left with the question: If the formal systems aren't causing individuals to grow, what is? We presented this dilemma to participants in six Fortune 500 seminars we were teaching at the time, asking them what caused their contribution to increase. We heard story after story of how these managers' and professionals' on-the-job experiences had led to their development and increased their contribution.

We decided to dig more deeply into how these individuals grew and developed by embarking on a study of managers and professionals at eight Fortune 500 organizations in a variety of industries—petroleum, banking, electronics, medical products, insurance, and telecommunications. From this study we discovered a wealth of information about the relationship between work and learning. Before sharing our research findings, we invite you to take the quiz on how people develop in Exhibit 2-1. Afterward you can compare your answers with our database responses of more than 900 managers and professionals from the Fortune 500 companies in the study.

Discovery 1: Development Occurs on the Job

Question 1 is false. We asked 900 survey participants to share with us three key developmental experiences, that is, activities or relationships that increased their ability to contribute at work. We found 74 percent of the experiences occurred on the job. Nineteen percent of those surveyed mentioned off-the-job experiences, such as college, military service, or personal trauma as being developmental to their careers. And a

```
┌─────────────────────────────────────────────────────────────────┐
│                  How People Develop at Work                       │
│                                                                   │
│ Circle True (T) or False (F)                                      │
│                                                                   │
│ T  F  1. Less than 50 percent of development occurs on the job.   │
│ T  F  2. Bad bosses can help your career.                         │
│ T  F  3. Most people have little choice in how they develop.      │
│ T  F  4. Older people report less current development.            │
│ T  F  5. Learning gives rise to uncomfortable emotions.           │
│ T  F  6. Most development takes months or years, not hours or     │
│          days.                                                    │
│                                                                   │
│ Circle the two most frequently cited characteristics of develop-  │
│ ment:                                                             │
│                                                                   │
│ Promotion    Challenge    Visibility    Novelty    Positive       │
└─────────────────────────────────────────────────────────────────┘
```

Exhibit 2-1. A short quiz to determine conceptions of how people develop at work.

surprisingly small number—only 7 percent—mentioned formal training programs.

Of the on-the-job experiences, we found 25 percent occurred within an assignment, 17 percent resulted from relationships at work, and 32 percent resulted from a transfer to a new assignment. These findings suggest that if managers want to grow and increase their contribution, the best place to look is within their jobs.

For example, one chemist ran a laboratory in an agricultural products plant that provided statistical quality information on products as they were being assembled. The work was repetitive and routine until he asked, "Why do we wait until the end of the run to take our measurements? Why can't we make our laboratory equipment mobile, enabling us to provide results during the run?" Learning how to accomplish that one task saved the plant more than $2 million a year in products that no longer had to be thrown out because of failure to meet specifications.

Another client told the following story: Until 3 years earlier, he had the reputation for being the toughest manager at his site. When his plant was under the threat of being unionized, he was selected to head the security division. This entailed supervising a staff that operated over an area of 1200 acres. "My management style was to kick ass and take names," he said, which seemed to work well as long as everyone was in the same location and he could see what they were doing. But in this new job, there was no way his former management style would work. The client continued:

"I realized you can't force people to do things when you can't see them," he said. "I became a manager who had to learn to trust my people. When I returned to my regular work, I decided to try the same management techniques I had just learned. I called a team meeting and told my people that they were now going to be responsible for running their part of the plant. And while I would help coach them, I would no longer direct them in every detail of what to do.

"At first it was painful for they would continually test me to see if they really had responsibility for running things. One of the first things I did was to begin sending them for specific training so they would have the knowledge to make good decisions. In fact, we had 20 percent of our people in training at all times, with each person receiving 100 hours of training a year. This was up from what had averaged 10 hours a year.

"I remember going to my office, closing the door and banging my head on my desk out of the frustration of having to delegate the authority to them, watching them make mistakes and then slowly take responsibility for themselves. It turned out to be an outstanding learning opportunity for them and for me as well."

Discovery 2: Bad Bosses Can Be Beneficial

Question 2 is true. Bad bosses *can* help your career! One common experience has surfaced in each of our management seminars: At least one person in each group cites having a "bad boss" as their most developmental experience. When we first heard this, we were stunned. We had never considered bad managers to be a positive developmental influence.

Prior to that discovery, we had been teaching individuals to go back and work with their managers on creating good development plans, assuming their managers were motivated and skilled in working with their subordinates. We thought bosses, effective and skilled in coaching, were the prime catalysts for growth. We were wrong.

In light of the comments from seminar participants, we also discovered managers' coaching abilities and interests vary wildly. In fact, it is the rare manager who is an exceptionally good coach. Many managers dread development discussions and having to deal with career expectations.

One manager we worked with had a unique way to avoid discussing development issues with his subordinates. He would tell his secretary to call him 45 minutes into the performance review and remind him of a meeting he had to attend.

"I could deal with anybody for 45 minutes," the manager said. "But so it wouldn't have to go too long and I wouldn't get in over my head, my secretary would call, I would apologize for having to leave, and I would promise we would pick up the discussion at another time. Knowing how rapidly we move people in this organization, I realized that by the time another year passed and it was time for another scheduled development discussion, most of the members in my group would have left to go on to other jobs, and someone else would have to deal with their development concerns."

Discovery 3: Individual Initiative and Choice Are Critical for Development

Question 3 is false. We asked each survey participant to check one of three categories to help us understand their developmental experience. We asked them to indicate whether they had initiated participation, whether they had a choice and decided to accept it, or whether they had no choice. The findings were contrary to the old paradigm advanced by management, which said employees should be aggressive on company business, passive in terms of their own careers, and management would take care of them.

Instead, 35 percent of respondents indicated they had initiated their developmental experience. This was far higher than we had imagined because of the prevalence of the paradigm that managers are responsible for the development of their subordinates. Instead we found that individuals already had taken development into their own hands.

We also discovered the importance of choice in development. The largest number of respondents, 40 percent, said they had a choice and decided to accept their developmental opportunity. This means that their development was not done *to* them but instead was done *with* them.

The smallest group, 25 percent, said they had no choice in their developmental experience. One woman's job loss during a flurry of company cutbacks proved to be a positive benefit when she landed a better, more challenging position at a bigger company.

Many people have a real desire to take the initiative and implement their own development. When discussing her career, an editor friend of mine used to fluctuate wildly between breathing fire and being depressed to the point of paralysis. Her pay and benefits weren't the issue. Although she was smart, talented, and energetic, her career was going nowhere. She produced good work but didn't get the kind of challenging assignments she wanted.

She was getting minimal feedback from her boss, and her job stopped being fun long ago. She saw herself as a victim, and in truth, she had become one—a victim of her own overreliance on management for job satisfaction. She had a misconceived notion that somehow the company would be more interested in promoting her career than she herself was.

One day while venting her anger at work she put her finger directly on the problem. "I'm not learning anything," she said. So she set about pursuing a new assignment within the same company. Within a few months she succeeded in landing a job she finds challenging and rewarding, which is reflected in her work and is noted by her superiors.

It is clear that some degree of control over one's development, whether initiated or a result of having a choice, is often a key characteristic for success. The developmental planning process, detailed in Chapter 3, will help managers plan most effectively and with the greatest payoff to themselves and their businesses.

Discovery 4: There Is No Mandatory Retirement Age for Learning

Question 4 is false. We asked respondents if they were currently developing. We found those who were older reported as much current development as their younger counterparts. In fact, participants in their early thirties reported the least development.

Our hypothesis is that in one's early thirties individuals are sorting through their career choices rather than working on their development. They also may be paying more attention to family issues than work issues.

The lesson is not to assume that older, longer-service employees lack the desire or ability to grow and increase their contribution. Many companies are too quick to put older employees out to pasture or to assume that some employees are incapable of growing.

"Interestingly, the belief that few can grow is self-perpetuating," say Bradford and Cohen in *Managing for Excellence.* "If a manager holds to this notion, he has little reason to confront supportively a poorly performing subordinate."[16]

Businesses can no longer afford to shuffle anyone aside or to allow employees to sit back and relax in a comfortable position. A few years ago we spoke to a group of senior technical people at a chemical company that employs about 900 scientists with advanced degrees. They were talking about how to handle people 50 years of age and older who had plateaued.

One manager said, "I don't think it's worth the effort to get them to grow. It's better to just let them sit there." When questioned, he acknowledged that the cost of employing these high-level scientists was about $250,000 a year.

"Okay," we said. "Let's say the guy's 55. You're telling us you're willing to pay $2.5 million to let someone sit there over the next 10 years and do nothing? By the time you add inflation, you're probably talking about $3.5 million. And then you have opportunity cost because you could have had a more productive person in there, so you're talking about $7 million. You're not willing to do something when you have a $3.5 million direct cost and a $7 million opportunity cost?"

He said maybe he ought to go back and rethink his position.

Discovery 5: Development Doesn't Always Feel Good

Question 5 is true. We asked respondents to tell us what emotions they felt during their developmental experience and gave them lists of words to check off. Their choices included pleasant feelings, such as happiness, excitement, challenge, or confidence, and uncomfortable emotions, such as anger, fear, frustration, or stress. We found that more than 80 percent of respondents said their experiences contained uncomfortable emotions.

No pain, no gain does contain at least a kernel of truth. Development is not easy. In fact, it's risky business. While going through a developmental experience one cannot tell precisely whether or not it will be successful. By realizing that negative emotions are a by-product of development, a person can use them as clues that growth is occurring rather than as a reason to give up.

As the authors of *The Lessons of Experience* point out: "The more dramatic the change in skill demands, the more severe the personnel problems, the more the bottom line pressure, and the more sinuous and unexpected the turns in the road, the more opportunity there is for learning....For future executives, comfortable circumstances are hardly the road to the top."[17]

Discovery 6: Development Doesn't Occur Overnight

Question 6 is true. Asked how long their developmental experiences took, 90 percent of the respondents said months or years. In fact, 57 percent said years, 33 percent said months, while 8 percent said days, and 2 percent said hours.

Obviously, development is not a quick fix. People need time to change and grow. Most training won't work because it follows the "sheep dip" approach. People are sent off for a few hours or days and are expected to come back miraculously changed. It doesn't work that way. Development and learning take time.

Discovery 7: Key Elements for Growth Are Challenge, Novelty, Relationships, and Responsibility

Respondents identified four key elements found in developmental experiences: challenge, novelty, relationships with others, and responsibility. See Exhibit 2-2 for a list of the 10 most frequently mentioned characteristics of personal growth experiences.

Challenge stretches a person's abilities. It causes them to learn a new skill, try a new approach, or to act or think in a different way. We define challenging work as a stretch assignment, or an assignment so large or different from what the person has done before that they have to learn something in order to be successful.

Novelty acts as a learning trigger. It signals that something is different about this situation and warns that past approaches may not work. Managers who fail to learn from a developmental experience sometimes indiscriminately apply successful past practices to a new situation, when the situation calls for another approach.

Development Characteristics	Percent of Respondents
1. Challenge	46
2. Novelty	45
3. Relationships with others	27
4. Responsibility	24
5. Exposure	19
6. Self-initiation	15
7. Risk	12
8. Instruction	12
9. Visibility	11
10. Introspection	10

Exhibit 2-2. The top 10 characteristics of developmental experiences as identified by managers and professionals in a Wick and Company study conducted at eight Fortune 500 companies.

Relationships with others are developmental when:

- A good boss entrusts the manager with important work needed for the manager's growth.
- A mentor guides the manager through the business jungle.
- A wise peer offers advice.
- An incompetent boss forces the manager to become more organizationally adept to make up for the boss's shortcomings.
- A bad boss, who is abrasive and operates with a high degree of conflict, teaches an individual how to survive in a difficult personal situation, the kind of situation a person is likely to find several times during his or her career.
- The unethical boss, who serves as a negative role model, constantly reminds the manager of what he does not want to become.

Responsibility involves accountability for the success or failure of one's actions where consequences are real and important. One reason training programs may fail to have impact is that managers don't feel any important consequences from their actions.

Proactive Learning: A Prerequisite for Success

In the new frontier, work and learning converge to present entirely new contours and possibilities for growing and developing through work experience. We must be the passionate pursuers of knowledge rather than the passive recipients.

It isn't always easy. In fact, being a proactive learner—that is, actually going out and learning something on our own—can be a frightening experience. Being forced to make decisions with no props, no multiple choice, no true or false, leads many of us to paralysis or, at the very least, irritability at being placed in such a position.

As one person commented on the active learning process we advocate: "I'm not sure I like this. First, you make me decide what I need to learn. Then you make me design my own way to learn it, and then you hold me accountable to see whether or not I learned it."

But it is that kind of involvement and commitment to learning that will define who succeeds and who fails in the workplace. Time and again successful managers point to experience, and not to classroom training, as their primary teacher. We must all become expert learners by taking advantage of the potential for growth at work.

As John W. Gardner noted in his book, *On Leadership,* industry continues to turn to leadership off-site training programs and graduate degrees for executive development. "But where leadership development is the goal, the most effective arena for growth continues to be the workplace."[18]

Unlike the days when Dad dedicated a career to one company, there now is no such thing as a lifelong employment contract, and no longer does it require a grievous mistake to end up on the unemployment line. Today's streamlined business world offers little room (even at the bottom of the ladder) for employees too lethargic to learn. They will certainly find no room at the top.

We can all grow and develop if given the opportunity, and we must recognize continuous learning as a condition of employment. Better managed companies won't settle for less than a person's best.

Yesterday's Managers

- Waited to be taught
- Thought learning occurred primarily in the classroom
- Held their boss responsible for their careers
- Weren't held accountable for their own development
- Saw education as completed or needing only minor adjustments
- Didn't see the link between their learning and business results
- Left their learning to intuition

Tomorrow's Managers

- Deliberately seek to learn
- Recognize the power of learning through work experience
- Are responsible for their own careers
- Are accountable for their own development
- View education as a continuous, lifelong endeavor
- See how their learning affects business
- Intentionally decide what to learn

With the tools in Chapter 3 you can map out a dynamic, rewarding work life for yourself based on a powerful foundation of learning.

PART 2
Taking Charge of Your Own Learning

3

Get S.M.A.R.T with Intentional Learning

Excellent learners work as if they are in two places at once. They are adept at completing their present work while anticipating the future and preparing for it. Excellent learners are like chess players who, while carefully moving a pawn, think four, five, and six moves ahead. They are like airplane pilots who, while flying the plane, must stay keenly attuned to upcoming weather conditions and approaching air traffic. Their flight plan changes as conditions dictate. Their current actions determine when and how they arrive at their future destination.

Chess players and pilots cannot ignore what they cannot see: they *must* anticipate the future. Managers rarely take the opportunity to think that far ahead. Too often they get so locked into the present that they can't see beyond their current assignment.

Make Time to Learn

The press of day-to-day business often drives out learning. It prevents managers from reflecting on where they and their businesses are and where they would like them to be in the future. Managers are often too busy trying to keep their heads above water to look around and locate the shore. Such unfocused busyness results in a lot of water turbulence but little forward movement.

The "I'm too busy" excuse, coupled with the erroneous belief that management is responsible for development decisions, can sink careers.

If you don't commit the time to learn, there's no way you can keep up with those who do.

"I think one consciously has to set aside the time [to learn] and value that time," says John Hardinger, a vice president at Du Pont. "I mean religiously value it. To learn something new and different. To go beyond their [the managers'] boundaries. In other words, not perfect a task that one knows how to do 95 percent."

Lazy learners rarely make leaders. Instead of seizing opportunities, they make a half-hearted grab at them. It is your responsibility to take the time—to make the time—to learn and develop your career in a way that adds value to the company as well as to you personally.

You're the best person to create your learning plan. Commit the time to make it happen.

S.M.A.R.T. Learning

To make the learning process easier, we've developed a model with five interlocking components, or steps: Select, Map, Act, Review, and Target. These steps can be easily recalled using the mnemonic S.M.A.R.T. See Figure 3-1. When all five components click, the learning process becomes like a rolling wheel, gathering momentum as it energizes and propels your career forward. Whether you're a CEO or a middle manager, this learning wheel leads to improved business results as you become a more capable performer. Each component is critical. If one is underutilized, the wheel goes flat and bumps along at a snail's pace or it goes careening off the career path.

Step 1: *Select* a Goal That's Vital to You and Your Company

To select what you need to learn, you must first look into the future and decide:

- What is important to your company's success in the next 2 to 3 years?

- What proficiencies do you need for success in the company as it will become?

Factors Important to Your Company's Success in the Next 2 to 3 years. You must anticipate customer needs and industrywide trends. Failure to do so can be costly, as we noted with the Swiss, who

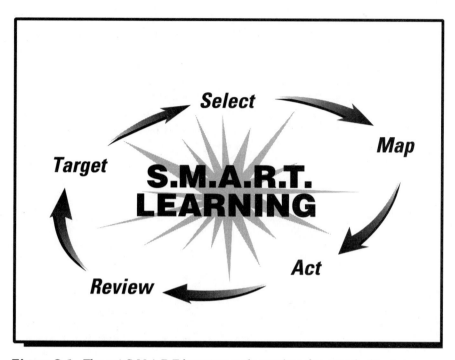

Figure 3-1. The get S.M.A.R.T learning cycle involves five interlocking steps.

went from leaders to losers in the watchmaking business because they were operating in a vacuum. They had no idea of the capability of other watchmakers and failed to recognize quartz movement watches as the key to their future.

The trick to spotting trends is to have multiple channels of information from both inside and outside your business. Assume the mindset of a commander on the battlefield who must absorb and process information from every possible avenue: satellites, reconnaissance aircraft, intercepted signal communications, scouts placed inside enemy lines, direct observation, eye witnesses, and information coming up through the chain of command. A business manager might look to *The Wall Street Journal* or trade magazines, talk to customers, talk to competitors, attend conferences, and build a network of key contacts. See Exhibit 3-1.

By looking beyond yourself and using all available channels of information, you'll get a clearer picture of the business climate and how your company fits in. You'll become adept at spotting those factors critical

Getting the Information You Need

When you enter a company at the top tier rather than working your way up through the ranks, you have to be a quick study. When Ted Hutton was hired from the outside as president of Waverly, Inc., he knew he had to learn a lot and learn it fast. During the first 6 months he used the following multiple sources of information to get up to speed at Waverly, a Baltimore-based publisher of medical and technical books.

He read:

- Books on emerging growth companies and the leadership role of a company president
- Trade publications
- Books published by his competitors
- Books that his company publishes

He talked to:

- His direct reports
- The chairman of the company
- The board of directors
- Individual employees, on a diagonal slice through the organization
- Group sessions with hundreds of employees
- Experts in the area of quality to help him change the way Waverly does business

He visited:

- The presidents of Waverly's key competitors
- His customers
- His suppliers
- His manufacturing facilities during each shift

Exhibit 3-1. Multiple channels of information for learning about a company and an industry.

for future success, and you'll avoid being blindsided by unexpected developments.

The following five questions can help simplify this trend analysis:

1. *Is your business or department clear about its mission, the customers it serves, and results that are needed?* If it is, you should choose a goal that complements and promotes the company's objectives. That way you're more likely to get corporate support and acknowledgement. For example, if your company wants to change from being product-driven to being market-driven, you may want to learn how to best identify the needs and values of your customers. If your company's vision is murky, then your task becomes more difficult but not impossible. You then determine the mission or objective of your particular segment of the organization and what it must do to be successful. (In fact, most companies lack a clear corporate vision, a problem addressed in depth in Chapter 5.)

2. *Are there technological trends that can put your company in a better position than your competitors?* If yes, you may want to choose a goal that would help advance your company's technology, thereby creating a competitive advantage. In the wake of airline deregulation in the early 1980s, Hal Rosenbluth, CEO of his own travel agency, spotted such a trend. Where there once had been three or four different fares on any given route, deregulation resulted in most routes being served by several airlines, each with dozens of different fares. By creating a private reservation data system that could call up all available routes and airfares, Rosenbluth gave his company a competitive advantage in the travel business. The result: Business boomed.

3. *What initiatives can your company take, such as improving quality or reducing cycle time, that can give it a competitive advantage?* A manufacturer of trucks required a lead time of 8 weeks from order to delivery. That was the status quo until a manager did an analysis and realized it took only 13 hours to actually build the truck. By streamlining the order entry process the company has cut delivery time from 8 weeks to 4. If, in your position, you can choose a goal that promotes such initiatives, it could have an immediate, identifiable impact on the company and your career.

4. *What steps might your competitor take to put your company at a disadvantage?* This is where your business can cut competitors off at the pass. You may want to choose a goal that could help counteract your competitor's initiatives. The Follett Corporation, a Pennsylvania-based maker of ice machines, realized that a competitor could gain a business advantage if it modularized its line. Instead, Follett decided to make the improvements in its own business.

5. *Do our customers have an unmet need or unfulfilled expectation?*
Toyota recognized the market value of a luxury car priced well below
cars of comparable quality and elegance. As a result Toyota created the
Lexus, a car designed for people who could afford the highest-priced
cars but recognize the Lexus as a bargain. Toyota saw a market niche
and filled it.

**Proficiencies Needed for Success in the Company As It Will
Become.**   Once you've determined what is important to your organization's future business success, you're ready to identify what you need
to do to increase your value to the company. Assess where you currently are in terms of where your company will be in the years ahead.
Ask yourself the following three questions:

1. *Will your knowledge and skills keep pace with the company?*   If you
feel unprepared for anticipated changes, try to ready yourself by seeking help before you need it. For example, if you expect your company to
downsize, hone those skills that make you uniquely valuable to a lean
organization and empower you to successfully assume more responsibilities.

2. *When working with people, do you have the ability to help them give their
best?*   If you aren't sure, try to get feedback or insights from coworkers
and friends. One of our clients sought such feedback and was surprised
to find that his coworkers found him a prickly bear of a boss. He worked
so diligently on changing his behavior that his employees gave him a
special achievement award for his changed demeanor. If you are not an
empowering manager, you may want to create a learning plan to
address that shortcoming.

3. *Are you learning as fast as your counterpart at your key competitor?*   If
the answer is not obvious, you may have to do some digging to find out
what your competitor is up to. When Ted Hutton became president of
Waverly, Inc., he wanted to know how he stacked up against his competition. He met with each major competitor's CEO and gained a good
sense of what he and they most needed to learn.

Selecting a Learning Goal.   Once you've determined where you
think your company is headed and what proficiencies you need, you're
ready to pick a learning goal. The most important learning question is:
*What should I know or be able to do that would give me and my business a dis-
tinct competitive advantage?* Your learning goal should be as clear and
concrete as possible so that you can formulate specific action steps and

measure your accomplishments. The goal should bring value to the business and to you, and you should be committed to achieving it.

The best development goal is one that will bring high value both to your business and to you. If you select a goal that provides value only to your business, you won't be motivated to achieve it. If you select a goal that benefits only you, your organization will view it as irrelevant. The Learning Value Index in Exhibit 3-2 can help you evaluate your goal.

Don't try to reinvent the wheel every time you go to learn something. Decide what is the best use of your time and be ready to make use of what other people have learned. When John Hardinger of Du Pont identifies a learning need he asks himself: "Is this something I need to learn, [something] that I need to get someone else in my organization to learn, or do I need to buy this expertise from someone who already has developed it?"

Brainstorming Learning Possibilities.   List each of your learning goals. Then brainstorm by pushing yourself to consider unexplored options. Ask yourself: What learning goal could I identify that is better than any goal I've identified so far? After you've brainstormed your list, star the two or three that have the greatest potential. Then go back and use the Learning Value Index to see which has the greatest value.

The last step is to write your learning goal in final form. It should be concrete enough that you will know when you have accomplished it, large enough so you will feel stretched in pursuing it, and small enough so you have a real shot at achieving it.

Where to Look for Learning Goals.   If you were to dissect your job, isolating the many components that are vital to your success, you'd find stimulating learning goals in almost every aspect of your work. Often a learning opportunity will leap out at you. You may want to examine your strengths and weaknesses to see if they suggest a learning target—one that either builds on your strengths or overcomes your weakness.

	Learning Value Index				
Learning Goal	*Low*				*High*
Value to Business	1	2	3	4	5
Value to Self	1	2	3	4	5
Your Commitment	1	2	3	4	5

Exhibit 3-2. The Learning Value Index—an aid in evaluating your learning goal.

Learning Goals Are Chosen to Enhance a Current Assignment.
In most assignments a manager must grow or derail. By being the first
to recognize where they need to develop a competence or knowledge,
managers can avoid career downtime and major headaches.

Peter Gilson recalled how, in 1972, with 9 years of sales and marketing
experience under his belt, Du Pont, the company he worked for at the
time, transferred him to Brazil to manage its emerging textile business.
He would be responsible for overseeing the construction of what would
be a $28 million Lycra manufacturing facility. And at the request of the
Brazilian government, all of his employees would be local residents.

"This was a very significant promotion for me," said Gilson, who now
is executive vice president of Physicians Support Systems, a Pennsylvania-
based health care management company. "The problem I faced moving
down there was, I not only lacked manufacturing experience and didn't
know one end of a spinneret from another, but I didn't speak one word of
Portuguese. So the issue was, `How do you confront what is an extraordi-
nary career opportunity and solve these two sizable issues?'"

To learn the language Gilson and his wife Peggotty attended total
immersion language classes for a month. "The day I arrived in Brazil we
had a presentations ceremony before 800 people, and I delivered it totally in Portuguese," Gilson said. "It probably was the worst speech anybody had ever given in their life, but in the end I got a rousing, standing ovation just for trying."

To learn the manufacturing skills he needed, Gilson spent 3 months in
Du Pont's Waynesboro plant where Lycra was manufactured in the
United States. He spent the first month as an operator, "and that's the
way I learned which end of the spinneret the fiber comes out of." The
second month he worked with an engineer, and the third month he
worked in cost accounting. "I was absolutely learning by doing."

Learning Goals Are Chosen to Prepare for Future Assignments.
Bill Hutton joined the Follett Corporation as director of operations and
was made president 3 years later. Even before he was hired, Hutton prepared for future promotions by identifying two potential mentors
within the company. Once he came on board, he frequently turned to
those mentors for guidance and inspiration. He developed a personal
reading and study program that focused on manufacturing, and he also
attended some of the premier training programs in the country. At the
same time he pursued a master's degree in business.

"To be honest with you, I'm continually preparing for the next assignment," he says. "I think in every position that I've ever held I've looked
for ways to really develop myself, and I've looked for various resources
to try and get that done."

Learning Goals Are Chosen to Eclipse the Competition.
Nothing in business is more fun than developing the ability to take market share from a strong competitor.

When Thom Harvey became CEO of a small waste management company in Delaware, he faced strong competitors. These included locally owned businesses and two national companies with deep pockets. He decided to take market share from his competition by offering excellent service and demonstrating positive ethics. He succeeded beyond his imagination. In the intervening years he bought out one of his major national competitors and acquired several local rivals as well.

Learning Goals Are Chosen to Improve People and Leadership Skills.   Many managers need to focus on the interpersonal side of their work. Jim Riscigno, an executive vice president with Club Corporation of America, decided he wanted to mold his senior managers into an empowered team. Previously they primarily were recognized or rewarded for their individual contribution. Riscigno fostered teamwork by forming small teams of senior managers to solve important problems. They met to reflect on how they worked together, and they were accountable to each other.

Most importantly, feedback from his senior managers led Riscigno to change his own leadership style. His senior managers identified how he needed to change to allow them to become empowered.

Learning Goals Are Chosen to Increase Awareness.   We all have blind spots. Even when you're an excellent learner in most aspects of life and work, there may be areas of awareness that need improvement. John Hardinger at Du Pont gives an example of how he was forced to increase his awareness by the corporate vision of Du Pont CEO Ed Woolard. Noting the growing diversity in a changing marketplace, Woolard insisted that his company put a high value on diversity.

To help achieve those ends, top managers were encouraged to join small discussion groups to address sexism and racial issues in the workplace. For Hardinger, it was like "walking into a new lake." At first he felt he was drowning, but he emerged a much stronger manager, more aware of the needs of all his employees, and more aware of himself. Hardinger tells his story:

> I have to say that I didn't want to learn, and I was pushed to do it anyway. Our chairman said that we were going to value all kinds of people and their capabilities. I thought we were already doing that.
> I thought it was somebody else he was talking to, but I signed up for what we call a core group, a small group of people from all over

the company who represent the wide diversity of men, women, and minorities we have within Du Pont. I didn't want to be the first one to test whether it was a career-ending event to say I already know all that, so I started going to the meetings.

I have to admit that I was closed-minded about it. I did not believe that there were problems and issues unique to women and minorities. As far as I was concerned, they picked out a group of militant women and blacks who were left-wingers and viewed Du Pont's role in life as a social institution to drive social change.

I mean, I was about as typical a conservative, white male, mid-westerner as you could find, and I just didn't believe it.

I've changed, but I had to be forced to change. I kept going to the discussion groups primarily because not going would have potentially damaged my career.

What a powerful experience it was. Then you reach a point where you go over the hill and you start letting go of a lot of your earlier perceptions because you realize that these people aren't left-wing militants because women in my organization are telling me the same thing.

My staff is all white men. I became very convinced that there was a real issue here. I'd come back from the core meetings to the staff of white men and say, `Do you think there's a problem here?' And they'd say, `Oh hell no. Our women—or blacks, or whoever it was—all love working here. They're all doing great.'

So I'd start again in an attempt to show that we had a real issue here on how people felt valued and how they could contribute.

It was absolutely necessary for me to be pushed [to deal with issues of women and minorities] and I've learned a tremendous amount from it.

Learning Goals Are Chosen to Meet the Customers' Needs. We said learning goals often will "leap out at you" during the course of your work. That's what happened to Peter Gilson, who gave this example of the importance of learning to meet customers' needs. After working at Du Pont, he joined W. L. Gore & Associates and had been there less than a year when a few customers started complaining about leaky Gore-tex. The complaints were sporadic, and Gore researchers were unable to duplicate the problem in the laboratory.

"The important thing to remember is having heard about this problem in isolated instances, and as a growing concern as the product matured, we had never been able to duplicate the phenomena of getting this Gore-tex to leak inside a laboratory," said Gilson, who was the business leader in the Gore-tex fabrics division. "The pore size of Gore-tex is 20,000 times smaller than a drop of water. So you need some sort of external pressure for water to actually force itself through this membrane. The final analysis indicated that although we couldn't duplicate the problem, we were sure it was real."

Gore thought the leaks resulted from customers who hadn't sealed the seams properly, but then Gilson got a letter from a mountain guide who was leading a small group of campers into the Sierras when they were hit by a storm.

"He had been trapped in a freak snowstorm in the Sierras and had come very close to freezing to death because our product leaked," Gilson said. "The guy said he had seam-sealed his garment perfectly, according to our instructions, and yet had horrible leakage problems. And he sent us his garment. It was at that point that we agreed to recall the product."

What Gore researchers discovered was that over a period of time the oils in perspiration clogged the pore structure of the membrane and caused the material to leak, a problem that was easy to solve in second generation Gore-tex.

Gore ended up taking back roughly $4.3 million in products, a huge, difficult decision for a small company that had about $6 million in sales.

"What I learned from the experience was that you have to listen to what your customers are telling you, and you have to listen very carefully," Gilson said. "If we had listened and had come to recognize that these problems were real, we probably would have brought our product off the market a lot earlier and at a lot less cost. But because we couldn't duplicate the phenomena, we were forced to wait. The lesson from all of this was, listen to your customers, work closely with them, and the problem solving is usually pretty simple."

Learning Goals Are Chosen to Keep Yourself on the Learning Edge of Your Profession.   A director of executive development for a high-technology company wants to stay on the cutting edge of her field. She participates in networks of peers from other companies, conducts research, writes articles, and continually explores the learning needs of her company's executive population. A rich stream of information and people flow through her work, enabling her to make a distinctive contribution and giving her a definite advantage over many other executives in her organization.

Learning Goals Are Chosen to Adapt to a Changing Business Environment.   Reduced cycle time is another example from John Hardinger at Du Pont, who says that for managers, this often means shortening the decision-making process. Hardinger recognized that he had to learn to make quicker decisions. He explains:

"Time is everything. And there are some people who have not learned to deal with the concept of a shorter cycle time. I don't know if they are unwilling to make decisions with less information and more risk, but they are not competitive in their professions.

"The decision-making process takes too long and some people are simply not going to learn to make a decision without all the support and information they have available to them.

"I don't mean to make it a reflection of age, but we all grew up *without* a sense of urgency. We could take a year to make a decision and it did not seem to make a lot of difference. Let's get all the facts and study, study. We don't have that luxury anymore. We have a cadre of people coming out of business schools who know how to get the relevant facts—not all the facts—and make decisions.

"I'm used to having a whole lot more facts available to me than I'm capable of having today, so I've got to determine what's relevant, get it, and decide. I'm used to having the luxury of reading a novel before I make a decision. Now I have to read Cliff Notes."

Time for Goal Achievement.   We have found that goals that take 4 months to accomplish work best. If the time required is shorter, that's fine. If your goal will take longer, then break it into smaller pieces and select a milestone along the way that you can attain in 4 months.

By committing your learning goals to an *annual cycle,* learning will more likely become a lifetime phenomenon. It helps to divide the year into three parts, beginning with January 1, May 1, and September 1. When people are setting New Year's resolutions, you can set a learning goal for your winter months. The second date can be the kickoff for your summer goal, and when school begins in the fall, you can begin working on your third goal for continued learning and development.

To serve as a reminder, at the beginning of each year highlight the three days—the first of January, May, and September—on your calendar and write: Begin New Learning.

One Goal at a Time.   There may be more than one suitable learning goal to choose from, but pick *one* only. Looking at development plans we often see managers working on three or four development targets at the same time. Pursuing multiple goals slows their progress and diminishes their commitment to each individual goal. This scattershot approach to goal setting results from a manager's inability to identify and crystallize what is most important to learn or improve.

Once you understand what is important to your business's success in the next 2 to 3 years and you have chosen a goal to promote your success in the company as it will become, it's time to move to the next step.

Step 2: *Map* Out How You'll Achieve Your Goal

At this point you may be saying to yourself: "Okay, I have the gist of it. I know what I want to do, so I'll get started." Don't. You *must* have a learning map and you *must* give it some thought. We've found that without a specific, detailed plan, learning remains accidental rather than deliberate, and too much time is wasted. It becomes difficult to measure progress, and the learning goal ultimately gets tossed aside.

The Plan for Learning.   Small details are important for the success of big ideas. Don't skimp on the particulars of your plan. Just as an explorer seeks to find or create the best map possible before setting sail, it is just as important to have an excellent map before you begin your learning journey. If you are unwilling to commit the time to mapping out a plan, you certainly won't commit the time to accomplishing your goal. When writing out your learning strategy, go into as much detail as you possibly can.

We've found that the good learners intuitively create a learning map or plan. Even if they've never verbalized it, they have a detailed plan in their head. We want you to carry it in your head *and* commit it to paper.

Commit it to your computer as well. By filing your learning plan in your computer system, you can easily refer to it, amend it, assess your progress, and check off what you have done. Just like a traveler, you can determine where you are in your trip, whether you are on track, and whether you need to change your destination.

After several years of trial and error and listening to what works, we have identified the most important elements in an effective learning plan. This learning plan is outlined in Exhibit 3-3. If any element is left out, the plan's effectiveness and chance for success diminishes. (An excellent example of a completed learning plan is presented in Exhibit 3-4.)

Your Learning Goal.   List the goal you selected in Step 1. Kay Whitmore, Kodak's CEO, cautions that it is essential to choose your goal very carefully:

"I think most people can distinguish important things from unimportant things, but distinguishing relatively subtle differences between the most important and the second most important is really a skill that needs to be developed. Only by consistently doing the most important thing do you get the most important work done. If you are forever doing the third most important thing, you'll finish your life having done a lot of the third most important things.

Learning Plan

1. Learning Goal

2. Specific Action Steps (with Completion Dates)

3. Resources Needed

4. Barriers Anticipated

5. Measurement of Results

6. Future Benefits to the Business

7. Future Benefits to Me (What will I learn or improve?)

8. Planned Completion Date _____

_____   _____
Signature   Date

Exhibit 3-3. This plan can be used to map out how you'll achieve your learning goal.

"You need to be a bit rigorous in asking, `What is the most important thing I need to do today?' `What is the most important thing I need to do over the next three months?' `What is the most important thing I need to do in this phase of my life?' A lot of that has to do with what you want to accomplish."

Specific Action Steps. Identify the action steps you need to reach your goal. Remember, it is important to *write down as many action steps* *as possible.* A high correlation exists between learning plans that are carried through to completion and those that begin with the most detailed action steps. You'll know you have enough action steps when you have a road map that can get you from the idea of what you want to learn to having actually learned it. You should have at least one action step, no matter how small, that you can accomplish by the end of the week. This will give you the incentive to get started. This is also a quick way to confirm your commitment and the fact that you can take charge of your learning.

It is very important to put a date by each action step. Setting completion dates will:

- Create time pressure to achieve each step
- Give you another way to set realistic goals
- Provide an excellent way to measure your progress

If you do not make a commitment to accomplishing each step by a particular time, it is likely that the press of everyday business will drive out your learning time. You may also want to block out a certain amount of time each week or month to focus on your learning.

Bob Hall, vice president of silicon solar cell development at AstroPower, is a wizard at simplifying complex projects. He breaks a large project down into the smallest pieces possible—action steps that are *manageable* and *measurable*, which he compares to bite-size M&M candies.

At this point, ask whether you have listed all the steps you will need. Art Beard of Du Pont asks the question this way: "What has to be true or be in place for your goal to be accomplished?" Look at the action steps you have just created. They should be detailed enough to guarantee success. You may find that you need to identify still more steps or to break a large step into smaller parts.

Anticipate the consequences of each action step. If you are successful and get the expected results, then you're on target. If you are unsuccessful, then you need to reassess your action plan and your commitment to it.

It helps to ask at the 1-week, 1-month, and 4-month marks:

- Did I accomplish the tasks identified as my action steps? If I did not, why not?
- Did my actions have the intended impact?
- Do I feel that I have learned something?
- Can someone else recognize an improvement because of what I have learned (i.e., new knowledge, greater revenues or reduced costs, bet-

ter morale, new use of time, change of behavior, number of people affected)?

The purpose of documenting your success as you progress toward your goal is twofold: To keep you from straying from your learning plan, and to further clarify your objectives.

Your Resources. Resources could include someone in your organization, a library, a particular course, a professor, a visit to another company, or whatever you find helpful. Be creative. For example, one senior manager wanted to improve his financial skills. During a 4-month period he used the following resources: two self-study courses; a week-long seminar at the Stanford University Business School; a tutorial from his chief financial officer; two books bought at a local college bookstore; and discussions with 10 people who had the kind of financial skills he wanted to learn.

Anticipated Barriers. Identify potential barriers, such as lack of time, organizational resistance, or resistance from a key person. By anticipating problems, you can construct action steps to overcome them or identify a resource that can help you get around them. In reality, a major barrier may be yourself and your willingness to commit the time and effort to accomplish the goal you set for yourself. To help make the time, block it out on your calendar and protect it from outside intrusions. Keep your learning in the "Must Do Today" file instead of relegating it to the "Can Wait Til Tomorrow" pile.

One manager I know refers to his learning days as "Chicago Days". When someone calls for him, his secretary says, "He's in Chicago." It's a shame that deception may be needed to counteract the persistent, wrong-headed attitude that learning should take place away from working hours.

Luckily, that attitude is changing. As we will see in Part 3, many forward-looking, admired companies are now asking managers to keep track of their learning time. You may want to keep track of yours. On a calendar or in a learning file created in your computer, you could note how many hours a week you devote to pursuing your learning goal.

Barriers to learning will be discussed in depth in Chapter 5. If your mind seems stuck on the problems rather than the advantages of learning, you may want to skip ahead to that chapter and then come back.

Measuring Results. Project yourself into the future and use your imagination to establish measurement standards before you actually get started.

For example, Jake Brown, a manager at AstroPower, wanted to build an innovative machine; he decided that his measurement would be a photograph of the machine in operation by his self-imposed deadline. The picture was to serve as concrete proof that he had achieved his goal.

The primary purpose for measuring results is for you to think through the impact of your goal. How will it make a positive contribution to specific people, solve a particular problem, or create a unique opportunity? You should be able to concretely visualize the completed goal and how you will measure whether it has been accomplished.

Benefits to the Business.   If you selected your goal well, it should be easy to identify the value it will bring to your business. You should be able to cite ways it will increase your competitive position, improve the satisfaction of those working in the organization, benefit your customers, reduce costs, or improve revenues. These benefits are also evident in the previous section, where you measure your success.

Benefits to You.   Here you can identify how you will change for the better. Indicate how you expect to improve your capabilities, feel a greater sense of confidence in your work, or increase your job security by becoming more valuable to your company.

Signature and Date.   Your signature at the end of the form is a symbolic way to acknowledge your commitment to accomplishing your learning goal within a fixed time limit.

Step 3: *Act* on Your Plan

The third step is to put the plan into action, starting with the first specific action listed on your learning plan. My grandfather used to say, "Thought without action is useless." You don't want your planning to be for naught. Begin working on your goal as soon as possible to reinforce your commitment to achieving it. Start immediately!

Within the first week you should accomplish the first task you set for yourself in the action portion of your plan. Measuring against your intermediate 1-month goal can keep you on track.

Refer to Your Plan Monthly.   Make sure to refer to your plan the last Friday of every month. Highlight it on your calendar. You should take a few moments and hold a progress meeting with yourself to review the past month and plan for the next. If your plan is kept in your computer, it's that much easier to refer to and amend.

Some people get as far as making a complete plan but then neglect to refer to it. Although the act of creating a plan can lead to more learning than would have occurred without it, you'll only get the full benefit if you keep the details fresh in your mind.

Get a Partner.   We recommend you find a learning partner. A partner can initially help you identify your best goal. You should share your goal with this person and tell him or her why you want to achieve it; and you should ask for advice to enhance your goal. As you work on your plan, your partner can provide encouragement. Commit to being accountable to your partner the first Monday of each month as a way to keep track of the progress you are making on your goal.

Use a Visual Reminder.   Again, ask, "What has to happen or be in place for my goal to be accomplished?" Make sure those actions take place. You should display some visible token in your office or home to remind you of your learning goal.

We give participants in our learning programs a small checkered flag to put on their desks as a symbol of their finish line. We also give out baseballs to remind people that it's time to play hardball with their learning, that learning will take a major league effort, that being successful requires teamwork, and that we hope each person will hit a home run.

Some managers carry a silver dollar as a symbol of their commitment to invest in themselves. Others type out their goals and display them in a Lucite frame on their desks as a daily reminder.

Keep a Learning Journal.   A learning journal can be an effective way to record and sustain your learning. At the end of each month, write a paragraph on what you accomplished during that time period and how you learned. By the end of the year you can go back and reflect accurately on the progress you have made.

It's best to keep your journal in a computer file. That way you'll have easy access and can make printouts as needed.

Your Learning Rate.   A month or so into your action phase, compare the rate at which you are learning to how you were learning before beginning the process. Ted Lingenheld, headmaster of The Tatnall School, a private school in Wilmington, Delaware, uses the image of a management team running on a race track. Although they begin as a group, the results of their learning initiatives become apparent as the pack begins to string out. The best learners achieve the most in the shortest period of time and lead the pack. Those who don't learn are left straggling behind.

By measuring your learning rate you can determine whether you are:

- A learning leader who is achieving results at a rate greater than your peers.
- A middle-of-the-pack learner who is learning at the same rate as others in your organization.
- A learning laggard who may be "lapped" by his boss and others. This is particularly true of those who do not commit the time to achieving their development goals.

The danger of falling into the learning laggard category is derailing. Learning at the same rate as others means that the opportunity for greater responsibility, promotion, and increased compensation may remain a dream.

Step 4: *Review* and Evaluate What and How You Learned

Next, evaluate what you accomplished by implementing your learning plan and, more importantly, *how* you learned. We rarely take time to reflect on our experience in a way that helps us become even better at it.

The evaluation need not take long, but it can be extremely powerful. For example, after each victory, Napoleon would walk the battlefield and view it from his opponent's perspective. At every point where his opponent made a significant decision, Napoleon would project himself into his opponent's position, asking himself what he would have done if the tables had been turned.

Napoleon took his mental exercise one step further by then imagining how he would have responded to the way he, Napoleon, would have fought the battle—not unlike trying to play chess by yourself. This critical evaluation gave him valuable insights on how to fight better in future engagements.

When you evaluate what you learned, the learning sticks. Jewell Westerman of Mercer Management Consulting tells of his son's experience in two classes at Harvard. He took one course on Russian society, taught by a very authoritative and dictatorial professor. Another course was on family abuse.

In the family abuse class, the professor came in one day with a large rubber doll and began yelling and screaming at the class, saying, "What the hell are you taking this course for? Who the hell do you think you are?" As the class gasped, he pulled the head off the doll and threw it against the wall. Then he threw the doll across his lap and started beating it.

After his tantrum, the professor stood before the class and asked, "What did you learn?" He went to the easel and wrote down everyone's response.

In the Russian society class, lectures were the standard delivery and learning was by rote.

"I remember my son had a test scheduled for the next day so I sat and drilled him," Westerman recalled. "He knew back to 1810 which revolution took place when and who led it. So the other day I said, `What happened in 1830 in Russia?' He didn't know.

"Then I said, `Well, why do people beat their kids?' And he knew the answer.

"Corporations are very much the same way. There is no substitute for sitting down with somebody and saying, `What have you learned from this job?'"

Step 5: *Target* Your Next Learning Goal

Lastly, target your next learning goal, making conscious use of what you have recently learned and accomplished. Incorporate these new skills into your repertoire of abilities and use them as an added tool as you begin your next learning project. You want your new learning to become so much a part of your business practice that it becomes automatic. Once it becomes incorporated, your new knowledge or capabilities will benefit you on an ongoing, spontaneous basis as you work toward future learning targets.

The progression of capability displayed in Figure 3-2 says that, initially, we may not be aware of a weakness we should overcome. We then become aware of the change we should make. Next, we begin to use the new capabilities in a highly conscious fashion, much like a golfer trying a new swing. Then the new swing becomes part of our muscle memory and we can use it automatically.

Once your new learning has been incorporated into your repertoire of abilities and you have completed your evaluation, you then can begin the goal-setting process again, confident that you now have a valuable way to increase your contribution, an approach that you can use for the rest of your career.

A Completed Learning Plan

Robert Moore is president of Bostonian Shoe, a $80 million company that makes and sells men's dress shoes. Although the company com-

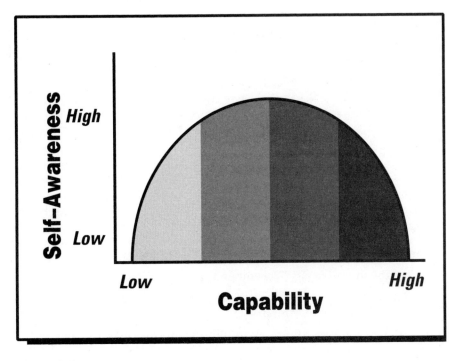

Figure 3-2. Learning curve.

petes in a stagnant marketplace, Moore is committed to achieving a 20 percent a year growth rate. The question is how? And that question led to his learning goal: to increase his expertise and his company's capabilities in point-of-purchase displays. Moore mapped out a plan to achieve his learning goal. See Exhibit 3-4.

The Results.   In June 1992, Moore sat down with me and reflected on his learning plan and the results. He had accomplished many of his objectives. Bostonian's point-of-purchase displays in the Macy's stores in the northeast improved dramatically, a change confirmed by the before and after photographs taken at each store. At each site Bostonian had achieved immediate brand identification, which its competitors had not. Because Bostonian began working more closely with store personnel, Moore's plan also brought about improved customer service and customer relationships.

What Moore had not anticipated from his learning plan was the tremendous business impact of creating a position he originally conceived as a "visual tech rep." The job called for someone to pay monthly visits to each Macy's store to make sure the display looked crisp and

Robert Moore's Learning Plan

Learning Goal

To learn the elements necessary to establish the finest, high-quality, point-of-purchase Bostonian Shoe displays in the industry at R. H. Macy's northeast division stores. There are 47 stores in the region, and Bostonian represents 25 percent of Macy's gross shoe sales volume and 10 percent of their total men's sales. We are a top supplier, yet our visual displays are second to other competitive brands, including Timberland, Cole Haan, Polo, Bally, Bass. My objective is to improve these displays to become the finest in their departments and serve as the benchmark for other Bostonian point-of-purchase improvement efforts across the country.

Specific Action Steps (with Completion Dates)

1. Establish objectives (December 1)
2. Benchmarking—store visits and photographing of top displays throughout chain (January 1)
3. Interview key competitors to understand process and tactics used to achieve their results and effective displays (January 15)
4. Interview R. H. Macy's visual staff to understand the policies and practices of their department (January 15)
5. Detail tactics and action plan (February 1)
6. Plan rollout (February 1)
7. Completion of program (March 15)

Resources I Need

1. Internal staff—store visits, photography
2. A public relations firm
3. My time commitment
4. Macy's management approval and support
5. Financial resources to support rollout of displays, materials, etc.
6. Cooperation of competitors during benchmarking process

Exhibit 3-4. A learning plan mapped out by Robert B. Moore, Jr., president of Bostonian Shoe.

Barriers I Anticipate

1. Macy's reluctance to rework or revise department visuals—local store management; New York City visual and merchandising staff

2. Bostonian sales support team, who focus on sales rather than other activities because of straight commission compensation program

3. Competitors' reluctance to supply information about their programs and practices

4. Time restraints

How Results Will Be Measured

1. Before and after photographs at each store

2. Sales performance before and after displays are established

3. Interviews with key Macy's visual executives after displays are set up

4. May 1 audit of displays and photography of each department

How Goal Will Benefit the Business

1. Improved brand awareness

2. Better in-store positioning and increased shelf space

3. More retail sales

4. Increased wholesale orders

5. Improved R. H. Macy's/Bostonian relations; strengthened strategic alliance

How Goal Will Benefit Me

1. Improved discipline of planning and program processes before implementation

2. Establish benchmark display program to rollout and deploy throughout major U.S. dealers for remainder of the year

Planned Completion Date

March 15 and maintain throughout year

Exhibit 3-4. (*Continued*)

attractive. But during the implementation of Moore's learning plan, the job expanded significantly. From benchmarking with a competitor, Moore learned that the visual tech rep could play an important role in training customers—in this case, Macy's shoe sales force.

Moore realized that this representative, who would be going to Macy's stores on a routine basis, had the opportunity to enhance the learning of the shoe departments' employees. He hired Martha Lemons, who makes a point of talking to the shoe sales force at Macy's to find out their most pressing business problem. As she travels to the retailer's other stores, she relates the problem and inquires about similar experiences. When she finds a Macy's employee who has faced the same problem and solved it, she serves as an intermediary by putting the problem solver in touch with the employee needing help. Because she is attuned to needs that don't necessarily impact her product, Bostonian is now seen as a valuable source of solutions as well as shoes.

Additional Short-Term Benefits.   The benefits to Bostonian and to Moore went beyond improved brand identification and customer goodwill. To measure the consequences of his learning plan, Moore kept monthly data on the impact of the new point-of-purchase displays. As a result, Bostonian has a breakdown of the number of shoes sold, including size and style, at each store. About a month after this initiative began, Moore got a shocking call. Macy's came to Bostonian with the news that total Bostonian sales had declined in the northeast region and Macy's wanted to order less for the next season. Moore and Lemons immediately turned to the store-by-store statistics they had been gathering as part of Moore's learning plan. Because of the significantly better factual data, they were able to detect the problem within 24 hours. Macy's had not ordered a full complement of core shoe sizes. Rather than sitting on the shelves gathering dust, Bostonian had actually sold out of the most popular sizes. The new displays had created demand that Macy's inventory could not meet! Because Bostonian had the right information at its fingertips, Macy's made an immediate decision that helped both companies. The retailer ordered 8000 more pairs of shoes for immediate delivery.

Long-Term Benefits.   The early success of this learning plan and a changing marketplace suggest a new configuration for Bostonian's future sales force. Currently the sales organization is divided into regions with salespeople calling on large and small accounts with samples of the newest styles. But large accounts, such as Macy's and Dillards, now do central buying, and the actual purchasing is done through electronic data transfer without the involvement of a salesperson. Consequently, most of Bostonian's future sales organization could operate like this: A few high-level sales directors call on major customers, with the actual purchasing done not through salespeople but through computer communication. Because fewer salespeople are needed, Bostonian can add value at the store level by hiring visual tech reps to provide all its customers with the service and attention that Martha Lemons is providing Macy's. The improved relationships would result in a competitive advantage for Bostonian, and everyone involved—Bostonian, the shoe salesperson, and the store—would benefit from increased shoe sales.

Moore's learning plan helped improve Bostonian's relationship with a major customer, and it is well on the way to transforming how the company will do business for years to come. Moore's experience demonstrates the tremendous opportunities available when managers enthusiastically take charge of their own learning.

The following learning tips summarize much of the discussion in this chapter. Some examples of learning goals are listed in Exhibit 3-5.

Learning Tips

- Make a commitment to maximize your learning at work.

- Identify a learning goal that stretches your abilities and makes you more valuable to your company.

- Write out your learning plan in detail. Don't skimp. Note your goal, all the steps needed to reach it, what resources you'll need, barriers you anticipate, and the benefits to yourself and your business.

- Begin working toward your goal right away. Don't let procrastination cool your enthusiasm.

- Create a "learning file" in your computer system. In it keep a copy of your learning plan, your learning journal, and the amount of time you spend intentionally learning at work.

- Work with a partner for needed feedback and to help you stay on track.

- Take time to evaluate what you learned and how you learned it. Such reflection makes reaching your next learning goal that much easier.

Learning Goals

CEOs

- To crystalize and communicate the future vision of the company
- To create an excellent strategic plan
- To change a leadership style to meet the demands of a company that has grown in size and complexity

Vice Presidents

- To learn to transfer responsibilities to others to create time for higher-value tasks
- To develop one's subordinates more effectively
- To work more effectively with women and minorities
- To gain skills in a new functional area
- To hire more effectively
- To gain a customer's perspective
- To correct an interpersonal problem that could cause the manager to derail

Managers

- To learn to influence the work of others in the organization
- To learn how to become a more effective leader
- To fill a knowledge void that prevents a person from making better decisions
- To soften an abrasive personality
- To learn how to sell both internally and externally

Exhibit 3-5. Examples of goals set—and met—by participants in planned learning sessions conducted by Wick and Company.

4

Your Learning Toolbox: Five Power Tools for Learning

Just as carpenters need the tools of their trade, managers need tools for their work—that is, specific tools for learning. In this chapter we present five powerful learning tools that you can use throughout the course of your learning plan:

1. *Visualization* to make your vision become reality
2. *The Learning Ladder* to help you identify which learning rung you are on
3. *Learning Star* to recognize your learning pattern
4. *Learning from Mistakes* to gain yardage from a fumble
5. *Benchmarking* to learn from the best

Visualization

Picture yourself being successful at work. Sit back in your chair and close your eyes. What is it that you've done? You've measurably increased quality, completed a major acquisition, resolved a complicated personnel problem, implemented a new marketing strategy, reduced cycle time, moved into a larger job.

Once you have your picture, ask yourself: *What has to be true or in place for this to happen?* It is a question we'll turn to again and again in this section. Your answer dictates how you go about achieving the success you visualized.

We all use spontaneous visualization everyday, whether it's picturing how we'll be greeted when we return home from a business trip or looking at blueprints and imagining how the new factory will look upon completion.

The tool we suggest is deliberate visualization, a concept that, under a variety of names, has long been used as a learning aid. *Guided imagery* is the term used by Dana Maxfield, a contributing author of *Learning to Learn Across the Life Span* (Robert M. Smith and Associates, Jossey-Bass, San Francisco, 1990). She defines it as "consciously created visualization, guided by information."

Guided imagery is frequently used in sports training. Baseball players imagine the ball to be twice its actual size. Jack Nicklaus always imagines the golf ball falling into the cup.

Here we offer visualization as a tool to promote learning. It is based on the ideas and visualization programs developed by Art Beard, an internal consultant at Du Pont Company. Beard joined the use of visualization and a planning process to bring what you visualize into reality. Beard has used his system of pictorial visions to promote and stretch learning, inside and outside of Du Pont, in this country and in Europe, with many companies and nonprofit organizations. He described the process to us in a series of interviews. We have condensed his comments as follows.

Don't Be Inhibited.   Beard's process requires that you actually draw what you've visualized, but don't let your lack of artistic talent steer you away from this tool. Maybe you're no Rembrandt, but you don't need to be. Many adults are embarrassed to draw pictures, equating drawing with child's play. They think adults should express themselves with words. Yet pictures have power, power both to illuminate and to stay imprinted on our memory. Pictures offer us a way to express something when we can't quite put it into words.

Pictures are easy for people to remember, whereas sentences are difficult to remember. Generally speaking, people can't recall more than a few simple sentences for a vision. Many businesses have complex verbal vision statements that no one remembers. Yet employees retain pictorial versions of the same visions with no problem.

A Picturing Exercise.   To get you in the right frame of mind, take out a pencil and sheet of paper and clear your head of other thoughts.

Now imagine your most important customer leaving work at the end of the day. First imagine that he or she, in a state of elation, walks into the door at home and says, "This was a really great day." Visualize what happened that day that brought on the happiness. What made it a great day? Draw the picture.

Then using the same scenario, imagine the customer to be in a state of extreme depression or discouragement and going home to say, "I really had a lousy day." Visualize what happened to cause that gloom. What made it so terrible? Draw the picture.

To do this exercise, you must first imagine the customer leaving, and then you must begin to image what happened to cause the mood. When you do that, videotapes of what might have happened start running through your mind. You are visualizing.

Then ask yourself, "Is there anything I could do, or the company could do, either to enhance the customer's positive experience or to reduce the negative experience? How can I cause more good days and fewer bad days?"

The questions lead to another visualization—a picture of the kind of superior value you or your company can deliver to the customer.

What You Should Try to Visualize

Beard's research has shown that the most powerful visions focus on providing superior value to your chosen markets or customers. Providing superior value may mean doing better than the competition, or it may mean doing better than what you yourself are now doing. Your chosen markets or customers may be external markets and customers, or they may be fellow employees, another department in your organization, or shareholders.

So before you begin, you must identify your customers and have a clear idea of what superior value you can provide. If you are working alone, a picture may immediately pop into your head. If not, you may want to talk to coworkers and those who will be affected by your learning plan. See Exhibit 4-1 for an example of visualizing.

Beard always suggests that customers participate in the visualizing process because creating a concrete vision requires an understanding of the customers' perspective. Since the customers themselves are the best source of information, their input leads to the most accurate picture of superior value.

Sessions to create a vision usually involve no more than 4 hours, and customers are happy to become involved. They are willing to participate because it is a novel experience for them and because they feel they can have an impact on the business.

Visualizing the Customer

Because the goal is to provide superior value, the visualization advocated by Art Beard always involves some aspect of marketing. One of the organizations Beard worked with, the Henry Francis du Pont Winterthur Museum in Delaware, wanted to learn how to reach a larger market.

Winterthur, the former home of Henry Francis du Pont, showcases American furniture and decorative arts from two centuries. It is surrounded by 200 acres of English landscape gardens.

One of the site's major market segments is the serious visitor who frequents the museum and expects to learn something useful about gardening or period furniture. In contrast, another market segment is the casual visitor who enjoys browsing for a couple of hours and goes home.

When asked to visualize the serious visitors receiving superior value from the museum, a local board member drew a series of pictures. Although he was no artist, he was uninhibited and prolific.

His first drawing showed a stick figure woman walking through the Winterthur grounds, observing the landscaping. Then he showed her attending a demonstration of furniture restoration.

The next scene showed the woman in her home giving her husband some ideas for restoring a piece that he had in his basement workshop. The next drawing showed the husband successfully completing the restoration project, while the woman went out and replicated some part of the Winterthur landscape on her own grounds.

The last scene was the key vision for Winterthur's marketing strategy. It made it clear to the museum's board and staff members that if they wanted to satisfy these serious customers, they had to provide not just historically interesting information but ideas that could be implemented at home.

Using the planning process, Winterthur developed a way to better serve those customers.

Exhibit 4-1. The customer must be distinctly identified to gain a clear idea of the superior value that can be provided.

The Current Client.   A recent experience I had with a bank illustrates the importance of a company recognizing its impact on customers.

The bank was managing money for my mother who had nurses around the clock. The lead nurse was given a checking account to pay the other nurses. Every month the bank put a minimum amount of money into the account, both so the rest of my mother's money could be better invested and so the risk of any misuse of the money would be reduced.

As a result of this policy, the nurses' checks bounced 10 or 15 times because the bank hadn't put enough money in the account. It came back to me that the nurses were frustrated and unhappy because of this. I went to the bank and told the person responsible that I wanted enough money put in the checking account so that not one more check would bounce!

Six weeks later it happened again. I got a call one night saying, "Cal, I hate to have to call you, but my check bounced, again."

The bank officer never understood that what made me happy at the end of the day was *not* getting phone calls from these people who were giving my mother superior service and who really counted on their paychecks.

Consequently, I didn't use that bank as the executor of the estate when my mother died, so their inability to visualize their customer hurt their bottom line.

The Internal Client.   Visualizing how your actions impact others inside your company—that is, your internal customers—has multiple benefits, from improving communication to creating better value for your external customers. This example comes from a session I held with sales and operations managers at Harvey & Harvey, Inc., a waste management company. The sales managers were asked what kinds of things would make members of the sales organization go home and say, "I've had a really bad day." They answered that they would say this when:

- They lost an important sale.
- A valued customer called up and said they didn't get their trash picked up at the agreed upon time.
- The billing for refuse pickup was incorrect.

When asked what kinds of things would make the operations people go home and say, "I've had a really bad day," the operations managers answered that they would say this when:

- The sales organization came down at 4 p.m. and said, "Schedule this for 8 a.m. tomorrow," and it had been sitting on the salesperson's desk since 10 a.m. Then all the scheduled routes had to be changed to accommodate the last minute addition.

- The sales organization wrote down the wrong address for the pickup, so a truck wandered around the countryside, chewing up valuable time.

After going through these exercises, both sides can look at the pictures and say, "Okay, how can we make each other's lives easier?" This process allows you to get down to very specific details.

The Potential Client.   One of Beard's visualization examples comes from a business that provides proofing systems to advertising agencies. Proofing systems simulate as yet undeveloped ad campaigns and make them real for potential clients. The purpose is to get the potential client interested in signing up with the advertising agency.

In this case, the picture of superior value shows clients asking for a contract with the ad agency three times as often as they currently do. Notice that the picture is entirely focused on the value to the customer. There is no sign of what the business is offering.

Now the question is, what has to be true or in place for this to happen? This leads to the question of how the business has to function, what components it has to have, in order to deliver that kind of value to the customer.

In this case, one of the questions Beard asked of the ad agency (the proofing systems' customer) was, "What would be the value to you, the ad agency, if our proofing systems resulted in your getting three times as many contracts with potential clients?"

The answer—in the millions of dollars—proved to be very motivational to the business providing proofing systems, because their company would clearly benefit from such a jump in their customers' revenues.

Creating Your Own Picture: Think Big

In the early 1980's Ron Zarowitz had a vision that stretched beyond what Chrysler Corp. could see. While grappling to put his 2-year-old daughter into a car seat, he came up with the idea of offering a built-in, fold-down version of the car seat as an option for consumers.

When Zarowitz became a manager at Chrysler in 1985, he constantly pushed for the built-in car seats, but the company wasn't interested. Zarowitz didn't give up. Finally, in 1987, top management agreed to at least discuss the idea. In 1991 the first built-in car seats appeared as a $200 option in 1992 Chrysler minivans. In December 1991, Chrysler said it was selling them as fast as it could make them. This is just one example of an opportunity delayed by the company's inability to visualize the market.

Zarowitz's vision proved to be one that differentiated his company. It was a vision he knew was worth fighting for.

Art Beard says that the best vision is one that has stretch in it. When using visualization, picture something that seems beyond what is possible. We are more inclined to aim for something we know we can achieve rather than to shoot for the stars. That way we avoid failure. "The single thing that inhibits us more than anything else is our own vision," Beard said.

Turning Your Picture into Reality

For your own vision, imagine the result you want and then work backwards, naming what has to be true or in place for it to happen. Once you get back to where you are today, you are ready to work your way through the steps consecutively.

This is contrary to most planning processes, which start with the present and work toward the future. In this process, you start in the future, visualizing yourself as having accomplished your goal, and work your way back to the present.

With your picture completed:

1. Get a large sheet of newsprint and a stack of gummed note pads.
2. Develop a time line, with vertical columns divided into either days, weeks, or months, depending on what is appropriate to your goal.
3. At the beginning of the sheet, write down the date that you begin the process.
4. At the end of the sheet write down your goal, which is the verbal summary of your picture.
5. Then, working backwards from your goal, write on the gummed notes each step required to accomplish your goal. Stick them on the newsprint at the appropriate spots. Be as detailed as possible.

The magic of the planning process is that it illuminates simply and in great detail what is needed to make your picture—your goal—a reality. It is easy to amend if new steps are recognized, and it provides immediate feedback as to whether you are accomplishing your steps on schedule.

For example, let's say your goal, 6 months from now, is to run a 10-kilometer race in under 50 minutes. You write down your goal at one end of the newsprint, and at the other end write today's date and your current status, which is 9-minute miles, or a 56-minute 10K.

Using vertical columns, divide your newsprint into months.

To run 6.2 miles in less than 50 minutes, you decide you need to do a trial 10K prior to your deadline, so you put "trial 10K" on a gummed note. Put it on month 5.

Prior to a trial 10K, you need to do speed work as well as long runs of at least 8 miles. So you write that down and attach it to month 4.

Prior to speed work and long runs of over 8 miles, you need to gradually build up your mileage and include some hill training to prepare for the speed work. That goes on months 1, 2, and 3.

Prior to hill training and increased mileage, you need to make sure to run at least 5 days a week, so that goes on every month.

As you look over your chart, you can fill in details as they come to you, such as setting intermediate speed goals and weekly mileage goals.

If you meet all of your monthly goals, in 6 months you're assured of crossing the finish line at a 10K race in under 50 minutes, for an average pace of 8 minutes a mile.

AstroPower, a solar energy company, used visualization to test, communicate, and teach its new corporate vision to all employees in less than 10 days. The picture was of each employee being familiar with the corporate vision and able to discuss how their specific work related to that vision.

The stated corporate vision was: Bringing solar electricity to everyone—at a price they can afford.

A team of people then asked, "What has to be true or be in place to make this picture come true?"

They came up with a number of steps:

- Prepare materials to be communicated to employees.
- Decide what to put on the materials.
- Decide whether employees should be able to comment on the vision.
- Decide who should receive the comments.
- Decide what response employees should get back from managers.
- Decide how vision should be communicated, written or orally or both. (They decided on both.)
- Decide who should lead oral discussions.
- Decide who should receive any written comments.

The team decided discussion leaders should meet with the president to discuss common questions and concerns. Then the leaders and president would identify the answers and send them back to employees within 24 hours.

AstroPower successfully communicated the vision within 10 days, and the company did it in a way that made the employees feel committed to a vision they had helped to create.

"Recent research says that entrepreneurs often have a picture of a future, desired state," Beard said. "It's one that they modify, but they always are working towards some kind of a vision. And that vision helps them sense what they should do in their business."

As you will discover in Part 4 of this book, the ability to create pictures is critical to the successful creation of a learning organization.

The Learning Ladder

When you are sick and drag yourself to a doctor's office, your doctor will diagnose your illness and prescribe a treatment. Similarly, you need a way to pinpoint trouble areas and take corrective action when your learning is lagging or failing. That way you'll remain a healthy learner.

The learning ladder is a diagnostic tool to help you understand where you currently are on your path to increased capabilities and how to get yourself back on track when you go off. See Figure 4-1.

Recognizing the Need

Learning begins with the recognition of the need to learn. Three situations commonly prompt people to admit they don't know it all:

1. Facing a tough challenge or problem they are not equipped to solve
2. Recognizing that something has not gone well, or expectations have not been met
3. Realizing they don't know enough to be successful in the future

Managers who are most gifted in their ability to learn and put their learning into action begin by recognizing what they don't know now but will need to know soon. Managers who are poor learners often miss loudly shouted cues from their environment that their learning is critical for future success and even survival. They fail to recognize the needs presented to them.

Tom Shaw, a vice president with Delmarva Power, faced a tough challenge when he moved from being head of utility production operations to vice president of the company's gas division. In his new position he was responsible not only for production but also for the functions of marketing, customer service, and distribution. In fact, he was running a

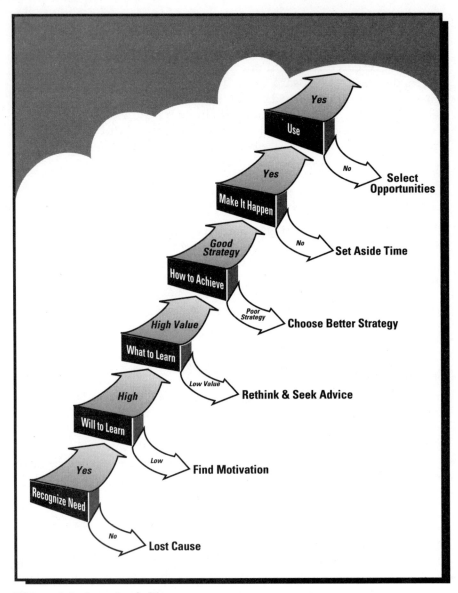

Figure 4-1. Learning ladder.

separate business line. Up to that point in his career Shaw had never run a free-standing business with its own profit and loss statement.

He recognized that without a more sophisticated understanding of finance, he couldn't run this business. Within 6 months he had learned so much about finance that he felt comfortable making presentations to the company's senior operating committee. He also had created a new financial information system that generated the cents per share his business unit contributed to the corporate parent.

Another example of recognizing the need to learn is Bruce Georgov, director of operations for Harvey & Harvey, Inc., a waste management company. Georgov correctly recognized that the roles were changing in his company's senior management. As the business expanded, the company's CEO no longer had time for daily business details, so he increasingly turned to his managers to assume leadership responsibility.

Georgov recognized the need to learn how to become a leader and to be ready to step into a significantly larger role than he had assumed in the past.

Diagnostic Questions

- Do you approach work with the assumption that you can learn something?
- Do you continually scan your work world to see what learning opportunities are out there?
- What currently frustrates you?
- What is not meeting your expectations?

Corrective Action

- Identify what you want to change and move to the next step.

If you can't identify anything you want to change and still don't see a pressing need to learn, your learning is a lost cause.

Demonstrating the Will

If you recognize the need to learn, the question is whether you have the will to learn. Here we offer examples of managers who display a continuing sense of curiosity, an urge to improve, and a desire to do things better or differently. These are managers with a high will to learn.

There are other managers who, even though they recognize the need to learn, appear to have little resolve to begin a learning process. For example, a vice president of finance knew that his company needed better financial reporting systems. The president and his colleagues clearly and continually told him so. He agreed there was a problem, yet he refused to take up the challenge. He had a low will to learn. Even though he was brilliant in other aspects of his work, his lack of will finally caused him to leave his company.

How you use your time can be a useful test of your will to learn. If you are a manager who works 50 hours a week for 50 weeks a year, you will spend 2500 hours at work. The question then becomes how many of these hours are spent in active learning, in investing in yourself so that you will become more valuable in the future. If you spend 10 percent of your time in active learning, you will have 250 hours to improve your performance; 5 percent would give you 125 hours.

Think of the impact if you conducted your work with time for learning built-in. Assume you and the manager who works for your best competitor currently have identical skills and capabilities. Further assume that during the next year you set aside 125 hours to learn something that will have a significant impact on your business. What would happen to your capabilities and your value to the organization?

We are not just talking about classroom time, but your will to spend time on improving the way you work. A national golf tournament is held each year at a country club near my home. Every day the pros are on the practice tee and putting green for hours before their match. Many more are back on the practice tee after their round as well. Compare this to the average golfer who steps up to the first tee without having put in the practice time, that is, learning time. Compare it again to the average golfer who goes directly to the nineteenth hole rather than return to the practice tee to work out what was recognized as a learning need on the course.

Diagnostic Question

- Do the hours you devote to learning indicate a robust will to learn?

Corrective Action

- Identify where in the past you have demonstrated the will to learn (i.e., sports, academics, work, hobbies). Try to discover ways to capture the same curiosity and commitment in your current work.

Deciding What to Learn

If you have the will to learn, next decide your learning priority. There always are many directions your learning can take. Some managers are unerringly good at deciding what is most important to learn. They can anticipate the needs of the future and thus get themselves ready to meet it. Others can't imagine what's around the bend.

The difference is in their ability to recognize the gaps between their current abilities and what is required of them now or in the future.

Diagnostic Question

- Are you working on the highest value goal?

Corrective Action

- Make a list of all the possible things you might learn during the next 4 months and prioritize them. To do this go back and review your most urgent needs. What can you work on to meet those needs?
- Seek out the advice of others whose judgment and savvy you trust. Ask them what they think is most important for you to learn.

Choosing How to Learn

While two managers may choose a similar learning goal, they may go about the task in very different ways. Some may choose a low-powered way, dabbling with their learning. Another may choose a high-powered strategy.

Bobby Moore, president of Bostonian Shoe, deliberately and energetically worked out his learning strategy. His goal (as detailed in Chapter 3) was to improve significantly the point-of-purchase displays at R. H. Macy's northeast division stores. He chose to learn by benchmarking, and by interviewing key competitors.

Diagnostic Question

- Have you chosen a powerful, time effective way to learn?

Corrective Action

- Use multiple channels to reach your goal.
- If you're not making the progress you had expected, go back and examine your strategy. Inject more energy.

Making It Happen

Presidents of the companies we work with say that when evaluating their managers, the characteristic they most often look for is the ability to make the right things happen. If you can make the right learning happen, you will increase the capabilities and skills you need for the future.

But you will have to be actively in charge of your work and your time. It means making tough time choices between urgent present demands and developing the skills you need to be successful in the future.

The best learners have this ability to "make it happen" built into the way they do business. They are able to say no to less important time demands and save time for what is most critical. They don't allow intrusions on their learning time. Their action overcomes the inertia of others and the systems they work in.

Poor learners continually let events and others set their priorities. Their good intentions remain intentions, not solid concrete achievement. Being passive means being passed over.

Diagnostic Question

- What are the barriers, either personal or organizational, that are keeping you from making your plan a reality?

Corrective Action

- Act with constancy of purpose. The drive to achieve what you want to learn must be greater than all the other distractions you face.

Using What You Learned

This is the acid test. Learning without action is a waste of time. It amounts to little more than navel gazing. Only by acting upon what you have learned will you and others see any concrete benefit. In addition to your main goal, you can use the many valuable auxiliary lessons you will have picked up along the way.

Bobby Moore, at Bostonian Shoe, said that before he even reached his goal he had learned that his company didn't spend enough time planning before jumping into action. Moore explained:

"We just start acting, and then it takes us much longer because we have to make so many course corrections along the way. What I'm already learning out of this is that by really thinking through what we want to happen and how to accomplish it, we will speed up a lot of future projects.

"Our next big project will be reducing cycle time in product development. So we will take what we've learned here and apply it in a new place."

Diagnostic Question

- Is your learning, put into action, making a business difference?

Corrective Action

- Reexamine what you have learned and how it can improve your performance. Don't let your new knowledge lie fallow.

Learning Star

Like a golf swing, learning happens so quickly that it often seems impossible to dissect and improve. In the late 1950s Ben Hogan wrote one of the great books on golf, entitled *Five Lessons, The Modern Fundamentals of Golf.*

In the book, Hogan breaks the golf swing down into four simple parts—the grip, the stance, the backswing, and the downswing. He goes into each part of the swing in detail so the reader can take the swing apart and put it back together again.

The learning star (see Figure 4-2) can do the same thing for your understanding of learning at work. It breaks down the learning process into five parts that you can examine and call on when needed.

Each part of learning has its own unique value. Some of us excel in certain aspects of learning, while others rely on other components. The parts do not operate hierarchically but as equals.

The Model for the Learning Star

The learning star is a slight modification of a theory promoted by Michael Lombardo at the Center for Creative Leadership. His theory of learning strategies is based on extensive research on the learning process and an in-depth look at the learning of 55 corporate managers. He identifies four elements as important to learning: *thinking, acting, self-system,* and *accessing people.* As a result of our work with executives, we have added a fifth learning element: *observation.* For clarity, we have labeled the element Lombardo refers to as self-system as *self-check.*

Lombardo discovered that one or two elements dominate most managers' learning style. He further found that the best learners are those who use, or at least consider, all of these learning elements. Finally, he discovered that most managers use the elements in particular patterns or orders.

While one manager might spend time thinking and then going to talk to people and then finally acting, another might observe something, act, and then talk to people to find out how it had gone. "We have strong, usually unconscious, preferences for how we go about our day-to-day problem-solving activities," Lombardo said. "For many managers, it is all in the think and act boxes. They access other people primarily for

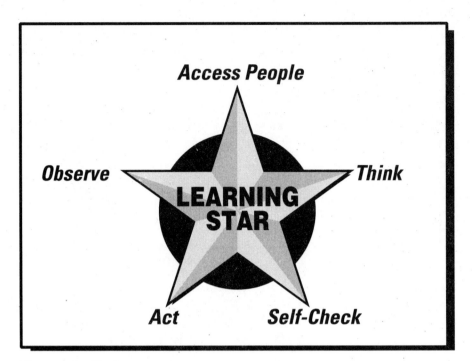

Figure 4-2. The Learning star.

information, and their reflections on self are close to nonexistent in many cases. That's a very common pattern."

When things go well, we happily stick with our preferred learning pattern. When things go askew, we still stick with our preferred learning pattern. Lombardo explains:

"What typically happens is that as long as we are at our best, or things are going well, or we can solve problems in our preferred ways, we usually do fine. We don't really question how we are doing what we are doing. What happens is that you run into a problem, you try to solve it your preferred way, and it doesn't work."

Lombardo said that then one of two things happens. People either get thrown into their least preferred modes of learning, or they keep banging their head against the wall, refusing to try another learning strategy.

For example, managers who prefer to think through problems may find they really need to access other people for information. Because they are not very good at enlisting the help of others, their attempts are half-hearted and ineffective, and the problem remains unsolved.

Or there's the head banging. As Lombardo says:

"Most of us grew up with the exhortation 'If at first you don't succeed, try, try again.' Well, a lot of people have that tape playing in their head. So when things aren't going well, they continue doing exactly what they are doing, only harder.

"Even when the only way to solve the problem is through other people, they don't do it. They just are going to think, act, think, act.

"So we find people either repeat their same pattern, whether things are going well or poorly, or they default to the least preferred learning pattern and get stuck there."

To avoid getting stuck when things go wrong, good managers need to master the five learning elements, or strategies:

1. Think

2. Check your present state

3. Act

4. Observe and study

5. Access people

Think.   Thinking is the conceptualization of a problem and its possible solution. It's any logical, problem-solving strategy, such as the interpretation of data and information to help you come up with a new idea or solve a problem.

It is the thinking side of learning that is most often engaged in a school or classroom setting. It is creating cognitive pictures of what the future can be like.

Self-check.   Take a hard look at yourself, your emotions, your motivations, and your personal history. Check your present state. Ask: Why am I doing what I'm doing? Where am I weak? Where am I strong?

I once worked with a senior manager who, by doing a self-analysis, recognized that his fear of failure caused him to fly off the handle at work and made him worry about small details that should have been left to his subordinates.

Self-analysis is perhaps the most underutilized learning element for managers, trained and rewarded for projecting a cool, controlled demeanor and not given to introspection.

Act.   For many managers, the proper sequence of events is to think first and then to act. But some managers find that they learn best through running experiments and discovering what happens.

Lombardo tells of one manager who was so controlled that he never took risks. He finally broke through his confining approach to work by acting impulsively, a behavior change that energized his group.

I reversed my pattern of learning something new at a recent conference. My normal behavior is to let others speak first and watch the reaction of the group. Instead, at this conference I stated my position first. I discovered that by acting first I had a major impact on the rest of the meeting. I now know that I can choose to initiate action rather than wait for others to speak first.

Observe and Study.   Benchmarking, a learning tool detailed later in the chapter, relies on careful observation to increase learning. By observing and carefully studying other people, other companies, and other techniques, you learn how your actions measure up and how you can improve.

A company president who was having trouble with his board of directors read a book on the excesses of the 1980 takeovers. From his reading he observed that successful CEOs cultivated board members to become their allies. He applied this to his board and found that, in a matter of months, his relationship with the board members had greatly improved.

Lombardo cautions that you must look beneath the surface:

"I'll never forget a guy who was viewed as very lacking in compassion by his subordinates. He said, `How can you develop compassion? Isn't it something you either have or you don't?'

"I said, `Well, tell me something. Who is the most compassionate person you know?' He said, two people: his wife and his minister.

"I said, `Do you know exactly what they do and why they do it?' And he didn't. Not even his wife. I mean he started answering the question, but it was just description.

"I said, `That doesn't tell me anything. That's just the *what*. Anybody can see *what*. Do you know *why* she does what she does, and why she does it at certain times and not others?' He didn't."

Lombardo said, "We have found a lot of people have never really examined why anybody did anything. So often, for the first time they would literally study a person instead of just observing them. They would begin to analyze them and appreciate their qualities."

Looking beneath the surface can open up endless learning opportunities. Lombardo explained:

"One thing we keep hammering on people is that knowing *what* happens doesn't tell us anything other than you have a memory. It doesn't mean that you could do it or that you have the vaguest idea how to do it or when.

"You need to know the *why* and *how* and *what*. What you're really doing is trying to help people come up with mechanisms to make sense of things that you could repeat in the future."

Access People.   Intentionally learning from other people is another of the lesser-used learning strategies.

Nev Curtis, CEO of Delmarva Power, discovered the importance of accessing people early in his career. As a young accountant, he was part of a team building a new power plant. Each Monday he asked a different engineer to describe his work plans for the week, whether it involved concrete work, the power generation system, electrical wiring, or monitoring systems.

Curtis would then take a copy of the plans and walk through the plant reading them. His learning began with the recognition that other people held the key to knowledge he needed for future learning.

A successful organization for accessing people is the Young Presidents Organization, a network of people who became presidents before the age of 40. They meet both formally and informally on topics of current interest and help each other solve problems.

Using the Learning Star

Here are three suggestions for using the learning star:

1. Become conscious of your own learning pattern. Think of a time in the past year when you felt you learned something. Identify the elements that you used to learn.

2. Determine if you overrely on one or two elements to the neglect of others. If this is the case, consciously try to bring into play the other elements of learning, thus giving yourself an enriched pool of information.

3. Help subordinates improve their learning. In thinking about the work of those whose learning you want to accelerate, ask if they have fallen into a particular pattern that keeps them from learning as rapidly as they can. Use the Learning Star to teach them that there are alternative ways of learning.

Learning from Mistakes

Nobody likes to make mistakes, but mistakes will be made. The best we can do is to see them as learning opportunities. See Figure 4-3.

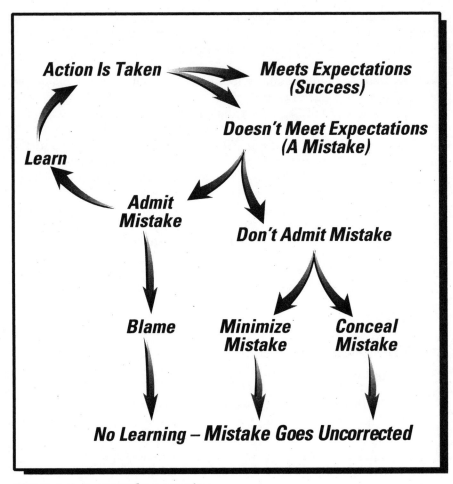

Figure 4-3. Learning from mistakes.

As young children, that's certainly the way we perceived our errors. If we tripped and fell down, we got up and tried again. If we batted at a ball and missed, we tried to correct our position so we could swat it with the next swing. No matter how flawed our efforts, they were, by and large, met with encouragement and praise.

Somewhere along the way, the scenario changed. Our mistakes began drawing more reprimands than encouragement. What previously was seen as adventuresome was viewed as troublesome and ill-conceived. We took note and adapted our behavior. In an effort to please, we decided it was better not to try something new than to risk failure.

As adults, it is often difficult to recognize a mistake when we make it. To admit it—to ourselves and others—sometimes seems more than our egos can take. But we must admit it, learn from it, and use the new knowledge to avoid future pitfalls. We need to regain a childlike attitude toward our mistakes: they are the predecessors of success.

A lot of learning takes place in problem solving. Charles W. Prather, the manager of Du Pont's center for creativity and innovation, has developed a simple model for learning from mistakes. Prather defines mistakes as "well-reasoned attempts at trying something new that didn't meet expectations." The model applies to individuals as well as organizations.

When someone attempts something new and makes a mistake, four responses are possible:

1. Admit the mistake and learn from it

2. Admit the mistake and place blame

3. Conceal the mistake

4. Deny a mistake was made

Admitting the Mistake and Learning from It

The most productive response is to acknowledge the mistake, try to learn from it, and share the learning throughout the organization.

Prather says that in order for learning to take place, management must encourage and support people to admit their mistakes. Then you can improve the action taken the next time. Prather explains:

"In Du Pont, as in many other companies, there already is an excellent model to follow, and it is the model for handling safety incidents.

"Typically, when a safety incident is uncovered, it is acknowledged, and great effort is expended to learn what went wrong and how to prevent the same incident from occurring again. The parties involved in the incident are always included in this process. The learning is communicated broadly throughout the organization, reinforcing the corporate value for safety.

"A critical point is that the degree of organizational learning is directly related to the degree of acknowledgment and discussion about the incident and about the learning."

Admitting the Mistake and Placing Blame

Another response is to admit the mistake but to focus on placing blame, rather than trying to learn from it. Such finger pointing results in humiliation for the person or group that made the mistake and increases the likelihood that future mistakes will be covered up rather than acknowledged. Prather says the responsibility of management is to "fix learning, not blame."

For example, at Harvey & Harvey, Inc., a waste management company, the sales and operations divisions have spent years pointing fingers at each other for performance problems. The sales people blamed the operations people for not providing the necessary pickup service. The operations people blamed sales for writing up incorrect service contracts.

Using the learning from mistakes model, we examined the behavior and asked, "What will it take for you not to blame but to work jointly and use mistakes to learn?" Incorporating the visualization tool described earlier in this chapter, I asked each person to draw a picture of what it would look like if there was no blaming and everyone worked together.

One person drew a star, with the points of the star representing people in both divisions. He said as long as everyone communicated openly, then the company operated at star quality, with each point connected. But if any lines of communication failed, then the star dissolved and its points existed in isolation.

By using that mental picture and recognizing how they used mistakes to place blame rather than to learn, they developed a planning process to identify where mistakes are made and focus on learning.

Concealing the Mistake

A third response is refusing to publicly acknowledge that a mistake was made. A low-level mistake, known only to the person who committed it, can be concealed. The result is no organizational learning.

Prather says that in the safety arena, this is sometimes referred to as the "bloody pocket syndrome." A machinist cuts his finger on a sharp part of a machine and, rather than tell anyone, sticks his hand in his pocket and goes home. He may have learned not to touch that part of the machine, but fearing a reprimand or embarrassment, he keeps it to himself. No one else gets the benefit of his lesson.

The only way the organization will learn from his injury is through acknowledgement and discussion. That rarely happens because businesses generally don't talk about mistakes.

If the mistake occurs at higher, more visible levels, the person who makes a mistake can simply refuse to mention it publicly or can choose to minimize it if public silence isn't possible. In this case, organizational learning is either absent or minimized as well.

Denying a Mistake Was Made

A fourth response is to totally deny that anything went wrong, even when all the facts show otherwise. In this case, those who make the mistake often continue in their erroneous behavior while the mistake is apparent to everyone else.

With the last three responses, no learning occurs and the mistake goes uncorrected. In order to increase learning, organizations must encourage and reward employees for admitting their mistakes and learning from them. The organizational climate must be one based on trust rather than fear—trust that being honest and admitting mistakes will not lead to personal damage. Prather says, "If the organizational climate is characterized by fear, there will be little perceived incentive for individuals to acknowledge mistakes."

So how do companies develop a climate of trust? Management must lead by example. In his workshops, Prather always asks, "Who of you has made a mistake in the past 60 days?" Nearly all of those present raise their hands. Then he asks, "Who would like to discuss a mistake and the learning that took place?" And all participants lower their hands.

Prather asks: "What would happen if you as the manager would lead by example and start acknowledging your own mistakes and lead the organization to focus on the learning?

"Once you had set the pattern of learning, how long would it be before others in your organization began doing the same? What would happen if you, as manager, would categorically refuse to fix blame, and not allow anyone else in your organization to do so?

"The power of this behavior is that small mistakes would be admitted early, before they turned into really big mistakes, and while they could still be remedied at very low cost."

If you fear that the mistake will have negative consequences, then you conceal it or minimize it. If you can blame someone else, then you can avoid all consequences.

Benchmarking

Benchmarking is an eye-opener. Goodloe Suttler, a general manager at Analog Devices, was one of 25 senior managers from five companies who were assigned to create a Center for Quality Management in Boston. Suttler says that during that 5-week assignment, the time he spent observing outstanding companies lit a fire under his learning.

"I learned more in that 5-week period than I had learned in the previous several years, at least with respect to some of the quality management issues. It was an intense learning experience that has helped me formulate an agenda not only for how this division should run but how the corporation should run, too," Suttler said.

"We thought we had done pretty good," he continued, and then we went out and saw some of these Demming and Baldrige prize winners and we were just blown away by what they had done. The practices that we observed both in Japan and the United States were incredibly motivating and moving. After I came back, I had enough to propel myself for several years."

Benchmarking Defined

Robert C. Camp, a leading advocate of benchmarking, defines it as "the search for industry best practices that lead to superior performance."[19] The idea is to use the best to become the best.

As it applies to your learning plan, we define benchmarking as seeking out people or organizations who are the best in their field and putting their knowledge to work for you. Again, using the best to become the best.

Benchmarking's popularity is due, in part, to the Malcolm Baldrige National Quality Award, which requires that all entries benchmark. But its growth is more directly due to fierce global competition that forces companies and individuals to seek out the best, wherever it may be, and, when possible, adapt it to their situation.

The word benchmarking originally was used as a surveyor's term, referring to a point of reference. Xerox Corporation is credited with popularizing the term in the business world in 1980 when it was used to describe a quality program at the company.

Then in 1982, Xerox's match up with L. L. Bean, a Maine-based retailer, became the first benchmarking case to gain national attention. Xerox was searching for ways to boost productivity in its logistics and distribution unit and looked to L. L. Bean as a model of excellence. The result was a 10 percent gain in warehouse productivity, 3 to 5 percent of which Xerox attributes directly to studying Bean.[20]

"What is fundamental is recognizing that benchmarking involves uncovering best practices wherever they exist," Camp says.[21] Wherever includes one's own organization, competitors, and organizations in totally different fields.

That kind of cross-pollination makes for odd couples. Who would have foreseen Xerox pairing up with a sporting goods retailer? Or Motorola benchmarking with Domino's Pizza in its effort to reduce cycle time between order receipt and delivery of its cellular telephones?

Many of the largest companies in America have some kind of bench-marking program in place. Books have been written on it, magazine and newspaper articles debate its virtues. Consultants scramble to help with its implementation.

Benchmarking for Individuals.   While benchmarking most often is used to identify best-in-class organizational practices, we have found that it can easily be adapted to provide a powerful tool in helping indi-vidual managers choose and achieve learning goals. You can use it to promote your own learning or, as a senior manager, to accelerate the learning of your organization.

Managers and organizations need to benchmark how much their counterparts know and the rate at which they are learning. If they dis-cover someone else is outlearning them, they need to find ways to increase the rate of their own learning.

By benchmarking the abilities of counterparts at major competitors, you'll gain insight into what you should be learning and where you stand in relationship to others in your field. By benchmarking best practices in your own company, you take advantage of information that's easily available. By looking across entirely different fields, you get a more com-plete picture of what is currently the best and what tomorrow's best will be: Problems and insights know no occupational boundaries.

Opening Your Eyes to New Ideas.   Theresa Eyre, education man-ager at Hewlett-Packard, said benchmarking has given her company "a different sense of what is possible as an organization."

"We were interested in understanding more about how the roles of managers, particularly middle managers, were changing in complex organizations," Eyre said. "We had read a lot about the new manage-ment roles, but we hadn't seen a lot of change in what our managers actually did at work. So we sent teams of middle managers to talk with their peers in other companies about how their jobs were changing."

Benchmarking helped Hewlett-Packard's middle managers in Cupertino, California, see other management models. "Because Hewlett-Packard is recognized for its successful management practices, it is tempting to believe that our way of doing things is the right way," Eyre said, "yet our success depends on our ability to continue to improve."

At Hewlett-Packard, benchmarking and learning go hand-in-hand. "Benchmarking management practices is an important component of our overall management-executive development process," Eyre said.

Typically, the company sends teams of two to four managers to meet with peers in other companies to exchange ideas about leadership and organizational practices. After the visits, the benchmarking teams exchange observations.

"We encourage the managers to look for ways to generalize beyond their specific observations, such as what conclusions can they draw about leadership in general? Then we encourage them to examine their own practices relative to these conclusions," Eyre said. "Benchmarking can help managers develop concrete mental pictures of people doing things that may be different from how we do things here."

Admitting You Don't Know It All.   The most difficult part of benchmarking is recognizing that you don't know it all. American companies, particularly those seen as industry leaders, have difficulty entertaining the possibility that they can learn something from a competitor or another organization.

"The idea that somebody out there might be better is a tough thing to come to grips with. Overcoming that myopia is very, very important," Camp says.[22]

If you want to become the best, or stay the best, you have to know not only what your competitors are up to, but where to find the best business practices, wherever they exist.

Benchmarking can be awe-inspiring. "I think that at some level, when you are there on the benchmarking trip, it can be overwhelming," Eyre said. "You feel like `Oh my gosh. There is all this out there that I never knew about or that I never gave credibility to before.'"

Kay Whitmore, chief executive officer of Eastman Kodak, says that being a globally successful company can make benchmarking more difficult. But being aware of external best practices is a must if a company wants to remain on top. He explained:

"One of our burdens at Eastman Kodak is that we have been very successful for a very long time. That has given us some habits and cultural entities that were an advantage at one time but, as the world changed, became disadvantages.

"In my mind, some of the more successful companies are those who walked right up to the edge of disaster and said there are two choices: over the edge or change. And they changed. Companies that have not been forced right to that edge are slower to change.

"Right now, in certain businesses, we have been pressed to the edge. Getting us to change was a problem, so we said `benchmark.'"

Getting started wasn't easy because the company had such a high opinion of itself. Whitmore gave this example:

"I asked the managers, `How good are you?'

"They answered, `Well, we're really great.'

"So I said, `How do you know?'

"And they said, `Well, we've always been great so we'll always be great and we just know that.'

"Then I said, `Let's benchmark.'

"They replied, `Yes, we'll go call somebody and check.'

"Then they go through the motions of looking like they are benchmarking when in fact they are not."

Instead, explained Whitmore, they just seek to reaffirm their own superiority. He speculates that the problem stems from a desire to create rather than adopt. "As a company, we have taken the `not invented here' syndrome to a rather high art," he said, meaning that if it's not invented at Kodak, they don't think it worthwhile. "And I don't think we're distinctive in that."

When a company is very good at what it does, the problem often is how to make managers recognize that another company may do it better, and then learn from them. Because managers at Kodak weren't ready to take that leap, the company decided to benchmark internally first. (See Exhibit 4-2.)

Other companies have a completely different mentality. Compare the mindset at Kodak to that of Corning, where a vice president of quality said, "We will `steal' any idea we can," meaning they are willing to adopt best practices from any source. Then he used the example of needing to improve Corning's process quality. They found that Westinghouse already had done a significant amount of work in that area and had a great program to do it.

"We just went out and bought it from them, which probably saved us 24 months of trying to invent our own, plus people's time. So it's better than we could have produced, and we're getting it 18 months to 2 years before we could have produced it ourselves."

Apple Found the Truth Hard to Swallow. In 1990 Apple Computer Inc. found out the hard way that they had been surpassed by a competitor. After the company introduced its first portable computer, weighing in at a hefty 18 pounds, Compaq Computer Corporation came out with a 6-pound notebook machine.

"We took it apart and we were stunned because we realized that Apple couldn't make anything similar," one Apple Executive told *The New York Times*.[23]

Although belatedly, they learned. In late 1991 Apple introduced its notebook computer, priced beginning at $2,295 and weighing from 5.1 to 6.8 pounds.

And Compaq Almost Choked on It. At the same time, Compaq was facing its own problems. Success had made the company smug.

Kodak Class: Internal Benchmarking

Being a very large company with many divisions and sections, Kodak believed that they did most things quite well somewhere in the company, but quality wasn't uniform. Whitmore tells what happened:

"Take an example out of manufacturing. We spool Kodacolor film in lots of different places. Some places we do that at higher quality and lower cost than we do at other places.

"So we can do some internal benchmarking. We have a thing called Kodak Class in which we go around and look at the Kodak world. We get some very tight parameters on how to measure quality and cost effectiveness. Then we provide that data for all locations. It shows where somebody does it better than somebody else.

"Benchmarking internally has gotten people started. It's been a methodology of first, `How do I learn from locations inside the company?' and then, `How do I learn from an organization external to the company?'

"It's the way you become world-class. If you are to be competitive long-term, you've got to do most things as well as anybody in the world, and you've got to do a few things better.

"We still assume we know everything there is to know about photography. If it is important to think about, we would have thought about it. So if somebody else thought about it, it must not be very important because we didn't think about it first.

"There is an arrogance in the learning sense of a successful organization that is really difficult to get past."

Exhibit 4-2. Eastman Kodak uses internal benchmarking to speed organizational learning.

Additionally, Compaq was focusing on the wrong competitor as `best in class.'

In 1991, Compaq saw its shares drop from nearly $75 to about $26 as its market share fell and domestic sales stalled. Late in the year Eckhard Pfeiffer, who was named chief executive after a management upheaval, told *The New York Times* that Compaq had been blinded by past success.

> "The company had been so successful over the past nine years that there hadn't been any doubt that the success formula was working, but it masked, in a way, the changes that were happening. The company failed to recognize the changes necessary to cope with the environment of the 1990's...."

"One other major flaw...was our almost exclusive focus on I.B.M. You know, `I.B.M. did this and how can we outdo them, how do we make it better, faster?' It was our total focus. The addition of second-tier pricing wasn't welcome because it deviated from that focus. We didn't recognize who the new competition would be."

That competition came from the upstarts like Dell, CompuAdd, and AST Research, and companies that didn't even register on Compaq's radar screens, like Northgate and Gateway 2000. A telling example was in the nearly simultaneous product announcements from Dell, AST, and Compaq the week before Compaq's upheaval.

Compaq introduced an 18-pound color portable that needs to be plugged into an outlet and costs $10,000. Dell and AST introduced 7-pound color portables that run on batteries and cost $5,000.[24]

Compaq had been exclusively benchmarking with the wrong competitor. By contrast, when Ted Hutton took over as president and CEO of Baltimore-based Waverly, Inc., a publishing and printing firm, he assumed he had a lot to learn. He made it a point to benchmark against as many competitors as possible and cull whatever knowledge he could.

"I found it very valuable to interview competitors," Hutton said. "Most of the time your competitors will be reasonably honest. In some businesses that's not possible because there is cutthroat competition."

The Benchmarking Process

We use a modified version of the benchmarking process described in Camp's *Benchmarking.*[25]

1. *Brainstorm what you need to learn.*   If you've completed your learning plan, as described in Chapter 3, what you need to learn already is crystal clear. To briefly summarize, you need to identify: what is important to your company's success in the next 2 to 3 years; what proficiencies you will need for success in the company as it will become.

2. *Identify the best.*   Studying a mediocre company or individual wastes time and results in lowering your expectations rather than lifting them. Equally disastrous is concentrating on the wrong company. The Compaq Computer Corporation example described earlier in this chapter offers a case in point.

Be creative in searching for best practices and who the best really is. It isn't necessary to go to large companies. Thom Harvey, CEO of Harvey & Harvey, Inc., the waste management company, benchmarked with George Clement, CEO of Clement Communications, to learn the best way to build a senior management team. In return, Clement benchmarked with Harvey to learn better ways to handle the disposal of chemicals used at his manufacturing plant.

3. *Discover everything you can about the company or individual you are studying. Never try to wing it. Keep your specific goal in mind.* You can choose one of many processes for benchmarking investigations. The object is to gather as much information as possible, remembering to keep it goal-specific. Eyre, at Hewlett-Packard, said that keeping a focus is crucial.

"It's almost too challenging of an experience to go into a company for a couple of hours or a day and expect to learn everything about the way they do business," she said. "So I think putting some structure on it and being clear on what you want to learn is important.

"Our managers return from benchmarking trips with a wealth of new ideas and are excited about sharing them. Yet, without clear focus, the benefits may be limited to hearing some interesting stories about how things are different in another company."

The key for encouraging organizational learning, Eyre said, is to work with the managers to establish goals and a method of reporting their findings back to their peers. That way, their benchmarking visits are more focused and key learnings are better defined.

If you are benchmarking with an individual, you should read everything you can about the person and the job he or she holds. Then arrange for an interview. Make it clear that the other person also will benefit from the exchange. Think through what you have to offer the other person, not only as a way to convince them to participate but to make the person feel they've gained something of value.

Camp writes that "It has been found from experience that the basic willingness to share—provided the information is not proprietary or confidential—is based on a mutual desire to uncover and understand industry best practices."[26] You have your professional experience and judgment to offer.

If your benchmarking culminates with an interview or an on-site visit, do as much homework as possible. Sources of information include magazine and newspaper articles, professional publications, annual reports, and internal publications such as newsletters. You also may want to talk to analysts who keep track of particular companies.

Also prepare a package of materials about yourself or your company, depending on whether you are benchmarking as an individual or an organization. Provide this package to your benchmarking counterpart ahead of time so that they, too, can expect to learn something about you and from you.

4. *Calculate the performance gap and how you can benefit from what you have discovered.* At this point in the process, you have gathered all of your information, made an on-site visit, if applicable, and are ready to analyze what you discovered.

There are times when you will realize that you outperform the person or organization being benchmarked. But because your purpose was to learn from someone else, usually you will find a negative performance gap. To close that gap, you must study what you have observed. What procedures or ideas can you adapt to your own work?

At Hewlett-Packard, benchmarking benefits to managers have been obvious. Eyre said:

"The individual managers who participate in the benchmarking trips find the experience highly developmental. It gives the managers new ideas about what is possible.

"Part of what I believe, and what studies have shown in the past, is that expertise is really just a collection of experiences. It's just building for yourself a very rich repertoire of experience from which you can draw.

"I think that benchmarking can accelerate the development of this repertoire and you can build it faster by building it deliberately."

5. *Have a clear idea of how you'll use your findings. Develop and implement action steps to close the gap and put your new knowledge to use.* You should give this step some thought before you begin benchmarking. Discovering best practices may be exhilarating, but unless you have a plan to put your new knowledge to use, it remains a mental exercise. This step is covered in your learning plan, which was detailed in Chapter 3. To summarize, write out your action steps, being as specific as possible. When listing each step, identify what consequences you anticipate. Be clear about what you want to get out of it. Erye, of Hewlett-Packard, said this is a step that often is shortchanged: "When you are benchmarking, you need to think through what you want to do with the information when you get back."

6. *Actually use the information you have gained.* Goodloe Suttler offers a good example from Analog Devices. When he went to benchmark with Florida Power & Light, Suttler was impressed with how they presented their quality improvement stories on 3 × 5 boards that were like displays at a state fair. In a step-by-step process, you could see the entire story, from the problem to the analysis to the solution. He said:

"We came up with a format that is on a metallic magnetic board so that we can add these nice story boards for the teams that go out and pick off a problem and solve that problem.

"We're trying to get out the idea that here is the process by which you solve classic cross-functional departmental problems. Here is the way by which you institute process control, and here is an example less than 3 days old as to how to do that, who did it, and who team members were.

"So it provides recognition. It provides a kind of closure on the process. And it spruces up the factory because it's a nice board. Quality story boards were a very specific thing I got out of Florida Power & Light that we are instituting here."

If you use the five learning tools presented in this chapter—visualization, the learning ladder, learning star, learning from mistakes, and benchmarking—you'll find new and creative ways to increase your knowledge and enhance your work. But inevitably there will be problems along the way. Chapter 5 tells you how to solve these problems.

5

When Things Go Wrong: Leaping the Hurdles

When I first met him, Frank was drowning in work. As the administrative vice president of an Atlanta-based company, he was a problem solver who found no task too small for his attention. Because he was the only senior manager who was readily accessible to employees, people literally lined up outside his door, seeking advice or solutions.

He ricocheted from one responsibility to another. He was the only person in the company trained to do estimations and specifications for special order products. And the other relatives of this family-held company relied on him to do the accounting to maintain a certain level of confidentiality.

He liked the feeling of being needed, of being a vital link in the company, but paying attention to so many small details was running him ragged. To keep up at the office, he was taking work home three nights a week; he was a pressure valve that was about to blow. His wife was about to start her own business, with Frank handling the accounting, so clearly the demands on his time at home would increase.

Frank realized he was in trouble. Somehow he had to regain control of his work. For his learning goal, he chose to clear his plate of smaller, individual tasks that were stealing time from his primary responsibilities. He recognized the compelling need to transfer some of his work to others.

"I'm completely overloaded," he admitted. "I can't get done what I'm supposed to get done now, and I don't know how to change. I'm afraid that if I hand over responsibilities to anybody else, mistakes will be made."

Frank wrote out a detailed action plan and declared his commitment to it. But at a follow-up meeting with top management several months later, he said he had made no progress toward his goal. When asked why, he started pointing fingers.

"I can't work on my learning plan because I don't have time. Nobody else knows how to do these estimations and specifications," he said. "And my family requires that I do the accounting."

The president of the company went absolutely nuts. "How do you think you learned how to do it? You have to take a risk and give someone else a chance to do it. I had to take a risk with you and you still don't do it perfectly."

More than a little taken aback, the vice president said, "I can't do it perfectly because I have too much to do. And there's nobody else in the organization who can do this."

The company president offered to reassign some of Frank's tasks, but Frank kept inventing reasons why the president's solutions wouldn't work. The argument went no place.

Although Frank said he recognized the need to delegate responsibilities, when it came right down to it, he didn't want to give them up. The truth was that he loved to solve small problems. He loved to have people lined up outside his door for help. And he couldn't distinguish between high-value tasks and low-value tasks.

He blamed everyone else for his inability to achieve his goal. He thought they were incapable of assuming some of his duties. In reality, he didn't want to give up any power or share responsibilities.

Later the president said: "I've been trying to get him to change for years from being a clerk to being a senior manager in this business. I want him to stop doing these lower-level tasks that other people can do and improve a number of our key administrative systems. I've got someone who can do the accounting who is acceptable to the family members, but Frank has difficulty giving that up. The vice president of manufacturing and engineering said he would take responsibility for estimating and making specifications, but Frank has trouble giving that up."

Frank faced some real hurdles to learning. But his biggest hurdles were those he created himself. They were self-imposed, yet he insisted they were beyond his control.

Like a bird banging against a glass wall, Frank refused to concede to reality. He had trapped himself.

Spotting the Red Flags and Identifying the Hurdles

The "I can't because..." excuse often appears when you first consider adopting a learning plan. It is one of many *red flags* that can pop up as you pursue your learning goal. They serve as warnings that you are approaching a hurdle to your learning.

The purpose of this chapter is to help you recognize the red flags and to identify the hurdles they represent, and to enable you to master whatever problems you encounter.

Don't expect smooth sailing. Everyone who decides to intentionally learn at work faces at least one or two hurdles. If you don't, it probably means your learning goal isn't challenging enough. One thing is sure. Your learning plan won't die without warning. Telltale symptoms will appear long before it reaches the critical stage.

We've singled out ten important hurdles that you may encounter. They are listed in Exhibit 5-1. The most common red flag excuses and the hurdles they signify are listed in Exhibit 5-2. Read through the checklist statements to see whether you've heard yourself saying the same thing. Then as you read this chapter, pay particular attention to the hurdles the statements signify.

Hurdle 1: Finding Time

Red Flag Excuse: *I am too busy. There's no time left for learning.*

Making a time commitment to learning is by far the biggest hurdle you'll face. Day-to-day demands take precedence over learning. On our list of things to do, learning often comes last. It should come first. A good example is found in Stephen R. Covey's book, *The Seven Habits of*

Ten Hurdles

1. Finding Time
2. Choosing the Wrong Goal
3. Wrong Approach
4. Blaming Others
5. Fear of the Unknown
6. Unsupportive and Downright Repressive Bosses
7. A Murky Corporate Vision
8. Good Intentions, Weak Follow-Through
9. Hitting the Wall
10. When You Can't Imagine Reaching Your Goal

Exhibit 5-1. These are the hurdles you must overcome for effective learning.

The Red Flag Checklist

Circle Yes (Y) if you've heard yourself say the same thing or No (N) if the statement doesn't apply to you.

Y N   1. I already have too much to do at work. There's no time left for learning. [**Hurdle 1**]

Y N   2. My learning goal is too challenging. [**Hurdles 2, 9**]

Y N   3. My learning goal is too small. [**Hurdle 2**]

Y N   4. Others keep me from achieving my goal. [**Hurdles 4, 6**]

Y N   5. Why try something new? I'm comfortable with the way things are at work. [**Hurdle 5**]

Y N   6. I can't learn because my boss is not supportive. [**Hurdle 6**]

Y N   7. My organization doesn't have a clear vision of what's important. [**Hurdle 7**]

Y N   8. My learning progress has fallen into the same abyss as most New Year's Resolutions. I lack motivation or willpower. [**Hurdle 8**]

Y N   9. I have hit a wall and just can't get through. [**Hurdles 3, 9**]

Y N   10. I've discovered a more important learning goal. [**Hurdle 2**]

Y N   11. I'm anxious about my learning plan. [**Hurdle 5**]

Y N   12. A major business change has made my goal obsolete. [**Hurdle 2**]

Y N   13. I am not making the progress I want. [**Hurdles 3, 8**]

Y N   14. My goal is not as clear as I thought it was. [**Hurdle 2**]

Y N   15. My learning plan seems like just another project. [**Hurdle 8**]

Y N   16. My goal is not at the core of what is important to me or my business. [**Hurdle 2**]

Y N   17. I started OK and then stopped working on my plan. [**Hurdle 8**]

Exhibit 5-2. Check to see whether you use any of these red flag excuses.

Y N	18.	I don't have a clear picture of myself achieving my goal. [Hurdle 10]
Y N	19.	I don't feel any urgency to accomplish my goal. [Hurdles 2, 8, 10]
Y N	20.	I feel I'm swimming against the tide. [Hurdles 2, 6, 7]
Y N	21.	I'm afraid I'll fail to reach my goal. [Hurdle 5]

Exhibit 5-2. (*Continued*)

Highly Effective People. In it he asks the reader to imagine coming upon someone working feverishly to saw down a tree.

"What are you doing?" you ask.

"Can't you see?" comes the impatient reply. "I'm sawing down this tree."

"You look exhausted!" you exclaim. "How long have you been at it?"

"Over five hours," he returns, "and I'm beat! This is hard work."

"Well, why don't you take a break for a few minutes and sharpen that saw?" you inquire. "I'm sure it would go a lot faster."

"I don't have time to sharpen the saw," the man says emphatically. "I'm too busy sawing!"[27]

Covey used the story to make the point that people must "sharpen the saw" by taking time for self-renewal.

At work, learning is how you "sharpen the saw." Cheryl Keith is a good example. If you had asked Cheryl Keith if she had time to devote to learning, the answer would have been a resounding "No!" In addition to being financial officer for AstroPower, maker of solar cells and one of *INC.* magazine's top 500 companies, she was, by default, director of administration and head of human resources.

Wearing her financial hat, she was asked to create sophisticated financial projections and analyses for venture capitalists holding a major ownership stake in the firm. In her administrative role, she found herself settling disputes or establishing policies. As the director of human resources, she was involved in hiring, firing, and taking care of the human side of a high-technology organization.

As if that was not enough, the company was in the process of moving into a new building, which was being built to their specifications. Keith's time was taken up getting the correct permits from the city and sign-offs on safety procedures.

Her learning goal was to take action off of her plate and give it to others. Here she faced a big problem. There was no one to give the work to. A recently hired administrative person had not worked out and had left the company. There was no human resources person in the company, and the rest of the company was going flat out as she was.

Keith faced multiple problems:

- She was out of time.

- She had few apparent resources.

- She faced urgent demands that required action.

- She had a boss who counted on her to produce results.

She did something unique. She took a day off and spent it at home analyzing her work and developing a solution. She spent the best part of a day and a night creating a new work plan. She wanted to arrange and distribute her work in a way that allowed her to focus on important financial tasks, tasks that were being shortchanged.

With some fear and trepidation she came into work the next day and met with her CEO. She went through her plan and was ready to fight for her solution when he said, without hearing her backup evidence, "Let's do it. I've been thinking about the same thing."

Keith dramatically changed the way she worked. She began to schedule her morning into large blocks of uninterrupted time, which she devoted to the detailed financial analysis that required great concentration. She kept in touch with employees by posting a sign-up sheet so that anyone with a problem could schedule an appointment with her in the afternoon.

And, after scrutinizing the company's employees, she was able to delegate work to someone else, a person whose abilities had been overlooked in the past.

Keith's productivity went up dramatically. Two months later she became the company's chief operating officer.

How to Clear Hurdle 1

- Block out learning time on your calendar and stick to it.

- Work accountability into your learning equation, whether it's by using a partner or frequently referring to your written timetable.

- Make learning the first thing you do instead of the last. It should be fundamental rather than supplemental to your work.

- If need be, move work off your plate and onto someone else's. Learn to delegate.

Hurdle 2: Choosing the Wrong Goal

Red Flag Excuses: *My learning goal is too challenging. My learning goal is too small. I've discovered a more important learning goal. A major business change has made my goal obsolete. My goal is not as clear as I thought it was. My goal is not at the core of what is important to me or my business. I don't feel any urgency to accomplish my goal. I feel I'm swimming against the tide.*

When it's apparent that you've chosen the wrong goal, give it up and find another one. Sometimes your goal may be too large and too ambitious, or too small and not challenging enough. Circumstances may make your goal obsolete, or you may realize there is a more important goal you need to pursue.

Some goals become obsolete for reasons beyond your control. For example, a plant manager chose to work on the development of his wage-roll people (hourly employees). He wanted to give them greater responsibility in their work. Three weeks into his plan his corporation announced a major downsizing. His goal of empowerment shifted rapidly to finding ways to save jobs.

A similar situation occurred with the director of training and organizational development at a large regional bank. His goal was to learn to create a new consulting service for senior line managers. The service would help managers deal with the major changes his industry faced. A month later his bank acquired a second bank, and his goal was washed away. His new goal was to design and deliver seminars for senior managers in both institutions on surviving the acquisition process, a project with a sense of urgency and challenge.

Don't bite off more than you can chew by choosing a goal that is too challenging. If you do, make midcourse corrections. A vice president of production in charge of four large plants wanted to improve the relationship between the production and maintenance people. As he began to work on his plan he realized his goal was too big. Each plant had unique relationships and problems. So he reduced the scope of his goal and decided to work with each plant sequentially.

How to Clear Hurdle 2

- If your goal is wrong or is not the best one, replace it with another one. Don't shut down and stop learning. Be flexible. Find a new goal that works.

- Identify why your first goal didn't work. Did circumstances change or did you overlook some crucial information?

Hurdle 3: Wrong Approach

Red Flag Excuses: *I have hit a wall and just can't get through.   I am not making the progress I want.*

Using the wrong approach to learning is not unlike starting on the wrong foot for the triple jump in track and field events. If your approach is wrong, you'll never jump very far. Your goal may be fine, but your execution needs work. The red flags are the same as for Hurdle 2. You have to use your judgment to determine if the problem is in the goal or in the approach.

John Cox, director of education for Club Corporation of America, wanted to use his time more effectively. He was responsible for training thousands of frontline people who dealt with customers.

Initially, Cox planned to have some managers take on leadership tasks around those training efforts on a part-time basis. The managers would benefit by learning more about the organization. Cox would benefit by having more time for strategic tasks.

But Cox's plan didn't get a warm reception. The executive vice presidents for whom the managers worked said they wanted the managers to focus on their work and not be distracted by getting involved in implementing training across regions. So, while Cox felt his goal—finding more time for larger tasks—was on target, he had to find a new approach.

As part of his new strategy he analyzed the way his company implemented training programs, and delegated more of the training responsibility to functional managers at the regional level.

As a result, he achieved his goal of gaining more control of his time.

How To Clear Hurdle 3

- Determine what part of your goal needs adjustment and massage it until it's right. When heavy air traffic dictates a change in flight patterns, pilots don't refuse to land. They simply adjust their approach.

Hurdle 4: Blaming Others

Red Flag Excuse: *Others are keeping me from achieving my goal*

For his goal, a vice president of manufacturing wanted to learn how to improve dramatically the quality of the plant's product. His quality initiative included the introduction of the new "Kanban" system to control production flow. It was a very complicated goal to implement, particularly at a time when the plant was having some immediate production problems.

When I talked to him about the lack of progress on his goal, he immediately started placing blame. "The engineering staff is not really behind what I am doing. Purchasing has really screwed us up by not ordering the particular supplies we need. The president keeps wanting me to solve specific problems before we move into a more general, systemwide quality initiative, and the workers don't know who is in control."

The finger pointing continued. "Those working on process development keep messing up the production line. I don't have time to adequately prepare for the training sessions I planned to have, and I can't get requisitions to hire more people."

As I listened, I realized that this vice president had created an iron-clad excuse as to why he was making no progress. By blaming everyone around him, he had effectively absolved himself of all responsibility for the lack of progress toward his goal.

He never took a hard look at himself. He didn't see how his behavior had alienated his people. He was unaware that his management shortcomings caused much of the production line's quality problems. He did not seek out others who could give him direct, honest feedback about his situation. It turned out that this blaming behavior was evident in almost every phase of his work. He soon was fired.

How to Clear Hurdle 4

- Before blaming others, look at yourself. You may be blocking your opportunity to grow.

- Turn to someone who is familiar with your situation and whose judgment you trust. Ask if your issue is real or if it's a roadblock you're putting in your own path.

Hurdle 5: Fear of the Unknown

Red Flag Excuses: *Why try something new? I'm comfortable with the way things are at work. I'm anxious about my learning plan. I'm afraid I'll fail to reach my goal.*

Sometimes the hardest part of learning is taking that first step. It's leaving the comfort zone of what you already do—and do well—and plunging into a challenge. Like diving into a chilly lake, the initial shock and discomfort give way to exhilaration.

Look for that sense of exhilaration instead of trying to avoid it. If the thought of your learning goal doesn't make your pulse quicken, you're probably not leaving your comfort zone.

Often you need to face rather than run from that which you fear. Bill McCabe, who was a fighter pilot in southeast Asia, described leaving North Vietnam one day when a supporting radar plane indicated three MIGs were in pursuit.

The strike force leader decided the best course of action was to turn back and take on the MIGs. "Check your fuel!" McCabe reminded his leader as they were about to turn around. Only two of the four fighters had sufficient fuel for a chase.

The leader still said, "We're going back!" The two fighters turned to face the oncoming MIGs. The MIGs, having banked on a easy kill, turned and ran.

McCabe recalls, "I learned, that day, the value of knowledgeably taking risks. You've got to be willing to face the challenge head on."

A senior line manager tells another story of turning into a problem and solving it. He wanted his direct reports to become an empowered team. It wasn't going as well as he wanted it to, so he had me interview each of his employees, focusing on what in this manager's behavior was helping or hurting them in their goal to become an empowered team.

They identified two things he did that prevented them from becoming an empowered team: (1) He frequently got too involved in the details of the organization, making his people feel he was intruding in their areas of responsibility. (2) He was emotional and given to outbursts that demoralized people rather than energized them.

When I again met with the senior line manager and shared what had been reported to me, he admitted that those were his faults and identified the underlying cause. He said:

"I have a fear of failure. I've been successful in my life and I've gone much farther than I thought I'd ever be able to. I'm basically pleased with the accomplishments of my group, but I have this fear of failure. What will happen if it doesn't continue to go well? That's what drives me to get overly involved in details and to blow up at inappropriate times."

Armed with the information from his employees, he did as McCabe did and turned right back and faced the problem. He held a seminar to discuss what kinds of things he, as a leader, could do to help them become an empowered team.

How to Clear Hurdle 5

- Recognize the stress and fear that comes with entering unknown territory and acknowledge its worth.
- Seek exhilaration rather than equanimity.
- Turn into your problem and see if it disappears.

Hurdle 6: Unsupportive and Downright Repressive Bosses

Red Flag Excuses: *Others are keeping me from achieving my goal. I can't learn because my boss is not supportive.*

The Unsupportive Boss.   Dealing with an unsupportive boss requires a critical judgment call. When a boss gives bad advice, you must decide whether to accept or ignore it, knowing that ignoring it could get you fired. But following your own sense of what you should learn, even if your boss is opposed or simply uninterested, could enhance your own development. It also could earn hard won support from the heretofore unsupportive boss.

Only you know if your learning goal is worth going head-to-head with your boss or if you should choose a goal that would win his or her support. A boss can be uninterested in your goal, or he or she can be downright hostile about it.

A participant in one of our programs was about to hold a career session based on what he had learned from us. When his manager saw him walking to the meeting, his manager asked what he was doing. When told, his manager said, "I'll tell you what your damn career discussion is. It's to go get your work done and stop planning for the future."

Not having alignment and agreement with your senior managers can completely negate the positive effects of any kind of learning. Without any organizational support, the odds are too great for the manager's new development to take root and produce results.

Confronting an unsupportive boss can have positive results. A vice president at Du Pont Company decided that becoming a global leader was an important learning goal, both for business reasons and his own development. Even though his boss wasn't supportive, the vice president stuck to his goal and did a masterful job of persuading his boss of its importance. When he completed his goal, his boss said, "I'm really glad you did it."

The Downright Repressive Boss.   There are also managers who are downright repressive. They don't want their best employees to grow because they might grow out of their position and out from under the manager's supervision.

So the managers intentionally hold on to workers who could learn something more in another job. If there were as much financial embezzlement as there is human resource embezzlement, no company would stand for it.

But most managers get away with it. There was one manager who intentionally held on to his people by increasing the performance ratings of the poor performers and downgrading the performance ratings of the excellent performers. That way he kept other managers from raiding his staff. No one wanted his "excellent" performers because they never measured up. And they never came after his truly excellent performers because they assumed no one in his department could perform.

How to Clear Hurdle 6

- Don't rely on your boss to promote your learning. Make it your priority.

- Seek advice from friends and coworkers as to whether your goal is worth alienating your boss. Ask if they think the boss is right.

- After you determine the wisdom of your boss, think through the consequences of your learning plan. Is it worth pursuing? Should you put it on hold, or should you drop it?

- Be political. Pick a learning goal that will have a positive impact on your boss. Talk to your boss about it and explain how you'll both benefit.

- Persist in learning. If your boss is not attuned to learning, he or she may not realize that it's going on right under his or her nose.

- Wait your boss out. Given the frequency of personnel changes, one of you may be moved to another department in the near future.

- If your boss is totally against your growth, you may want to change jobs.

Hurdle 7: A Murky Corporate Vision

Red Flag Excuses: *My organization doesn't have a clear vision of what's important. I feel I'm swimming against the tide.*

If your company doesn't have a clear vision, then your task of choosing and pursuing an appropriate learning goal becomes more difficult but not impossible. In fact, most companies lack a clear corporate vision. Most people don't push senior management to clarify their vision, and most senior managers think their vision is apparent, even when it isn't.

Often it's a matter of mixed messages. People don't know what to work on because the company doesn't know what it wants to be. One day it's one thing. Another day it's something else.

The research and development department of a billion-dollar business found itself in such a quandary. In addition to several mature products, the company had promising research in the pipeline for products that could be future blockbusters. Managers in the organization found themselves torn between the two. They were never sure whether they should try to make incremental improvements to the mature products or throw their efforts into the research needed to hit a future home run.

Several times a year, depending upon whom they talked to, the focus of their work would change. First there would be a directive to do those things that would bring improved short-term profits. Then they were told to go on a crash program to create future products more quickly. Work was like a yo-yo. Because they never knew what was most important, they never knew where to focus their learning energies.

In another case, two top executives in a small grocery store chain didn't agree on the primary focus of their business, leaving the employees totally confused about their own focus.

When I met the president of the grocery company, his chain had grown from one to four stores. His great strength was customer relations. He prided his stores on providing excellent personal service and making sure each detail was just right. His weakness was in keeping his costs under control. To compensate for his lack of financial skills he hired a chief operating officer to manage the stores and bring costs under control.

But the strengths of the two men—excellent customer service and minimal costs—seemed in direct conflict. To bring down costs, the new operating officer did away with a lot of personal service, such as bag boys carrying groceries to the car. The messages from the two executives were so mixed that employees no longer knew whether to focus their learning on the service side of their business or on cost control. It's a problem the president continues to work through.

How to Clear Hurdle 7

- Try to get senior management to clarify the company's vision.

- Determine the mission or objective of your particular segment of the organization and what it must do to be successful.

- Study people in your area of expertise to see what could make you distinctive, regardless of what the company's vision is. This increases your marketability when and if you change jobs.

Hurdle 8: Good Intentions, Weak Follow-Through

Red Flag Excuses: *My learning progress has fallen into the same abyss as most New Year's Resolutions. I lack motivation or willpower. I am not making the progress I want. My learning plan seems like just another project. I started OK and then stopped working on my plan.*

The general manager of a business generating $500 million a year wanted to learn how to create an empowered team of workers. He focused attention on one plant and began with a bang, visiting with workers on the production floor, listening to their needs, and planning with his managers how best to create the empowered teams he envisioned.

But between planning and action he began to lose energy for his goal. It began to feel like just another project rather than something distinctive. It began to feel like duty rather than a voluntary commitment to his own growth.

He was still in a state of malaise when we met a few months later. Upon analysis, he realized that he had another major change effort under way in his organization and had simply run out of gas. He worked through his lack of action by teaming himself with one of his managers who was excited about the prospect of working on the learning goal. Together they learned how to create empowered teams in a way that benefited each of them and the workers on the factory floor.

Even when you realize the importance of learning, circumstances and old behavior patterns can ambush your development plan. I've seen it happen time and again. One of the most striking examples occurred in Ohio during a meeting with a company president and his 10 direct reports. See Exhibit 5-3.

How to Clear Hurdle 8

- On your calendar, highlight the last Friday of each month as a time to reflect on your learning progress. Also mark the date by which you want to complete each of your action steps. That way you can keep track of your progress.

- Use a partner as a motivator, or work with someone who has a stake in whether you accomplish your goal.

- Go public with someone. Announce your learning goal and ask the person to hold you accountable.

- Analyze what is holding you back.

Hurdle 9: Hitting the Wall

Red Flag Excuses: *My learning goal is too challenging. I have hit a wall and just can't get through.*

Ira Kaplan, CEO of Servolift Eastern, a food equipment manufacturer, wanted to write a strategic vision for his company. He had grown up with his family business, worked there for 23 years, and thought it would be easy to write the focus of the company, which he then would communicate to his employees.

About 2 months into the process Kaplan hit a wall. He realized how difficult it was to put the company's vision into words. The company was more complex than he realized and had a wide variety of people with a stake in the company, all with different expectations.

Keep Your Eyes Open for an Ambush

When we gathered one morning in the conference room of a posh hotel, the executives were attentive and enthusiastic. They had flown in from around the country and had been working on their learning plans for 4 months. That morning we were to audit each person's progress toward his or her goal. In the afternoon everyone would set new learning goals.

As we discussed each person's plan and progress, the president was particularly effective in getting the group to clarify their most urgent business issues as a senior management team.

I felt the meeting was going well...until the midmorning break told me I had misread my audience. Rather than using the 10-minute break to reflect on our discussion, half of those present grabbed their portable phones and made calls to their home offices.

It was clear that their minds had been only partially focused on what was being said in the seminar. The senior managers had not been able to tear their thoughts away from the daily grind of their business. They felt compelled to check in at the office, even though they were quick to acknowledge the importance of a higher-level learning.

Their divided attention was disconcerting, but the crippling blow came at the lunch break, when the president approached me with a crestfallen look. The company CEO had just called and said he wanted to see the president and the vice president of marketing about an important deal that had just come up. The president apologized and said he would try to be back by 3 p.m. When we left at 5 p.m., the president still had not reappeared.

Here was a man committed to his own learning and the learning of his people. He knew the value of focusing his senior managers on development and improved performance, yet his example said otherwise. By leaving a meeting where he had gathered people from all over the country, his message was clear: Learning was *not* his top priority. Why, then, pretend that it was?

Did he ask his CEO if it was possible to push the meeting off until 5 o'clock? Or was this a meeting that could have been postponed until the next day? I don't know. He never told me. But the meeting fell apart after that.

Both the president and his senior managers crashed into the time hurdle, which is, by far, the most difficult to maneuver. We are so busy doing that we rarely take time for improving.

Exhibit 5-3. If follow-through is inadequate, there will be no learning: good intentions are not enough.

To break through the wall, Kaplan first teamed up with his vice president of manufacturing and engineering, who had done extensive quantitative industry analysis. They jointly considered the needs and expectations of those with a stake in the business, including major customers, stockholders, and employees.

After 4 months Kaplan had gathered, analyzed, and tested the information he needed to write his company's vision. He then hired an outside consultant who had experience in writing strategic plans. The result was Servolift's first strategic and operating plan, which now guides the work of the senior management team and the rest of the company.

Cause and Effect Diagram.   If you find yourself hitting a wall, mapping out a cause and effect (see Figure 5-1) diagram may help you analyze the problem. A cause and effect diagram is useful in identifying the causes of a particular result. In this case, we identify why Kaplan was not able to create a written vision for Servolift Eastern.

The causes of Kaplan's lack of progress include himself, his method, others, and materials and machines he did not use. In successfully writing his company's vision, he addressed each of the causes that had kept him from being successful the first time through. The results on the right and the causes on the left give the appearance of the bones of a fish.

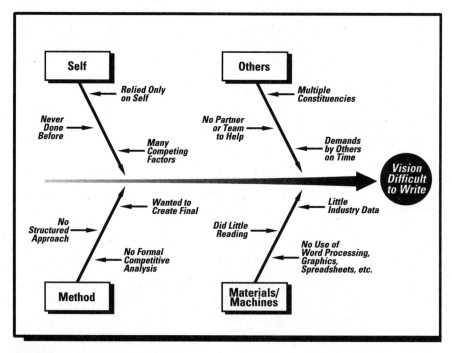

Figure 5-1. Cause and effect diagram.

If you feel you have hit a wall, you can use similar analysis to understand what is keeping you from achieving your learning goal. First identify the major categories that might be holding you back. Then along the "bones" add the specific causes, which are the details of what is blocking your progress. The final step is to then identify action steps to address those barricades.

How to Clear Hurdle 9

- Just put one foot in front of the next and keep going.

- Examine your approach to see if there's an easier way to reach your goal.

- Try breaking down your goal into smaller pieces. That way you can achieve a sense of momentum as you successfully complete each step.

Hurdle 10: When You Can't Imagine Reaching Your Goal

Red Flag Excuse: *I don't have a clear picture of myself achieving my goal.*

When people talk about jobs or feats they consider impossible, they all begin the same way: "I can't imagine..." (I can't imagine running a $6 billion company. I can't imagine writing a dissertation while working full time. I can't imagine running a marathon. I can't imagine doing what you do.)

Fact is, if you can't imagine it, you'll probably never do it. If you're serious about succeeding at something, you must be able to visualize yourself achieving it. You must be able to project yourself into the future and see yourself successful at whatever it is you hope to accomplish.

We do it all the time without even thinking about it. Our projections and visualizations have been a vital part of who we are since we were first asked, "What do you want to be when you grow up?"

It's a question we're still asking. And it's a question your learning goal can help you answer. What is it that you want to be? What is it that your learning goal can help you be? Name it. Picture it. Work toward it.

How to Clear Hurdle 10

- Paint a detailed mental picture of yourself achieving your goal.

- Draw a picture of yourself having reached your goal.

- Identify how you'll feel when you accomplish your goal, and if others are affected, imagine how they'll respond.

- Plan to reward yourself in some way once you reach your goal.

After You Clear the Hurdles

Once you recognize the red flags to learning and identify the hurdles they represent, you can master whatever problems stand in your way. The best learners are able to hover over a situation like a helicopter and garner a clear picture of the problem. They then can descend to the ground and take corrective action. The rewards are great. Once you've cleared your hurdles:

- You will rely more on your own judgment. You will have successfully determined when you needed to persevere in pursuing your goal and when you needed to be flexible.
- You will feel crafty at having gotten the best of the situation.
- You will have sold your ideas to those who may have initially resisted.
- You will be more in touch with your feelings about your job.
- You will have a clearer picture of what is important to you and your work.
- You will be more confident of your ability to slice through problems.
- You will be a better steward of your time.

PART 3

Leaders and Learning Organizations

6

The Complete Formula for a Learning Organization

Lear Seating Corporation is a Michigan-based company that supplies seating systems to the automotive industry. For the last decade, they have experienced a 30 percent compound annual growth rate from just over $100 million to over $1.25 billion in sales. And despite a stagnant industry, they see their major growth in front of them.

With a focus on just-in-time manufacturing, the company can manufacture and deliver a car seating system within 2 hours from the time it is ordered. (In 1991 they made 3.5 million seat sets.) Their least efficient plants turn their inventory 50 times a year, their average plants turn their inventory 80 times, and their outstanding plants turn their inventory 120 times a year.

The company originally sold car seat springs to the automotive industry but now designs, develops, manufactures, and delivers entire car seat systems to automobile assembly plants in the United States and Europe. When I called Lear Seating's CEO Ken Way to ask for an interview, I explained that I wanted to discuss his role in creating a learning organization. Way was quick with his response: "You don't want to come see us," he said. "We don't have a training department."

Of course, that was all the more reason to pay Lear Seating a visit. Although Way's comment reflected the old paradigm of learning occurring only in a classroom, it was clear that he had discarded that formula long ago. His company offers a clear-cut example of a *learning organization, one that continually improves by rapidly creating and refining the capabilities needed for future success.* Learning organizations are in constant flux: revising, strengthening, and creating simultaneously.

In a *Sloan Management Review* article Ray Stata asks, "What is organizational learning, and how does it differ from individual learning?" Each is a process that entails new insights and modified behavior. But he says they differ on at least two counts:

> First, organizational learning occurs through shared insights, knowledge, and mental models....Change is blocked unless all of the major decision makers learn together, come to share beliefs and goals, and are committed to take the actions necessary for change.
>
> Second, learning builds on past knowledge and experience—that is, on memory. Organizational memory depends on institutional mechanisms (e.g., policies, strategies, and explicit models) used to retain knowledge....
>
> The challenge, then, is to discover new management tools and methods to accelerate organizational learning, build consensus for change, and facilitate the change process.[28]

Learning is fundamental to growth and progress. It undergirds all the current theories on how to improve business, be it total quality or just-in-time manufacturing. Learning is the foundation without which any attempts at improvement would fall flat.

As Peter M. Senge says in an article in the *Sloan Management Review*, learning organizations are required to be not only adaptive, which is to cope, but to be generative, which is to create. He states: "The total quality movement in Japan illustrates the evolution from adaptive to generative learning. With its emphasis on continuous experimentation and feedback, the total quality movement has been the first wave in building learning organizations."[29]

In citing their evolution from adaptive to generative learning, Senge points out that in their early years of total quality, the focus of the Japanese was on making a reliable product. The focus then shifted to understanding better what the customer wanted and providing it. Now the Japanese have taken another leap forward by seeking to understand what the customer might truly value but would never think to ask for. That's generative learning. That's how companies get on the cutting edge.

Looking for Learning Organizations

Every year I read dozens of annual reports, looking for companies that display the telltale signs of a learning organization. By analyzing what is presented—and researching what may have been left out—I find many companies have latched onto learning as a way to transform themselves into industry front-runners. Each of the following companies has discovered ways to significantly improve performance in areas critical for business success. Studying these companies provides insight into how businesses can use intentional learning to achieve exceptional results:

1. Corning's quality-driven turnaround
2. Analog Devices' creation of a learning organization
3. Kodak's transition to a new technology
4. Boeing's commitment to a new product
5. Lear Seating's high growth

It came as no surprise to find that Lear Seating had a clearly stated, challenging companywide vision. The annual corporate profile says the company's mission is "to provide exemplary service, superior quality, cost leadership, and leading-edge technology."

In reading Corning's annual report, I again was struck by the clarity of the company's vision and by its constancy of purpose to quality and diversity. On quality, CEO Jamie Houghton wrote: "Total Quality is a theme common to everything we do, from strategic planning to processing an invoice. There's a clear understanding at Corning that, in the merciless business world of the 1990s, quality is the only enduring competitive edge."

The annual report of Analog Devices, a Massachusetts-based high-technology company, told a different story. Here was a company in the throes of major changes: from being technology-driven to customer-driven, from having highly autonomous business units to aligning businesses so they can learn from each other. Analog CEO Ray Stata wrote:

> Organizational restructuring is just part of the change we must bring about. More importantly, we must accelerate the rate of improvement in all that we do. In the '80s, as part of our quality improvement thrust, we made significant progress in improving on-time delivery, defect rates, yields, and cycle time. Today, 96% of our shipments are made on time, compared to 75% to 80% just a few years ago.
>
> While that represents real progress, it is not nearly good enough to be a winner in the '90s. We have therefore renewed our commitment

to quality management and improvement, with top management taking a much more active role in learning new improvement skills, applying them in their own daily work, and gaining the knowledge and understanding to competently diagnose the work and progress of others.

Kodak's annual report began with a firm commitment from CEO Kay Whitmore, who wrote: "From my perspective as the company's new chief executive officer, the most significant development of the past year was to declare in no uncertain terms our strategic intention to be the world leader in imaging and then, with the announcement of Photo CD and new digital copier-duplicators, to show the world that Kodak has the technology, the will, and the reach to realize its vision."

The centerpiece of Boeing's annual report is the design and development of a new project, the 777 long-range twin jet. It describes the new challenge in this way: "Our commercial airplane business is to push forward with the development of the 777 model in an efficient, cost-effective manner. We have assigned many of the company's most talented managers and engineers to this program. I fully expect our 777 team to deliver a cost-competitive product that will set a new industry standard for engineering excellence."

Alan Mulally, vice president and general manager of the 777 Division, said in an interview: "If we learn well, our reward is to stay in business and keep our name in the phone book. And if we learn really well, we grow and create opportunities for our people, customers, stockholders, and community. If we don't learn, we are out of business."

In these companies, learning goes far beyond simply training and developing individuals. For them, learning permeates the processes used throughout the organization, with the goal being to produce the best possible product for its customers. Such learning, put into action, creates new competencies, new capabilities, and improved performance.

The Formula for a Learning Organization

In studying businesses across the country, we've found that the most successful companies, both small and large, employ the same basic elements to create their own unique learning organizations. From our research, we have devised a formula for creating a learning organization. This formula is given in Figure 6-1. Each element of the formula is absolutely mandatory. If one element is missing your organization will either learn the wrong things or learn at a rate less than its full potential.

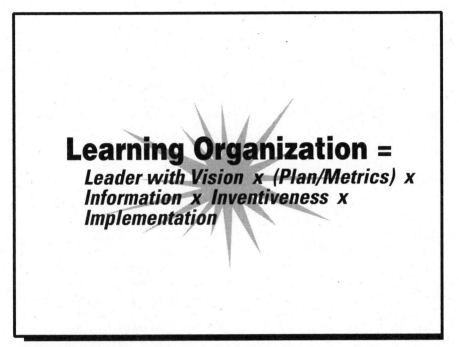

Figure 6-1. Elements of a learning organization.

But how you go about realizing each element is completely up to you and the distinctive personality of your organization.

For example, in the companies we discuss in this chapter, Corning invests heavily in training and Lear Seating has no training department at all. Boeing creates an organization starting with a clean sheet of paper while Kodak must foster learning inside a highly successful, very focused 90-year-old business. And while the concept of a learning organization is new to each of the above-mentioned companies, Ray Stata at Analog Devices has been working for 15 years to create a learning organization.

Using these companies as examples, we hope to provide a framework for understanding the key elements for creating a learning organization; elements that you can apply to accelerate learning in your organization. In studying successful learning organizations, time after time we saw:

1. A leader with a clearly defined vision

2. A detailed, measurable action plan

3. The rapid sharing of information

4. Inventiveness

5. The ability to implement the plan

When these elements are present, an organization gains the capabilities needed to break out of the crowd. Each front-runner reports that leading the pack may be exhausting, but it is a hell of a lot more fun than being stuck in the back. Let's look at each element of the formula in turn.

Learning Organization = *Leader with Vision*

Without a leader committed to learning, an organization will never approach its potential for success. Only the leader can commit the organization to facing reality head-on. From his or her vantage point, the leader is the one best positioned to see and articulate the performance gap between what the organization currently achieves and what the organization needs to achieve in the future. A strong learning leader has the ability and the will to close that gap despite internal skeptics and external difficulties.

The leader must have a clear vision, deeply held and consistently communicated. That seems simple enough, but how many of us have worked for a company with no vision that anyone could ascertain? As John Kotter, an author and professor at Harvard Business School, points out in a *Harvard Business Review* article, "What Leaders Really Do," a vision isn't a mystical or magical concept. It is born from the needs of important stakeholders, from senior managers to wage roll, from stockholders to suppliers and customers.

> What's crucial about a vision is not its originality but how well it serves the interests of important constituencies—customers, stockholders, employees—and how easily it can be translated into a realistic competitive strategy.
>
> Bad visions tend to ignore the legitimate needs and rights of important constituencies—favoring, say, employees over customers or stockholders. Or they are strategically unsound. When a company that has never been better than a weak competitor in an industry suddenly starts talking about becoming number one, that is a pipe dream, not a vision.[30]

A vision should energize those striving to bring it into reality. Because a vision generally is quite different from the one that went before it, it often faces skeptics who are comfortable with—and sometimes addicted to—the old vision. Old habits die hard. They always have. Moses faced a rebellion when leading the children of Israel into the wilderness after they fled Egypt and the tyranny of Pharaoh. Many of the Israelites wanted to return to the slavery they knew rather than journey on to the unknown promised land.

Vision enables members of the organization to anticipate what they can contribute to help achieve important results. As Ted Hutton, president of Waverly, Inc., a publishing and printing company, said, "If you don't have a clear picture that guides everyone, they either focus on the wrong thing or wait to be told what to do. In either case the business will not produce the results it is capable of."

Jamie Houghton pointed out another valuable role of a clear vision. Pointing to a diagram of the four key business segments served by Corning, he said, "By clearly defining what businesses we want to be in, we then know what not to do. Time after time someone will come up with a good idea, but one that is not central to the success of one of our four businesses. Because we are clear about our purpose, it is easier for us to say no. By knowing when to say no, we better focus our efforts."

When we work with companies that are not up to speed in their learning, the learning organization formula quickly pinpoints the problem areas. Often we find they lack any stated vision, or the vision isn't consistent between corporate and operating units, or the companies lack good ways to measure progress.

We have a simple test that reveals the degree to which a vision has been communicated. When meeting with a president and his or her senior team, we ask each to write down the company's vision and how it is measured. They then read what they have written. Many presidents are horrified at the divergence on their staff. When asking the same question at an operating level, we often find pens never touch the paper because the vision has not been communicated or because it is so complicated that it cannot be remembered.

Compare that to the clarity of purpose for those working on Boeing's newest project, the 777 long-range twin-jet. The vision is "Working together to produce the preferred new airplane family." Sound too simple? The best visions usually are direct and uncomplicated.

To set the vision and lead a learning organization is to be on a never-ending pilgrimage. The question is always, "What more can we do?" It is never, "Have we done enough?" To be a learning leader is demanding. It requires insight, strength, and perseverance. But it is crucial if businesses and organizations are to be successful.

Because of their importance in shaping learning, Chapter 7 is devoted to learning leaders: how to identify one, how to become one, and examples.

Learning Organization = Leader
with Vision × (*Plan/Metrics*)

With a leader and a vision in place, an organization next needs the ability to develop a plan of action with detailed metrics. How will you achieve what you have identified as your goal? How will you measure your progress? How will you gauge the effectiveness of your processes? Planning and a system of measurement keeps the vision grounded in reality and prevents it from becoming an esoteric exercise. The larger vision for improvement and change must be turned into specific action steps.

How you measure your progress depends upon the vision itself. Time lines are important to the accomplishment of any vision, with intermediate goals to be reached along the way. Whether your vision involves quality improvement, reduced production time, a reorganization, or a changing business focus, establish a time line and a completion date. Learning organizations rigorously measure their progress and hold themselves accountable. The breadth of the vision, the detail of the planning, and the feedback from the metrics drive the inventiveness and implementation in the final factor of the formula.

Learning Organization = Leader
with Vision × (Plan/Metrics) ×
Information

To be uninformed is to be vulnerable to threats lurking *outside* the company and missed opportunities *inside* the company. Learning organizations don't assume that management knows it all or that the rank and file can read the corporate mind. And they certainly don't pretend to have an innate knowledge of what's going on outside their doors with customers, competitors, and world leaders in particular competencies.

A learning organization is hungry for knowledge. Information that flows with speed, honesty, and openness is at the heart of the organization's ability to be quick and canny in any business environment. It is important to take a good hard look in the mirror, noting your flaws and your attributes. But don't be too taken with yourself. For businesses, narcissism is the road to ruin. You also have to look out of the window.

Outside Information.   What happens outside an organization often determines its success or failure. If internal achievements—no matter how great—don't meet the demands of the external environment, you're spinning your wheels. Companies must interface with the rest of the world. Despite the obvious importance of external information, ideas that originate outside a company are the most underutilized source of knowledge.

At Du Pont Merck Pharmaceutical, tapping that source of knowledge is one of their primary learning tools.

"We conduct probably 120 symposiums a year," said Gil Berezin, director of clinical development and education. "We have 20 field-based people whose major responsibility is to gain access to the major thought leaders and form partnerships so that we can learn from them and they can learn from us."

The initiative to become a learning organization usually follows a strong dose of outside reality. Corning's quest began when Jamie Houghton saw true quality during a visit to IBM. Analog Devices began with the Center for Quality Management where it learned that companies can learn faster from each other than trying to learn alone. Boeing got on the learning bandwagon when it became clear that unless it learned to build significantly better airplanes at greatly reduced costs, customers would defect to major competitors. There are three rules in seeking outside information:

1. Court the customer.

2. Steal shamelessly.

3. Check out competitors.

1. *Court the customer.*   Customer service and satisfaction are given lip service throughout the business world. In learning organizations, they aren't empty words. Customers are sought out early and often. While customer requirements often are maddening, companies that listen well gain a powerful competitive advantage.

Customer requests can lead companies into unexplored territory. At Boeing, an airline customer said he wanted an airplane with a fuselage that could change size. The aeronautical engineer told the customer that the request was impossible. But the engineer then asked the key question: "Why do you want such a plane?"

The customer replied, "Because we don't know 10 years from now what size plane we will need. If we had the flexibility to shrink or expand the size of the plane, it would help us meet future travel demands, even those we cannot anticipate." You can read how Boeing accommodated this customer request later in this chapter (see Exhibit 6-1).

2. *Steal shamelessly.*   A learning organization must not fall into the trap of trying to reinvent the wheel. If another company is terrific at something your business needs to know or do, enlist their help. A major paradigm shift going on today is that companies are no longer holding

their organizational processes as secrets but are willing to share what they have discovered. Such sharing is built into the Baldrige Award for quality, which requires winners to actively share with other businesses the knowledge that led to their winning entry.

The isolation companies once operated in is breaking down. As David Luther, senior vice president of quality at Corning, said: "Steal shamelessly. Have you heard the term `steal shamelessly'? I encourage people to adopt it. It's absolutely crazy to reinvent something that somebody else has done.

"We looked at Westinghouse for instance. They've got a fabulous course on process management. We went out and bought it from them. We brought it in, and I think we were on the gun and running within 60 days.

"For us to write that course would have been 18 months. Who cares that we didn't invent it? Approach, deployment, and implementation. Nobody pays for approach. There are a million approaches out there. Many of them are brilliant. Most are adequate. Spend your time on deployment and going after results."

In learning companies, benchmarking and learning from each other's best practices are common occurrences. When I met with Goodloe Suttler of Analog Devices, he was just back from observing organizational strategies at Milliken. Corning had recently been to IBM to discover how it was measuring the effectiveness of training. Lear Seating trades product design information with a Japanese ally to gain the ally's best thinking on ways to improve Lear's manufacturing processes.

The tentacles of a learning organization reach far and deep, supplying a constant stream of new information and ideas. Any hesitancy to seek outside information disappears once an organization recognizes the advantages of utilizing the knowledge of other companies.

While I was talking to Phil Condit at Boeing, he mentioned a problem they were trying to resolve. I suggested he contact Hewlett-Packard, who had already solved it. And because I knew that Boeing had solved a problem Hewlett-Packard was wrestling with, it only took a 10-minute phone call to start the process by which they could learn from one another.

Compare this to a recent conversation I had with the president of a multibillion dollar company. As we discussed learning strategies, I suggested he and his senior managers take a look at other companies that excelled at the very competencies that he sought. His response was lukewarm at best: "I am not sure what someone who is not part of our industry can teach us."

3. *Check out competitors.*   Competitor information is critical. First, you need to identify your key competitors because they may not be who you think. (In the case of Kodak, it is not only Fuji but also Sony.) Second, you

need to take seriously the threat of present and future competitors rather than assume they will go away or are unworthy of consideration.

The U.S. automotive industry continues to pay for its past disregard of foreign competitors. Even after it became apparent that Toyota was able to manufacture cars of better quality at lower cost, it took General Motors more than a decade to adopt flexible manufacturing technologies.

The move from stovepipe organizations to teams that included designers and builders took more than 15 years. Thus Honda designed and built three generations of its Acura while GM was still working the bugs out of its first-generation Saturn production.

Once you gather competitor information, be prepared to act on it. An organization needs to empower its members to continually ask, "What has our competitor learned to do better or differently that we should adopt or leap frog?"

Arrogance cannot be tolerated. When someone is caught defending a current practice against the better practice of a competitor, he or she should be asked to switch roles and take on the argument from the side of the competitor. A learning organization values good ideas, no matter where they originate.

They live the motto of the Virginia Theological Seminary, which is, "Seek Ye the Truth, Come Whence it May, Cost What it Will."

Inside Information.   When looking internally, companies must get an accurate read of their working climate and be quick to share information across departmental lines. There are three rules for seeking information within your company:

1. Know who you are.
2. Share information freely.
3. Don't hoard information for personal power.

1. *Know who you are.*   Know thyself is fundamental for learning organizations. Problems and solutions are shared with a degree of trust missing in many companies. Information is not tightly held by a person or team to gain an internal competitive advantage. It is relayed quickly to those who can use it to improve performance in any and every part of the organization.

Whether you are a CEO or a middle manager, you must know what is going on inside your organization. You may not be in a position to know firsthand what issues and problems are percolating throughout the company, but you had better have a handle on it.

In trying to keep abreast of internal goings-on, be honest about how much you want to know firsthand. Many executives like to project an image of availability and empathy to fellow workers. But if you don't have an open door, don't pretend that you do. Most managers are too busy dealing with their own day-to-day problems to take on someone else's. By all means delegate the problem-solving responsibility to a direct report, but keep informed and don't send mixed signals. Many managers say they want to know what's going on, but what they mean is this: Come to me with the good news and keep the problems to yourself.

I knew an editor at the now-defunct *Charlotte News* (North Carolina) who made it clear to all reporters that his door was open. "If you have a problem, don't hesitate to come and talk about it," he said at one staff meeting.

One young reporter, not yet well-versed at double-speak, took the editor at his word and marched into his office the next day. The reporter stayed for about 15 minutes and then returned to her desk. Shortly thereafter the editor came out, marched across the newsroom, and in a stage whisper to the city editor growled, "Can't you take care of your own problems?"

This time, the editor's unspoken message was clearly understood by everyone: "My door is open, but you'd better not cross the threshold."

Learning organizations must be who they say they are. Double-talk only heightens apprehensions and feeds the grapevine. Make no mistake about it. What grows on the grapevine can have a tremendous impact on the well-being of your organization. When unchecked and unanswered, the grapevine becomes more like kudzu, blanketing the workplace with uncertainty and obscuring the company's objectives.

At Du Pont Merck, a worldwide pharmaceutical operation, they've used open communication to beat the grapevine in speed and accuracy. Executive Vice President Kurt Landgraf communicates monthly by voice mail with every one of his 2200 employees, telling them what's going right and what's going wrong.

"They absolutely love it because they feel part of what is going on," Landgraf said. "They hear things from us first and it is very important that they don't get information through the rumor mill.

"One of the things we did was to end the rumor mill. We made it not valuable because no one had the need for it. I tell people, `When you hear something that concerns you from the rumor mill, call me up and I'll tell you the truth. I'll tell you whether it's right or wrong.'"

And unlike the newspaper editor, he meant it. Landgraf got calls asking if it were true that the corporate headquarters was moving to Rahway, New Jersey, or that the sales incentive compensation program was changing, or that quotas were going up.

He said answering such questions was time well-spent. "When you stop the rumor mill, people feel more secure in their jobs," Landgraf said. "They feel more comfortable that they have the information they need to make decisions in their own lives."

There are all kinds of ways to stay in touch with employees. To get an accurate assessment of the day-to-day work climate, some companies use sophisticated internal surveys that provide year-by-year trends on organizational attitude and climate. But one of the most effective tools is face-to-face meetings between leaders and workers. Both Corning and Boeing employ techniques that enable people to raise sensitive issues without disclosing their identity. By equalizing the power between leader and worker, the leaders were able to gather better information about what really was going on versus what they hoped might be going on.

2. *Share information freely throughout the organization.*   Promote companywide learning. Good internal communication requires transmitting and implementing ideas from one section of the company to another. Analog Devices has a fundamental belief that shared information is vital to business success. The company went from ten autonomous business units to a globally managed manufacturing function so that their plants in Japan, Ireland, and the United States might learn from each other more rapidly.

CEO Ray Stata says: "When you start thinking about learning organizations, you begin to see that structure can be an impediment to organizational learning. Or the way you structure the company can facilitate learning.

"Tom Urwin, our vice president of manufacturing, was interested in organizational learning. He brought together councils of people who began to compare notes and learn from each other. The way we structured the manufacturing organization causes a lot of learning to take place."

Kodak, through its Kodak Class benchmarking process, identifies best practices throughout the company and uses them as a source of knowledge and inspiration for other parts of the company. Their Australian plant went from worst to best in efficiency. It eventually became the benchmark for teams of workers who wanted to improve efficiency in the Rochester, New York, plant.

Solectron, a Malcolm Baldrige award winner, has daily updates on the quality of each product. It uses computer systems to alert workers on the factory floor when a process is about to go out of control.

Learning organizations go to great lengths to structure themselves in a way that speeds the flow of internal information. At Analog Devices and Boeing, the organizations are structured primarily to move information more rapidly across internal organizational boundaries.

3. *Don't hoard information for personal power.*   Make it clear that you're in business for the good of the entire company, not personal gain. Create cultural norms that place a high value on honesty, even in the face of difficulty. Instead of covering up problems or fixing blame, make problems visible so that solutions can be found quickly.

A Learning Organization = Leader with Vision × (Plan/Metrics) × Information × *Inventiveness*

Once an organization has a leader with a vision, a strong, measurable plan, and accurate information from both inside and outside the company, it's time to get the creative juices flowing.

When it comes to solving problems, the best learning companies spend little time trying to adapt an old solution to fit a new problem. They face the issue with new eyes open to fresh ideas and theories. They see problem solving as a real learning opportunity.

New ideas or approaches can be threatening when a manager or company has invested heavily in old ideas that either have outlived their usefulness or never were particularly successful to begin with.

The point must be made, early and often, that the organization has yet to reach its potential. It's the image of the pilgrim who never arrives. You may be good but you can be better. You may be fast, but you must be faster. You may be smart, but you will be smarter. There is no finish line to cross. You simply keep trying to better your best. It's not unusual that two recent Baldrige Award winners used the image of a journey to communicate their continual improvement process to employees.

There are numerous catalysts for inventiveness. It can be driven by the recognition of the performance gap between where the company currently is and where it wants to be. Sometimes inventiveness is triggered by customer requirements: see Exhibit 6-1 for an example. Still other times inventiveness is driven by competition, such as Kodak's entry into digital technology, which is discussed in Chapter 9.

Reframing the problem or task to view it from a new perspective can be the best stimulus for inventiveness. In a speech to business leaders during a workshop on work and learning, Victoria Marsick of Columbia University and Kathleen Dechant of the University of Connecticut described this reframing as a critical process in learning. It is what allows you to see in a new light and discover a new path for action. In Exhibit 6-2, Phil Condit describes how he reframed the way he manages his organization at Boeing.

As Charles Handy said in *The Age of Unreason:* "The learning organization is constantly reframing the world and its part in it.…The quality

---

Boeing's Flexible Fuselage

Boeing's inventive answer to a customer's request for a plane with a flexible fuselage was to reframe the way Boeing viewed the interior of an airplane. As a result, they created a plane with a flexible interior, quick-change seats, and movable galleys.

Overnight, the interior of the 777 can be reconfigured from vacation-travel, family-style seating to business travel seating for fewer higher-paying passengers. Without customer involvement, the paradigm of a rigid interior would not have been broken. Based on past experience, it would have been easy to say, "Flexible fuselage? You are nuts!" But by being inventive, Boeing won a customer and created a new prototype.

Exhibit 6-1. A customer's request leads Boeing into new learning.

circles in manufacturing organizations are, at their best, examples of reframing at the shop-floor and office-floor level. They are, actually, the wheel of learning in action, with problems to be raised, ideas suggested, tested, and reviewed. They will always work best, however, when the problem can be reframed."[31]

Normally, technical organizations would not consider using quality principles to improve their research and development. Yet Analog Devices did, and it took real inventiveness, a reframing of what they had done in the past, to make it work.

Using quality principles and tools to improve the research and development processes may sound simple until you have worked with bright, world-class researchers who value their independence. Ray Stata explained:

"Dennis Buss, our head of technology, has taken the initiative to convert the technical community into believers in quality management. It turns out that the technical community are the most avid resisters to many of these learning and change phenomenon. They resist because the technical community values the lone ranger, star performer whose genius creates a great idea out of the blue, all without any bureaucracy. For them, bureaucracy is the anathema of inventiveness, so they are the champions of the antibureaucrats.

"Now to some extent, quality management has an aspect of organization to it, in that teamwork is important, methodology counts, and a belief that it isn't only pure genius that creates innovation, but that you can create structures that facilitate innovation. All those things that are alien to where the technical community is coming from.

Reframing Your Management Style

Phil Condit, president of The Boeing Company, describes the process he went through in changing his fundamental assumptions about how to structure the work environment of the Boeing 777 program. When he led that division, he used an organizational coach to reframe the way he managed his people. He tells the story:

"I have almost always worked in a bureaucratic environment. Very structured, very organized. You just can't have 160,000 people without a big bureaucracy. So I've spent a lot of my career trying to break down boundaries and loosen up organizations. I rattle around, I shake them, and I move people around. Don Krebs, my organizational development expert, came in and warned, `You've got to be careful.' He got out a piece of paper and drew pictures of two kinds of organizations.

"He said there is an overbounded organization typical of a bureaucracy. Lots of structure. Everybody knows where the power is. They know the formal routes of communication. They know who can get things done and who can't. They are very comfortable because they know where they belong in the organization. They may bitch a lot but they are comfortable. They know where all the pieces are. The greatest danger of the overbounded organization is that it can't move. It will collapse inward on itself.

"Then there is an underbounded organization. Very free form, very entrepreneurial, but very insecure. They are not sure where they belong. They don't know what their role is. They don't know who really has the power or who makes the decisions. The danger of the underbounded organization is that it will fly apart.

"Krebs said that in our division, we had an underbounded organization because it was brand new with lots of new people. He said, `You're in here rattling around, shaking it up, and it's in danger of coming apart simply because you're causing motion when it needs stability.'

"I cooled it for a while and let things settle down. He was dead right. There were lots of people in the organization who just didn't know where they fit.

"This learning process of looking anew at a situation continues to go on for me and for some of my key people. Just being able to sit and talk to Don and understand another view of something that we don't normally think about is most helpful."

Exhibit 6-2. A keen understanding of the company's working climate is essential for the learning organization.

"So the technical community points to the dichotomy between wanting continuous improvement and bureaucracy or breakthroughs and inventiveness. They say to their boss, `You have to make your choice but you can't have it both ways.' I think breaking that dichotomy and saying these are not either/or phenomenon is the unsolved problem, and Dennis Buss has taken that on. He saw that dichotomy and found a way to solve it." The result has been a significant productivity increase.

An arthritic organization lacks this inventiveness and remains deeply rutted in the same path. A learning organization is inventive, supple, and responsive to change.

Learning Organization × Leader with Vision × (Plan/Metrics) × Information × Inventiveness∇*Implementation*

Now it's time to *act*. Without action, the other elements in the formula are only a mind game. All the learning and creativity in the world is worthless if it does not get implemented through action. If the rest of the formula is in place, this should be the simple part of the equation, but many companies seem to get stuck just before the final prize. Sometimes it is the risk of trying something new that pulls them up short. Sometimes they just get so caught up in the learning process that they forget the end purpose—to actually use what they have learned. They are great at huddles but poor at executing plays.

Learning organizations have an urgency to act. These companies are excellent at executing their learning. The one company that declined to be a case study for this book stands out as an example.

In looking at the company's financial performance, I was struck that its stock had gone up by 950 percent in 5 years. It had experienced an average growth five times greater than its industry and had annual sales of over $2 billion. From having read its annual reports for a number of years, I had a good idea where learning had played an important role in the success of its business. I called a senior manager to ask if the company would participate in my study of learning organizations.

He said no, explaining, "Whether it's entering markets or how we train our people, the only competitive advantage we have is execution. We have spent years refining that process, and I don't see any reason to tell one of our competitors how we do it. We have declined a number of business school studies and case writing efforts. I apologize for not being helpful on this, but, unlike other companies, we don't have anything we can put a patent on."

The ability to execute, to implement, is the final payoff. It enables Lear Seating to deliver a car seat system ready for installation within 2 hours of the time it was ordered. It enables Boeing to find design conflicts 10 months earlier because of its paperless, computer-driven design process. Corning's ability to implement what they learned enables you to talk on a telephone using fiber optics.

To implement requires perseverance. Because companies like those mentioned above are being inventive and working to achieve such high goals, they sometimes will go down the wrong path or come up short. They have an incredible tenacity and sense of responsibility to achieve the goals they have set for themselves. They never give up.

Creating a Learning Organization

If you want to create a learning organization or measure your company's strengths and weaknesses, hold your organization up to the learning formula. If an element is missing or is weaker than the others, then you have identified a potential learning opportunity.

A new Japanese business strategy, described by Peter Drucker in an article in *The Wall Street Journal*, is a perfect example of the learning formula in action. He describes the process by which Japanese companies are organizing the systematic abandonment of their own products. Their research and development departments are simultaneously producing three new products in the time normally taken to produce one.

On the first day a product is sold, the Japanese set a deadline for abandoning the new product, a deadline that forces them to work immediately on replacing it. Drucker says they work on three tracks: (1) improving the product with specific goals and deadlines; (2) developing a new product out of the old, which they call *leaping*; and (3) pursuing genuine innovation.

"The idea is to produce three new products to replace each present product, with the same investment of time and money, with one of the three then becoming the new market leader and producing the `innovator's profit.'"[32]

In this business strategy, the *leader* must have a *vision* to create the new market pacesetter. Specific goals and deadlines supply the *plan* and the *metrics*. In order to pursue three tracks simultaneously, *information* must flow freely internally and be constantly updated externally. Tremendous *inventiveness* is required to make the leaps in imagination needed to get beyond today's capabilities. The end products are the *implementation*, the tangible results, the successful completion.

You can use the quiz in Exhibit 6-3 to see whether your organization measures up to the learning formula.

The Learning Organization Quiz

Step 1: Decide what entity you want to rate. It can be your entire company, department, or working group, as long as the entity has an identifiable leader. Write the name of the organization below.

Organization: _____

Step 2: First rate your organization according to how true each statement *currently* is. Next select the preferred condition. Total all circled numbers in each column. On the scale at the bottom on the page, put a * by your organization's current score and a + by the preferred score.

	Current						Preferred				
	Not True				Very True		Not True				Very True
1. Our leader has a clear vision.	1	2	3	4	5		1	2	3	4	5
2. Our leader's vision is clearly communicated and understood by all.	1	2	3	4	5		1	2	3	4	5
3. Our leader is admired by the troops.	1	2	3	4	5		1	2	3	4	5
4. Our leaders walk their talk.	1	2	3	4	5		1	2	3	4	5
5. We have a clear plan to transform our vision into reality.	1	2	3	4	5		1	2	3	4	5
6. We effectively measure our processes, progress, and results.	1	2	3	4	5		1	2	3	4	5
7. Results of our metrics are shared rapidly and widely.	1	2	3	4	5		1	2	3	4	5
8. External and internal customer requirements are clearly understood.	1	2	3	4	5		1	2	3	4	5
9. Our customers are involved in the design and development of our products or services.	1	2	3	4	5		1	2	3	4	5

Exhibit 6-3. This quiz will help you rate your organizational entity in terms of the learning model.

	Current						Preferred				
	Not True				Very True		Not True				Very True
10. We routinely learn from the best practices of other companies whose capabilities are better than ours in critical areas.	1	2	3	4	5		1	2	3	4	5
11. We avoid the problem of "not invented here" by using the good ideas of others.	1	2	3	4	5		1	2	3	4	5
12. Other companies learnings are quickly transmitted and acted on.	1	2	3	4	5		1	2	3	4	5
13. We rapidly identify a best practice in one part of our organization and share it so it can be used by another part of our organization.	1	2	3	4	5		1	2	3	4	5
14. Our people readily share their good ideas with others to help our organization be more successful.	1	2	3	4	5		1	2	3	4	5
15. The training we do is actively supported by the work environment.	1	2	3	4	5		1	2	3	4	5
16. We often accept challenges even when not sure how to meet them.	1	2	3	4	5		1	2	3	4	5
17. We are inventive in how we meet our challenges.	1	2	3	4	5		1	2	3	4	5
18. We hold people accountable, but do not punish "mistakes."	1	2	3	4	5		1	2	3	4	5
19. We are a "make it happen" organization. We have a bias toward action and take pride in our accomplishments.	1	2	3	4	5		1	2	3	4	5
20. We find work fun.	1	2	3	4	5		1	2	3	4	5
Totals											

Rating scale: 0————|————20————|————40————|————60————|————80————|————100

Put a * by your organization's current score and a + by the preferred score.

Exhibit 6-3. (*Continued*)

7

Leaders Who Promote Learning

Everybody watches when you're the boss.
You have this important personal responsibil-
ity to come to grips with. How can I increase
the contribution of others? What is my
unique contribution? What is the example
I've been trying to set? What is the message?

ALAN MULALLY
Vice President and General
Manager of the 777 Division, The
Boeing Company

Business leaders bear tremendous financial and organizational responsibilities. How well they live up to those duties is fairly easy to measure
with facts and figures. They get out the charts. They run a financial
analysis. The bottom line tells the story. Those obligations are enormous, and an executive's success often is measured against them.

But if you truly are a leader, those aren't the responsibilities that tear
at your heart. It is the knowledge that you have been entrusted with the
livelihoods and fulfillment of others. You can't measure your success by
doing calculations on a sheet of paper. It's not something that gets high-
lighted in quarterly reports, yet how you live up to that trust is felt
immediately by those who report to you, as well as by customers and
stockholders. If you never agonize over your personal responsibility as
a business leader, your chances of becoming a learning leader are
minuscule indeed.

Leaders in all walks of life are called upon to elevate and energize those around them. Usually dynamic and always articulate, they have a clear vision of where they want to lead their organizations. They boost rather than degrade those around them. They unify rather than divide. They inspire. And they push an inspired organization to become a powerful, profitable one.

Leaders who promote their own learning as well as the learning of others have a special style of leadership. They keep their goal—their vision for the company—constantly before them, but they also pay attention to others' concerns and new ideas. They continually absorb information from inside and outside the company. They keep their eye on the bottom line, but they never lose sight of the importance of each individual's contribution. They realize that to increase each person's contribution both empowers workers and brightens the bottom line.

After clearly communicating their vision for the organization, learning leaders try to bring everyone on board but don't hesitate to fire those who refuse to make the transition.

They may not be knights in shining armor, but the learning leaders we interviewed have accomplished some amazing feats. They have taken the reins of organizations on the brink of disaster and have brought them around to increased profitability and prominence. They have used their positions to promote learning and increased job satisfaction. They have conscientiously managed as well as led.

Much has been written about the difference between leaders and managers. Kay Whitmore of Kodak said people should not malign those who are good managers but aren't necessarily good leaders.

"Fortunately, there are some people who are simply good managers," Whitmore said. "They are not too hot as leaders, but they are the people who get the work done. They need somebody else to help expand the horizons, help set the framework, take the leaps forward, but you still have to have people with a variety of skills."

Phil Condit at Boeing characterizes them as the "visionaries" and the "soldiers."

"The best organizations have some of both," he said. "If everybody's a visionary, trying to keep them on track is really tough. You can stand a couple, but you need some soldiers, too; some guys who keep the post lines up and things marching along. What you really try to do is sprinkle both throughout the organization. A few to keep it loose and a few to keep the organization from running off a cliff."

Successful companies do need both—leaders who create the vision and managers who administrate it. Here we are not concerned with how to manage a learning organization but how to create it, nurture it, and drive it forward with a sense of urgency, exhilaration, and inspiration.

Here we have grouped some of the most important characteristics of learning leaders under five rules of thumb:

1. Create the vision.
2. Set an example.
3. Cultivate a supportive environment.
4. Don't be a tyrant.
5. Hear what you don't want to hear.

Creating the Vision

This is where it all begins. By creating the vision, you are determining your organization's future. The vision dictates the shape your organization adopts, the speed at which it grows, and the path it takes.

Recognize the Performance Gap

The core of the vision is recognizing both your company's current performance and how you want it to perform in the future. By measuring one against the other, you identify the performance gap, the gap between today's performance and tomorrow's potential. It is the leader's job not only to articulate the gap but to motivate the entire organization to close it.

Often the first problem the learning leader faces is an organizational belief that the company isn't doing that badly. The company sees itself as better than it really is, as needing to make small improvements rather than major changes. The leader's job is to accurately describe reality by saying, "We're not as far along as you think we are. Back here is the starting line. This is where we are today, and there, out in the distance, is where we have to be if we want to survive." As shown in Figure 7-1, a leader must define the playing field.

Identify Current Capability

Self-delusion haunts us all. It is particularly obvious in any major foot race. In the New York Marathon, for example, about 26,000 runners show up each year to race 26 miles. The masses of people are grouped according to ability. Those who anticipate being among the first to cross the finish line lead the pack. Those who anticipate averaging under 6 minutes a mile come next, then the 6-minute, 30-second milers, and so

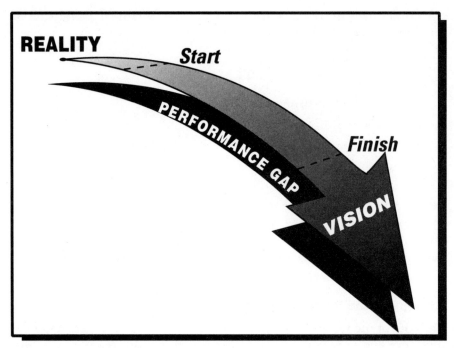

Figure 7-1. Defining the playing field.

on. Theoretically, those who anticipate taking more than 4 or 5 hours to finish should be at the back of the pack.

But inevitably, hundreds of runners have self-images that outstrip their abilities. And they position themselves near the front, only to get jostled in the beginning as swarms of runners maneuver around them. Positioning themselves with the fast runners doesn't make them fast: Only by improving their own capabilities can they run a better race.

Smart runners recognize their abilities. If they want to be in the front half of the pack, they know what they have to do. They assess where they are and work toward improving their speed and position for the next race. To get ahead, they must improve their capabilities.

In the workplace, a leader must provide a reality check by making sure the organization recognizes its current abilities in relation to the rest of the business world.

While identifying current capabilities, the leader is careful not to crush the spirit. Instead, a leader motivates people, makes them really want to reach the finish line, or whatever the vision or goal may be.

People enter the workplace with varying degrees of ability and preparedness, just as they do in a marathon. Some finish. Some must drop out. But no one stays on the starting line.

Ted Hutton of Waverly, Inc. recalled the horror of crewing for a sailor who clearly had a vision but didn't share it with anyone else in the boat:

"This guy was a raving maniac in the boat and it's the last time I've ever crewed in a race because it was horrible. This guy was a superb sailor but he barked out orders at you left and right, and he never told you where he wanted to end up. Therefore, you never could anticipate the next move. You had to wait to hear from him, and by then, valuable time had passed and it was too late.

"In a company, you must make people understand where you are going so they can anticipate the future. Then, if they believe in it and feel that they have a part in developing your course of action, they are going to work to the best of their ability."

Stretch Capabilities

For a company, the vision must be one that stretches the capabilities. Without pressing against the boundaries of their abilities, organizations will fall short of their potential and behind their competitors. It is the leaders' responsibility to discover the leading edge of whatever their companies want to accomplish, and to set about surpassing it.

But the vision shouldn't seem impossible to reach. Don't set a vision that will be shrugged off as a pipe dream. If your delivery time is 6 weeks and you declare your goal is to reduce it to 4 hours, you are going to lose all credibility with your people.

Not that such a reduction in delivery time is impossible, but your workers will certainly think you're living in a fantasy world. Learning leaders avoid that kind of cynicism by setting intermediate milestones to achieving the vision. They make the goal something that conceivably can be attained, and then they keep moving that goal a littler farther away.

Ultimately, the vision for the organization should be infinite. It should be one that continually expands the horizon, a barrier described in a prayer as "nothing save the limit of our sight."

Take Care of the Customer First

No matter what the business orientation, visions have one common purpose: to make the organization and its product the customer's first choice. As Boeing's Alan Mulally said, "Everybody makes it so esoteric, but the customer will either choose you or they won't."

So the vision must be customer-oriented. "I've really come to the conclusion that one of the fundamental problems of business in the United States today is that many, many people have lost sight of the function of business, which is to produce a product or service for customers," said

Nev Curtis of Delmarva Power & Light Company. "We have to take care of customers first, then everything else will take care of itself."

Change From the Top Down

To achieve a vision requires change. A learning leader's chief role is managing that change at optimum speed. "The role of the leader in managing change is key, and that applies to leadership at every level," said Stata at Analog Devices. He explained:

"The whole notion now is that of the leader as being a learner, as the coach and counsel, as the teacher and learner, as the walk and the talk, and as creating the expectation as well as the demand that subordinates become learners. In the last analysis, the leader must draw the line in the sand, saying, `There it is. As much as I love you and despite all of our past history and experience, you've got to get over that line in the sand or you're finished.'

"It does come down to that in some cases, and it's only when people understand that there is a line that they will face up to it. Otherwise organizations or people won't change."

The rate of change cannot be ignored. As Theresa Eyre of Hewlett-Packard said, it is like swimming in a river against the current. If you only swim at a slow pace, the current will take you backward. To gain ground you have to swim at a fast pace and then, in relation to the shore, you may only make slow progress.

Kodak's Kay Whitmore recognizes the rate of change as being vital: "Why do you get into a learning environment where you can learn faster than other people? Because if you don't keep your rate of learning up, others will catch you and pass you."

By articulating and handing down the vision, the leader puts the learning wheels in motion.

"I would say that number one, the leader has to accept that if it is going to become a learning organization, it will be largely as a result of what he or she does to make it happen," said Stata. "The transformation into a learning organization can only be achieved from the top down."

Setting an Example

Be an aggressive learner. It is the most powerful message you can send.

"A childhood friend once told me: `Never listen to what people say to you; only watch what they do to you,'" said Kurt Landgraf, executive vice-president of Du Pont Merck. "People don't really care what management says to them. They discount that. What they are looking for is what management does in real-life situations."

So learn. Don't pretend that you know everything. Leaders don't need to appear all-knowing to keep the respect of their people. Leaders who admit their own shortcomings command greater loyalty and respect. Those who pretend to be the Wizard of Oz eventually are exposed.

Alan Mulally at Boeing said that the ability to admit you don't know everything and to respect the ideas of others often requires a change of attitude. "We all had to go to class to figure out how to listen," Mulally said of the management at Boeing. "We've gone to class to learn not to say, `That's the stupidest idea I've ever heard,' or `You want to do *what*?'" Mulally explained further:

"We've gone to class to stand up and be able to say in a meeting, `You know, I don't understand what you mean.' These are competent engineers who know a lot, and you're not going to find many people who will stand up and say, `I don't understand what you mean.'

"That's not received as competent. We have reminded each other [to be honest] and we have practiced being honest. It's back to enabling us and letting us be free to say, `I don't get it.'

"The other day the financial officer was going over some figures, and three times I said, `I don't get it.' I'm capable of understanding, and I don't get it the first time. I don't get it the second time. Could you go over it one more time: What do you really mean? What does the data really tell us?

"Well, it doesn't take many times for my boss, or me to say that for the message to get across that it's okay to admit what you don't understand. A large organization is watching us, listening to us, and they recognize that it's okay if you don't have every answer and together we will figure it out."

Those who lead organizations must become the epitome of the teacher/learner model. They must learn by teaching, and teach by learning.

"To some large extent, they have to demonstrate through their personal behavior and through their demonstrated acquisition and implementation of new knowledge and skills that there is something new and different about them," said Ray Stata of Analog Devices. "That's one of the harder things to do because the whole change phenomenon has to be demonstrated through their change in behavior."

Leaders can't just bring in experts and say "Listen up. This is what I want you to learn. This is how I want you to behave." Leaders must go through the paces themselves. They can't be the cheerleaders standing on the sidelines of learning. They have to be active learners. As Whitmore of Kodak explains:

"The trick is to pick an appropriate subject to work on. I've tried to resist the temptation to know something about everything. So I work on a list of four or five specific things. Right now two issues Kodak is working on—broad, corporate issues that we're trying to learn more about—are globalization and creating a learning organization.

"Actually there are multiple lists. There is a list of the four or five items that Eastman Kodak as an institution ought to work on. Then there is a second list of the four or five items that I personally want to work on. So I help set the corporate agenda, but I also have to set a personal agenda, and that's a different list."

In setting learning agendas for themselves and their organizations, each of the learning leaders we interviewed has become a sponge for information, a practice we repeatedly stress. To lead and manage effectively requires a broad education and a propensity for critical thinking. Get the best information you can from outside of your organization by benchmarking and reading everything you can get your hands on. (Benchmarking is described in detail in Chapter 4.)

Benchmarking provides top executives a unique opportunity to develop learning between and among companies. It's a practice encouraged and demanded by the Malcolm Baldrige National Quality Award. Ray Stata explains the importance of benchmarking:

"I think that there is some data around that suggests that the "monkey see, monkey do" phenomenon is quite operative at the CEO level, and the most important way to influence behavior change amongst organizational leaders is to have them exposed to an environment where there are success stories and success phenomenon that are not occurring in their organizations.

"That becomes the shock treatment that leads to the CEO saying, `Oh my God. If I don't do something I'm going to be left behind.' That helps create learning across institutions. It may be that is the most important phenomenon in terms of leadership learning. We must promote collective societal learning. We've got to get experiments going across a lot of companies and then have a systematic way to share that learning experience in order to accelerate the whole process of learning. That's probably the greatest deficiency that we have in the United States today."

The Center for Quality Management in New England facilitates learning across organizations, Stata said, by bringing together companies that are committed to quality management and that recognize they can progress faster in an environment of shared and mutual learning than they can by learning on their own.

When it comes to getting accurate information about what is going on inside your organization, your best method is to promote open communication, as discussed in depth in Chapter 6.

Too many senior managers think they have a fix on the internal workings of their company. But they don't have a magic one-way window into the workers' attitudes and opinions. What these managers often see is a reflection of what they want to believe. In a learning organization, the leader takes pains to develop multiple sources of internal information.

Don't think you can get good inside information by meeting regularly with the next tier of management. Seek out people up and down the organizational chart. Ask for their opinions and ideas. Really listen to them. Their experience makes them a valuable learning resource, which leads to rule number three.

Cultivating a Supportive Environment

A work environment that buoys rather than debases employees results in a double gain: people are fulfilled and the company is more profitable in the long run. Such an environment fosters diversity, promotes a sense of security, makes people feel optimal, and encourages risk taking.

Foster Diversity

At Corning, CEO Jamie Houghton has made it clear that the company's future is directly tied to how well it promotes diversity within the work force. He said that in 1987, he decided the company needed to reignite its diversity efforts. Houghton said:

"We were losing women and blacks at twice the rate of white males. The baby boom was over and statistics said only 15 percent of the people entering the work force in the year 2000 were going to be white males.

"If you only want to deal with 15 percent of the talent out there, that's fine, but we realized that we had to do something different because Corning has never had a hard time hiring women and minorities. The problem was we didn't keep them. They were leaving because of the `glass ceiling.' They didn't feel their careers were being fully enhanced. We can do something about that."

One of the things Corning has done is to set and publish numerical goals of minority hiring and promotion. They've also hired a chief diversity officer. That's really the easy part, Houghton said. The hard part is trying to assess people's attitudes.

"A lot of people in Corning thought that just because top management sent down this bulletin saying, 'We are going to be a diverse company,' that it was going to happen overnight. Of course, it didn't. We have to educate people."

Many managers have realized, at least intellectually, that diversity will play an important role in their organization's future success. And their commitment goes beyond an intolerance of overt racism and sexism. They make it clear that it is the differences, not the similarities, that lead to new ideas and fresh approaches, adding a depth and dimension that can't be achieved in a company of clones. Nev Curtis of Delmarva Power & Light gave us his views:

"All levels of an organization should reflect as much diversity as possible, and by that I mean that it is very desirable to have somebody without a college diploma at the senior levels. To have someone who has actually been in a union.

"You can't ask a lineman about dividend policy, but you can ask a lineman what's the best way to climb a pole so you can use that knowledge when you create a training program. Or when you buy trucks you get the person who is going to use it involved. (See Exhibit 7-1.)

"One of the problems of upper management is that we filter by our own experiences and our own biases. The cynic would say it's for our own personal advantage, but I think we're honestly not aware of a lot of it."

Promote a Sense of Security

At Du Pont Merck, Landgraf has found that providing a sense of security has been a key ingredient for creating a supportive environment.

"A core belief I have is that the very first prerequisite for learning and growth is security," Landgraf said. "Without that, people operate suboptimally in every way. If I'm concerned that my job will not be here next week, or if I believe that my boss will treat me poorly based upon emotions, then I will spend more time worrying about my future than is appropriate. I'll try to protect myself by saying I'm not going to grow and I'm not going to bond with other people."

Landgraf said he has structured his organization to minimize insecurities. He explained:

"I try to set up an organizational structure that is bounded by shared values. The bottom line is, I say to people, 'I care about you. We care about you. We trust you. We want you to grow. We want you to be better. We want this organization to be better, and if you'll interact with us

Breaking Down Barriers

Nev Curtis, as a new 6-month employee and 2-week president of Delmarva Power & Light Company in Wilmington, Delaware, knew he had a lot to learn, and he knew his employees could become his best teachers. So one morning, before the sun was up, Curtis headed 100 miles south to talk to a lineman. He recalls what happened:

"We were shooting the breeze. I didn't have a tie on. Finally, he looked down on me—because I'm so short I look up at most everybody and most every lineman—and he said, `Nev, what do you do for the company?'

"I said, `Well, I'm the president.'

"He said, `The hell you are.' Then I got out my ID card and proved that I was, but I asked him why he reacted that way. He said for two reasons: `Number one,' he said, `is that presidents don't get out of bed at 6:30 a.m. and number two, there's no way a president of Delmarva Power would be on a line dock asking a dumb lineman like me what was wrong with the company.'

"That really made me so aware of the barriers between management and workers. Right then I decided that one of my objectives would be to break down barriers. Both between workers and managers, but also between managers and managers.

"If you're going to do that, you must recognize that every person has value. Too many times organizations allow barriers to grow up. `I'm better than you because I wear a tie and you don't.' Or `I'm better than you because I'm white and you're black,' or `I'm male and you're female.' Those barriers should not exist. You've got to act to find some way to knock them down."

Exhibit 7-1 Learning is fostered when barriers are broken down.

in a caring and open and honest, decent way, we'll do the same thing back to you.'

"Now as extraordinary as it may sound, that is the single, most important factor to the success of this company. This organization was a loser. The single thing that has turned the organization around is that it has bonded together in a productive way.

"We have eliminated the hurtful things that people do to each other. Now I say eliminated. I'm not stupid enough to believe that people don't think hurtful things, but it's not acceptable here to exhibit racist behavior or to do things that overtly hurt other people. To make this organization optimal, the people have to feel optimal."

Make People Feel Optimal

In an article in *Sloan Management Review,* Hanover Insurance CEO William O'Brien described the importance of making people feel optimal, saying, "In a learning organization, the manager shoulders an almost sacred responsibility to create conditions that enable people to have happy and productive lives."[33] Landgraf of Du Pont Merck agreed, saying:

"My strongest belief from all of this is that people want to be happy. People want to treat each other with respect. People want to work in an organization where they feel teamwork. It's not the human condition to want to be mean and miserable and nasty.

"The human condition is to want to be happy and cooperative, and if you set up an environment where people can do that, they run in and fill every other void."

While we recognize the value of a workplace where people feel optimal, leaders are not liable for the happiness of everyone who works for them. Happiness is a highly subjective condition that relies heavily on a person's own spirit. We do think that leaders can cultivate an organization that, by its challenging, supportive, and equitable nature, becomes fertile ground for happy employees.

It doesn't happen without a great deal of planning and personal investment. A leader can't send out a memo saying, "OK, from now on we're going to be an open, supportive place to work." The leader must become the prototype.

Alan Mulally of Boeing describes it this way:

"It's pure leadership by example. You can't talk and you can't walk any differently than anybody else. If I suppress a piece of data, or if somebody asks for help and I say no, everybody knows. So what do they do the next time? They don't ask.

"So if you believe in your heart that this environment will result in a competitive business plan, then you have to create the environment. A lot of people have been brought up in an environment where they think giving orders, kicking ass, taking a stand, that's what the leadership contribution is.

"To me, the most honest thing that you could ever do as a leader is to keep asking yourself everyday, `What is the biggest contribution I can make to establish a creative learning environment, an environment where everyone is contributing to the business plan?'"

Encourage Risk Taking

In a learning environment, inventiveness and risk taking are highly valued elements of the organization's culture. Learning leaders set the tone by being fearless in trying new approaches and new ideas. By being creative in their own solutions to problems, they provoke others to do the same. Because the leader dares to act boldly even when the outcome is uncertain, others in the organization are also willing to take risks.

"Risk means to potentially make a fool of yourself," said John Hardinger of Du Pont, "and I've done that hundreds of times, skiing or what have you. You must find a way to make people understand that that is part of growing. It shouldn't be viewed as a failure but as a success because you are bound to learn something if you just go try. The vast majority of innovators around the world have been looked at as the town idiot when they started out. But if it hadn't been for those innovators, nothing would have changed. Nothing."

Not Being a Tyrant

While not being a tyrant ties in with creating a supportive work environment, it is more directly linked to the leader's demeanor, style, and personality. No, being a leader is not a personality contest, and yes, it is more important to be respected than liked. But we found almost all of the leaders we interviewed to be immensely likable and genuinely concerned about the welfare of their employees.

Are they just good actors skilled at making a good impression? Are they interested in their employees solely because happy employees are good for profits?

Maybe so. We're not psychologists and can't read minds or motives, but interviews with managers throughout their organizations led us to believe that these leaders are respected and generally liked by their people. The reverse also is true: learning leaders generally like and respect their people. (See Exhibit 7-2.)

Excite and Motivate

Learning leaders must project a sense of excitement and possibility. If you can't excite and motivate your people, your organization will remain stuck where it is.

"I think one of the most telling statements I've heard, and one that really stuck with me, was from an interview with Roger Smith just before he retired as chairman of General Motors," said Ted Hutton of

---

Tyrants Not Allowed

In a letter to shareholders in a recent annual report, General Electric Company CEO John F. Welch, Jr., wrote that to remain a leader at GE required more than a bottom-line fixation: It required working with people instead of mowing them down. Because the pronouncement came from an organization whose leadership strategies were widely admired, and because it came from a CEO who had cut down his share of employees on the road to increased profits, the business world sat up and took notice.

Welch described four types of leaders: Type 1 "delivers on commitments—financial or otherwise—and shares the values of the company." He wrote that the employment prospects for that person is "onward and upward." Type 2 is the leader who doesn't meet commitments and doesn't share the company values. Those are soon fired. Type 3 are leaders who miss commitments but share the values, and they usually get a second chance.

But Type 4, he wrote, "is the most difficult for many of us to deal with. That leader delivers on commitments, makes all the numbers, but doesn't share the values we must have. This is the individual who typically forces performance out of people rather than inspires it: the autocrat, the big shot, the tyrant. Too often all of us have looked the other way—tolerated these 'Type 4' managers because 'they always deliver'—at least in the short term."

Not anymore. Welch wrote: "In an environment where we must have every good idea from every man and woman in the organization, we cannot afford management styles that suppress and intimidate."

Exhibit 7-2. A learning organization does not accept autocratic managers.

Waverly, Inc. "The question was in the context of why things hadn't gone so well for GM and the interviewer asked Roger Smith what he would have done differently."

Roger Smith told *Fortune* magazine:

> I sure wish I'd done a better job of communicating with GM people. I'd do that differently a second time around and make sure they understood and shared my vision for the company. Then they would have known why I was tearing the place up, taking out whole divisions, changing our whole production structure. If people understand the why, they'll work at it. Like I say, I never got all this across. There we were, charging up the hill right on schedule, and I looked

behind me and saw that many people were still at the bottom, trying to decide whether to come along. I'm talking about hourly workers, middle management, even some top managers. It seems like a lot of them had gotten off the train.[34]

You can't be a leader without followers. If you look around and you're alone, something is seriously wrong.

Allow People to Change

One of the most difficult concepts to accept is that people can and do change. Stata said:

"Within organizations there is a tendency to get typed. There gets to be a `tape' on individuals that often gets written quite early on. That becomes the mythology of that individual and becomes a tremendous obstacle to that person ever changing or being accepted in their changed behavior. I think it's why, very often, you see people who have to leave companies and go to other companies to be able to realize their potential. They get typed and nobody accepts the fact that they can learn to change.

"An incredibly important aspect of the learning phenomenon is getting people to throw out their tapes and accept the realities of what people are, month-to-month, and year-to-year, as opposed to what they were 5 years ago."

Give Responsibility, Share Blame

Leaders must be generous in handing out responsibility and miserly in placing blame. To encourage risk taking, which is vital to growth, you must appreciate a good effort even if it fails.

Learning from mistakes is one of the learning tools discussed in Chapter 4, but because it is so important, we wanted to say again: Placing blame will smother learning. When mistakes draw more reprimands than encouragement, people stop trying anything new rather than risk failure.

When someone attempts something new and makes a mistake, the most productive response is to acknowledge the mistake, try to learn from it, and share the learning throughout the organization.

Ed Chambers is director of the Long Island–based Industrial Areas Foundation, which was created to empower community groups to act in the political arena. He cites persistence and patience as significant leadership qualities. A leader is unwavering in the pursuit of the organization's vision. But along with persistence, true leaders have the patience to let others develop along the way and learn from their own mistakes. The goal is progress, not perfection.

Hearing What You Don't Want to Hear

There's a wonderful children's book called *The Enchanted Flute.* In it a princess is given a magic flute that, when she plays it, produces the sounds most dear to the heart of whoever is listening. Her fussy mother, Queen Pernickety, loves the sound of the flute because all she hears is the admiration and praises of her subjects.

But the queen's delight turns to horror when the enchanted spell is altered. Instead of hearing the sounds most dear to their hearts, listeners hear the sounds their hearts most fear. For Queen Pernickety, those are the voices of her tired, groaning subjects telling her the truth.

It is not easy to hear the truth when it isn't what we'd like to believe. Ted Hutton of Waverly, Inc. said: "I'll be the first to admit that I don't like hearing criticism or about things that went wrong. Quite frankly, sometimes I don't listen because I'm so convinced that I know the way to go. But I have to listen and talk to people and, in a sense, argue with them as to why I think I'm right. Now if they are persistent and keep coming up with good reasons, then I'll back off."

Once or twice a year, Hal Rosenbluth, CEO of Rosenbluth Travel, asks the vice presidents in his company to evaluate how he and the company are doing. What he hears isn't always pleasant, but it is a valuable learning tool. Rosenbluth explained:

"We look on constructive criticism as a gift from a friend, and here it's like Christmas time every week. It has to be looked at as a gift from a friend or the company is not going to progress. They are written, and then we get together and discuss them. In one way or another they expose to me my shortcomings and where I need improvement.

"We also have quality assurance teams that go out to different offices and ask our associates about the performance of their leader. Another fun time. So as leaders, we are accountable to our people."

Characteristics of the Learning Leader

Learning leaders embody characteristics that go beyond those commonly found in typical leaders. Learning leaders are concerned not only with their own learning but constantly are prodding and provoking others around them to learn. The learning is never for its own sake but is always focused on meeting the challenge at hand and achieving the economic results needed for business success. These leaders anticipate change, and manage it at optimum speed. In Exhibit 7-3 Hal Rosenbluth explains his commitment to learning.

All of the learning leaders interviewed for this book have identified a chasm they want their organization to cross, whether it is to create a better product, expand into new territories, or reduce costs. And they all have presented a compelling reason for their followers to jump the chasm, even if the leaders themselves are uncertain how they will reach the other side.

By consistently stretching the abilities of those who work for them, learning leaders create a dynamic environment that not only places a high value on innovation and knowledge but generates the energy needed to move the organization from contemplation to action. Peter Senge explains the role of the learning leader this way:

> In a learning organization, leaders' roles differ dramatically from that of the charismatic decision maker. Leaders are designers, teachers, and stewards. These roles require new skills: the ability to build shared vision, to bring to the surface and challenge prevailing mental models, and to foster more systemic patterns of thinking. In short, leaders in learning organizations are responsible for *building organizations* where people are continually expanding their capabilities to shape their future—that is, leaders are responsible for learning.[35]

Taking Learning to Heart

Hal Rosenbluth, CEO of Rosenbluth Travel, a privately held, $1.3 billion travel management company headquartered in Philadelphia, and coauthor of *The Customer Comes Second: And Other Secrets of Exceptional Service* (Morrow, 1992), says that his commitment to learning flows from his vision for the company. He describes this vision as a chain of people, service, profits. He explains, "We focus on our people, our people focus on service, and profits result." He goes back again and again to the importance of valuing your people and treating them with respect. Happy employees make for happy customers, who make for healthy profits.

In hindsight, says Hal Rosenbluth, he was never much of a student. He wasn't motivated or inspired to learn, so he didn't. Because the right environment wasn't there in school, he wasted a valuable learning opportunity. He doesn't intend to allow that to happen again—to him or to anyone who works for Rosenbluth Travel.

"One of the ways to create a positive effect on someone's life is through learning," Rosenbluth said. "I've heard others refer to their companies as lifelong learning universities. It was key to me that we have the same kind of environment where learning would happen both consciously and subconsciously on a daily basis."

In 1974, when Rosenbluth first went to work for the company founded by his great-grandfather, the organization was totally customer-focused. This focus was so extreme that people were stressed out by customers' demands and by the pressures of internal politics. The company was doing quite well, but Rosenbluth didn't like the working atmosphere or the way people were treating each other. He recognized the gap between the reality of the working environment and his vision of how it should be.

When Rosenbluth was promoted to a position of authority, one of the first things he did was to begin getting rid of people who, although they produced, created unpleasant working conditions. Long before John Welch, CEO of General Electric, wrote in his annual report that Type 4 managers can't be tolerated, Rosenbluth was cutting them loose from Rosenbluth Travel. As Rosenbluth said in a *Harvard Business Review* article: "I started systematically getting rid of the prima donnas and the political manipulators. The whole organization took a dim view of my actions because the people I

Exhibit 7-3. A learning organization values its employees, treats them with respect, and cultivates a learning environment.

removed were seen as indispensable—even after they left and the company failed to fall apart."[36]

Rosenbluth said he sees his leadership role as that of a gardener, weeding out undesirable elements and cultivating the best in those who remain. "I just walk around and sprinkle different seeds and put some water on them. I make sure that they have the right environment to grow. My responsibility is to ensure that the environment is there for everybody to be creative and innovative."

Giving people the opportunity and impetus to learn, he said, may be the greatest gift the company can give to its workers. "We try to develop each other as human beings and use learning to help us develop our personal lives as well as our professional lives," he said. "Learning and training are the most important vehicles for us to have a positive effect on our people's lives."

Rosenbluth said he learned early on that to create a culture where people are supportive and fulfilled, learning has to be fun. He explains:

"We have a director of training who, many years ago, said something that has had a tremendous impact on me. He said that the education system takes the fun out of learning by the fourth grade, and from that point on, your retention, your desire to learn, your inspiration to learn as much as you can, wanes.

"I see it with children. They love going to school up through the first couple of grades, and after that they don't like to go anymore. Why is it? It's usually because the fun has been taken out. So we try and put the fun back into learning in a professional way, but a way in which we tend to retain more as a result. Even when we began to train all of us in total quality management, we had to come up with an organization to train us that had a sense of humor. We knew we would retain a lot more if it was taught in a fashion that was somewhat fun."

Rosenbluth said his own intentional learning continues daily. "A lot of it goes on through vertical reviewing where people review my performance and then they help identify for me my shortcomings that I need to learn to overcome," Rosenbluth said. "Then from that I will sit down with our director of training and have him identify for me what I need to do. He also teaches me how to listen. He does that every month because I know I have a problem with it."

One way Rosenbluth "listens" to his people is with pictures. Every 6 months his human resources department chooses 100 people and

Exhibit 7-3. (*Continued*)

sends them paper and crayons. They are asked to draw a picture of what Rosenbluth Travel means to them and how they would like to represent the company. People aren't asked to sign their names, but most do.

"I learn so much from these drawings," Rosenbluth said. "Problems within the organization. Where things are good. Where things are bad. Where there is good leadership."

Many of the pictures refer to learning, depicting the company as Rosenbluth College or University. Others portray a sense of security. In picturing his career, one respondent drew a man climbing steps leading up to heaven. But he had a computer shackled to his leg.

"I called this person and said, `What's going on?'" Rosenbluth recalled. "He said the response time on our computers was terrible and we're never going to get anywhere in the company unless we speed up the response time. From that we found out that there was a telephone line communication problem in one of our systems."

"People express themselves in different ways," explains Rosenbluth, "and this is just one of the ways that I can keep tabs on whether or not the environment is right for learning and for being involved."

Exhibit 7-3. (*Continued*)

PART 4

Learning Strategies That Work

When I went to interview Corning CEO Jamie Houghton, I arrived about 10 minutes early and sat waiting in the reception area of Corning's New York City headquarters. Houghton walked in a few minutes later and apologized. "I'm sorry I'm late," he said. "I was on an international call." I looked at my watch. It was 1 minute after 10. I couldn't believe it. I said to myself, "Here is a very busy man who was just on the cover of *Business Week* under the title 'Class Act.' He's good enough to give up some time to see me for my book, and here he is apologizing for being 1 minute late!"

During the interview, I realized that Houghton's apology spoke volumes about his management style and about Corning. His commitment to quality colors everything he does. He truly walks his talk. For him, being 1 minute late was not acceptable behavior. Commitments are taken seriously. Doing things right the first time, on time, every time is not a slogan but a way of life.

Houghton is an exceptional manager running an exceptional organization. There are many others. Here we highlight five companies whose learning is in high gear. They represent a broad spectrum of industries and situations. We hope you will find ideas that can be adapted to your needs.

Offered for stimulation are:

- Corning Inc., a company that, guided by Houghton's vision, took the first steps to becoming a learning organization more than 10 years ago.

- Eastman Kodak Company, which is being pounded by global competition and whose survival depends on learning new capabilities.

- Rosenbluth Travel, a privately held service company that uses fairly outrageous tactics to promote individual learning.

- J. P. Morgan & Co. Inc., a respected financial services institution that is persistent in its belief that individual learning is critical for employees and for the organization as a whole.

- Motorola, Inc., which has developed a new model for senior executive development that involves solving real-life, critical problems and teaches its top executives how to learn on the job.

At each company we interviewed several top managers about their own learning and how their organizations learn. Because outsiders rarely get such frank insight into other businesses, we let them speak for themselves. In the following five chapters we present these managers' own thoughts in their own words.

8

Corning Inc.

A Decade of Learning

When Jamie Houghton took over as Corning's chairman in 1983, he had a clear vision of what he wanted the company to become: a world leader in quality; a champion of work force diversity; and a better financial performer.

He didn't know how it would happen, but he knew what he wanted. Now, 10 years later, Houghton's long-term, focused vision is reaping substantial dividends. The $3 billion worldwide organization has made measurable progress in quality and diversity, and in 1991 had a return on equity of 15.6 percent, up from 8.5 percent in 1983.

Headquartered in Corning, New York, the company has four broad market sectors—telecommunications, laboratory sciences, consumer housewares, and specialty materials—and more than 100 locations around the world. All of its 29,000 employees are encouraged and expected to be active participants in the company's quest for improved performance.

Interviews with several top managers give insight into what has worked for them and underscore the importance of learning as the foundation for any new initiative.

Instilling a New Vision

The importance of Jamie Houghton's vision for Corning cannot be overemphasized. Today, it doesn't seem so risky or exceptional: quality, diversity, customer satisfaction, increased profits. So, you ask, who wouldn't include all of those elements in a company's vision?

In 1983, nobody else did. And even 10 years later, few companies are aggressively pursuing those goals. Fewer still are achieving them. When Houghton took over, Corning was very cyclical, and the 1982 recession had taken its toll. The company was in the process of restructuring, downsizing, and divesting. It was more than enough to demand the full attention of any CEO. But Houghton realized that the company's future was riding on something more fundamental than day-to-day business decisions. If the company was to be successful, those decisions needed to be grounded in a vision.

One of the first things Jamie Houghton did in 1983 was outline a vision for 1995. Ed O'Brien, corporate director of Corning's education, training, and recruiting, said: "I was in the meeting when he delivered that talk and I bet 70 percent of the managers in the room rejected his talk and wondered what he was smoking. Now people look at it and say, `Well, obviously it makes sense and obviously it's the right thing,' but it was not obvious when he did it, which, to me, makes it courageous and more important. Two years later, the vision was formalized, along with our statement of values, purpose, and strategy.

"Then there's the fact that he gave us a 10-year vision. I never heard of anyone coming up with a 10-year vision. It was so well done that nothing has had to be changed. It's as true today as it was in 1983 when he came out with it, and managers are still saying it's the right thing. It's still achievable, but boy, there is still challenge in it.

"His vision has turned out to be critical, and it certainly was for education and becoming a learning organization because it told us what direction we were going.

"The two major elements of his vision that were unique were his commitment to total quality and his commitment to valuing diversity. Managers at the time were saying `What's this quality stuff? We don't have time. We have hard business decisions to make.' And the commitment to diversity is a critical competitive issue. It is not a nicey-nice thing. Jamie does it because it's the right thing and he knows it helps business.

"When you bring blacks and women into an organization that was white male, it is very disruptive unless you manage it and learn to understand the differences. Unmanaged change diminishes organizational effectiveness. Jamie has forced us to deal with the issues at an accelerated rate—to understand them so that we don't lose organizational effectiveness. In the end we probably will be more effective. I think an organization's culture can provide more of a competitive advantage than technology does. Technology can be copied quickly through industrial espionage and other things. If you see what's on the other person's drawing board, you can duplicate it or pass them very quickly.

"However, when you have a cultural advantage they [competitors] can know precisely what you're doing, but in my opinion, a significant cultural change takes a minimum of 8 years to accomplish to have a significant effect. So someone looks at Corning and where we are now with some of our cultural advantages, like in the area of diversity, and they are 8 years behind us. If we keep doing a good job, they can never catch us. If they have unmanaged diversity changes—there will be diversity changes because that's what the demographics say, whether they want it or not—it will be very disruptive. Their organizational effectiveness will go down. Ours has not gone down; if anything ours is going up. The net result will be a significant competitive advantage. Jamie drove valuing diversity for all the right reasons."

Four Key Training Strategies

In 1986, Corning established a corporatewide goal for the amount of time each employee would devote to training and education. Each employee was to devote 5 percent of his or her working time to training by 1991. In 1991, the new goal was to sustain a minimum level of 5 percent for 5 years, and at the same time, double training effectiveness. It's a goal that applies from the top to the bottom, from Houghton on down.

That 5 percent goal was "very important in moving us towards becoming more of a learning organization," O'Brien said. Worldwide training had been taking place at about a 3 percent rate. "Jamie and the management committee were concerned that we didn't value education and training enough, and without meaningful education and training to support the ongoing change process, we were not going to keep up."

O'Brien took over as corporate director of education, training, and recruiting right after the 5 percent goal was implemented.

"I assume one of the reasons that I came in was they started to get nervous about that 5 percent training rule and that we were going to waste a lot of money on training for training's sake," O'Brien said. "So I had to have a fresh education and training strategy that had the highest impact on Corning's ability to compete worldwide."

To do that, O'Brien developed four key training strategies that Corning still uses:

1. Shift emphasis to achieve high impact. That is, focus on those things that drive fundamental change throughout the organization.

2. Create a lean, purposeful organization by cutting course administration and delegating some training programs to external resources,

such as the College Center of the Finger Lakes, a local college near Corning's headquarters.

3. Focus on a few vital priorities, such as values, philosophy, innovation, and high-performance work systems. Delegate other courses.

4. Target a 30 percent return on investment as a way to determine the highest priorities for training, a strategy used initially to establish credibility.

While Corning relies heavily on training, it is training that is reinforced by workplace experiences. It is training that is made valuable by application. O'Brien explained:

"I am challenging the traditional concept of corporate education and training. Most people think of education and training in terms of courses. But it takes a paradigm shift. We are saying our charter is really to have high impact and drive fundamental change. To do that we must shift away from thinking that it's just a traditional course.

"I had heard that when Moses came down from the mountain with the 10 commandments, he had another tablet that said, 'Thou shalt not have an interactive workshop with more than 25 people.' It's one of those truths you just accept and never challenge. Then we heard of a woman, Kathy Dannemiller, who was running what she called large-scale interactive workshops with 500 or 600 people. I was cynical but not enough that I didn't send someone to watch one of the workshops. The person came back and said 'Gee, it really works.' I still had a lot of doubts but we applied this concept and it worked. It truly challenges the old concept of a class as we traditionally know it."

Strategy 1: High-Impact, Fundamental Change

Managing change is the key to success for any organization. O'Brien said the change formula Corning uses was developed by Dick Beckhard in 1969. It is shown in Figure 8-1.

The formula reads this way: *Dissatisfaction* with the present state *times vision* of the future *times* putting the *first steps* together must be *greater than* the *resistance* to change.

O'Brien said that the mistake most managers make is in not making sure their employees are on board. "They assume that by lecturing and telling others, everyone is just going to buy in. And they don't."

O'Brien used this formula as a learning tool when he heard that the consumer products division was going to make a major organization change. He knew that the division manager and nine key people had been cloistered for about 9 months, putting the whole picture together.

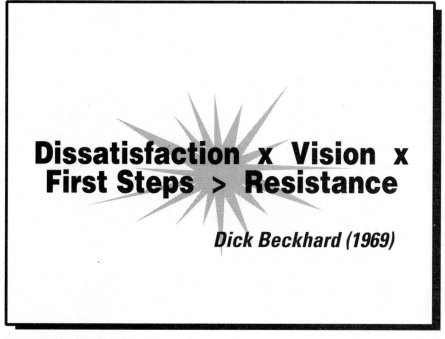

Figure 8-1. Change formula.

O'Brien knew the announcement of the change would come soon, so he went to the division manager and said, "When you say, `Follow me and go over the mountain,' you're going to have nine people with you, but how are you going to get the hearts, the minds, and the souls of the others to come over the mountain with you?"

The manager said he planned to have a traditional communications meeting, spending about 2 hours explaining and answering questions. O'Brien told him a traditional meeting would produce the traditional results, meaning nobody else would buy into the new plan. Traditional meetings, he said, don't address the individual's biggest concerns, like "What's in it for me?" "Will it affect my pay?" "What's going to happen to my career?"

"I told the division manager that he must apply the change formula," O'Brien said. "Every individual you want to change must be dissatisfied with the way things are now. They have to see a desired future. Then they have to agree that the first steps for them make sense, and they have to believe in it enough to do it. All this has to be greater than the normal resistance that everybody has to change. The only way to get them there is by their involvement, their meaningful participation."

Large-Scale, Interactive Workshop.   To set the formula in motion,
O'Brien and the division manager developed a large-scale, highly structured, 2-day workshop for 400 people.

The division manager explained his vision and how he got there in a
20-minute introduction. ("You never let a person talk for more than 20
minutes. That's about all the people can listen to," O'Brien said.)

Then there was time for interaction. The 400 participants were divided into groups of eight and seated at tables. Each group chose a facilitator, a recorder, and someone to ask questions and speak for the group.

After the 20-minute vision statement, the participants were asked two
questions:

1. What did you hear? "At the beginning of the session we give them a
3-minute view of selective listening. We explain why, although the same
words were uttered, everyone's going to have heard and interpreted different things, and why that can be healthy and constructive," O'Brien
said. "So they talk about what they heard and record the key points."

2. What questions or concerns do you have with what you've heard?
What might cause it not to work?

Then the division manager got back on the stage, and portable micro-
phones were distributed. "People felt very free to say exactly what was
on their minds because it wasn't their opinion, it was their table's,"
O'Brien said.

He said the leaders were coached ahead of time to not be defensive
and not come down hard on people. Above all, the leaders were to come
back with an honest, thoughtful answer.

Another element of the workshop was the inclusion of three or four
external customers. They were told that "Now is not the time to be tact-
ful or diplomatic or to smooth over real issues." They were told to be
blunt about what they liked and didn't like.

"A lot of the information was not new, but it isn't what was said. It
was who said it," O'Brien said. "When people heard it directly from a
customer they said, `Oh my goodness, we've got to do something about
that.' You talk about motivating a group of people. It was marvelous."

Another part of the workshop focused on better internal communication and cooperation. O'Brien explained:

"One work group will say, `We can't do our job if people over here
continue doing what they are doing. We don't get their support, so we
can't do what we need to do.' Then they would write down their concerns and send them to the other functions. Then that functional leader
had to get up and say, `OK, here's what we are going to do about your
concerns. Here's our action plan.'

"They had a breakout session to work out their answers first. We had
coached them—at first I thought this was corny, but it was very effec-

tive—to hiss as a group whenever the person speaking was defensive or rationalizing, defending their position. So if someone said, `Well, I really couldn't do anything...,' you heard 400 people hissing. So it was also a very dramatic learning experience for us. They never forget that lesson. They have follow-up sessions later and say, `Here's what you told the group you were going to do. Now what did you do?'

"When we got through, the division manager truly had the hearts, minds, and souls of those people. They still had to make some things they promised happen, but it was one of the most effective change events I've ever seen. It saved them, in my opinion, at least a year from the normal time schedule and maybe longer.

"Since then we've done it for our television business. There we took 1200 people. We divided them into three workshops of 3 days each, which included all of their hourly employees. Ken Freedman was the president of the organization, and he did a wonderful job. Talk about leadership. At the end we had tears, cheers, shouting. You talk about commitment. They were ready to tear through the wall. You can say, `OK, what about the next day? Whoops! I got carried away.' No, it was a real change process. It may save that business because that business was very, very shaky."

O'Brien said Corning has used the same process with a number of organizations, from a class of 25 to several hundred. "It was high impact and it drove fundamental change."

Strategy 2: Identify and Use External Resources

"Our second training strategy is how we get things off our plate," O'Brien said. "The old 'work harder and smarter' just doesn't take you very far. So the question was, how do we free up resources to work on high-impact training? The key to what we did was we identified and leveraged external resources."

The answer was phase out and farm out: phase out what wasn't working and farm out those courses that focused on individual learning and didn't have high impact on institutional learning. For Corning, one of their primary external resources is the College Center of the Finger Lakes (CCFL), a local college founded by the Houghton family in 1961. O'Brien had inherited about 84 training courses at Corning. He immediately transferred 62 of those courses to the local college, courses such as stress management and formal presentations. Corning also enabled CCFL to install a satellite system that now receives about 1000 courses, developed by some of the world's leading experts, designed to meet individual needs.

Strategy 3: Focusing on Corporate
Vital Few

By moving a lot of courses and concerns out from under the training department, O'Brien has been able to focus on vital, corporatewide concerns, such as quality, diversity, innovation, and high-performance work systems, which is another way of saying empowered teams of workers. O'Brien explained:

"High-performance work systems are almost the ultimate in employee involvement. Employees have an input in how the work is designed. With self-directed work teams, you can get rid of levels of supervisors and managers. The self-directed work teams are properly qualified, properly trained, and are awesome in terms of what they can do. They are really the ones that have the knowledge and are closest to what's going on.

"It's another industrial revolution. Where before the concept was that hourly employees should check their brains at the door, and when they come to work, don't think. If an employee felt the urge to think we'd say, `Check with your supervisor so they can handle it.' Now we are saying what a waste. It's like the NAACP says, that the mind is a terrible thing to waste. That's exactly what we've done with our hourly work force for years.

"Now we're saying we need those minds, every one of them, and we've got to train them," O'Brien said. "It's just exciting to see the power of that. Talk about going back to the golden rule. It took us a long time to discover human beings. It's kind of embarrassing, but it's exciting now to be a part of the change."

Strategy 4: Achieve a 30 Percent
Return on Investment

At Corning, this final training strategy already has outlived its usefulness. It was implemented to establish credibility for the training initiatives that O'Brien proposed, but the return on this investment already has passed 30 percent. Now the goal has become to double training effectiveness in the next 5 years. O'Brien said a formula he developed with Barbara Bunker, a professor at the University of Buffalo, has been helpful.

The formula is TE = P × R × WE. That is, *training effectiveness* results from three factors. If any of the factors are missing, the training is ineffective. *P* stands for *program* or course. *R* stands for the *right person* attending the course at the *right time*. And *WE* stands for *work environment*. If the training isn't supported by the work environment, it is useless.

"Meaningful experience at the right time, in the right environment, is the most powerful learning that there is," O'Brien said, "and it has nothing to do with the correct number of courses. It's a variety of different experiences that challenge a person. That's where the most powerful learning takes place. Effective education and training supplements job experience."

Learning from the Bottom to the Top

David Luther, senior vice president of quality, said that while Corning expects and supports learning, it doesn't dictate how people go about it. Luther explained it this way:

"The company is saying, `I'm not going to tell you what you ought to be taking. I am telling you, however, that it should be related to your job in some way. We are telling you it is a job responsibility, but we are not telling you what it is. You have to figure that out for yourself.'

"So if you are a forklift driver in Germany, I want you to go out and learn how to drive forklift trucks better. If you are running a division in Corning, I want you to go to Harvard or wherever and learn about strategy," Luther said. "Jamie learned about computers."

Luther said Corning's egalitarian approach to training is important. He makes it a point to see that correct information reaches those on the bottom of the organizational chart, and that management listens to their concerns. Luther explained how he does this:

"Many managers have a somewhat elitist view that education is really for the top people, and that's baloney. The only difference in many cases for those people on the bottom of the organizational chart and us is we got to go to college somehow. We sort of caught the wave and went with it.

"The people down in the organization are very interested in what they do. They want to win. They want to do it right. They want to learn how to do it.

"Companies always say people are their most important asset. Everyone says that, and no one believes it. Most companies generally treat their machines better than their people.

"At one time, in the original quality awareness training, we were training 900 people a month. We brought them out of their work environment and put them in classrooms. They said, `They must think we're important. Look at how much money they are spending on us.' It was the first real, visible sign that we thought they were worth anything. It was the first visible investment in them. We could have been teaching anything. The subject wasn't important. It was the fact that we were bringing them out.

"We decided early on that on quality awareness training, everyone was going to get the same stuff. There is a certain value of going to the welder and saying that you're getting the same information as the chairman."

Luther said time and again that when asked what's right and what's wrong with the company's quality program, the work force said it wanted training that helped them become better workers. He explained further:

"One of their themes is `I love training. I enjoy being in class, but I'm getting sick to death of concepts. Tell me how to do my job better.' They are very pragmatic and they've got the finest of intentions. They don't seem to seek out items that you might consider peripheral to what they are doing. They want information that 100 percent hits on their day-to-day task.

"I have a great deal of confidence in the work force. They are much more pragmatic sometimes than their management. Much more honest in many ways. I don't know whether it's a function of viewpoint, or where they are, or a function of what they've got at stake. A manager is a little more reluctant, I suppose, to call attention to the way you are supposed to fix something. They are at the other end. They are supposed to be the receivers of the process, to do the work.

"I had a great example the other day. We had a union-management quality review at the Fall Brook plant. We send out workers to our customers, and they look at what the customer does. One case involved little pieces of glass tubing. We handle them with gloves. We pack them separately, and we pay a great deal of attention to avoiding scratches.

"Well, our workers went to the customers and watched their box arrive. This guy reached into the container, wrapped his arms around a whole ton of the glass and walked over and dropped it into a hamper. Our workers went crazy. They said, `You can't do that. You're scratching the glass.' The guy said, `So? Nobody cares. Why are you bringing that up? We don't care if it's scratched. We scratch it all the time.'

"Our workers said, `Well, we thought scratches bothered you.'

"`No,' he said. `You never see it.'

"Our workers were really upset. They asked their managers `Why are we spending all this time making sure they're not scratched? How could you let this happen? You say you're out talking to the customers. Why didn't you know that? Why are you wasting our money and our time doing something the customer doesn't want?'"

Luther smiled as he relayed the story and said, "I think that's wonderful."

Diversity: a Multitiered Approach

Corning's emphasis on diversity dates back to 1986. Houghton recognized that women and black employees were leaving the company at twice the rate of white males, costing the company as much as $5 million a year for hiring and training. In 1987 he established two company-wide quality improvement teams, led by senior managers, that continue to address issues faced by women and blacks.

"Those groups were charged to define their charter, identify issues, propose solutions, make recommendations, and, where appropriate, make things happen," said Dawn Cross, who was hired in 1990 to head Corning's cultural diversity program. "Essentially, my job has been to move the needle for the corporation in the area of diversity."

The needle is moving. From 1987 to 1990, attrition for blacks dropped from 15.3 percent to 11.3 percent. For women, the drop was even greater, from 16.2 percent to 7.6 percent. And more women and blacks are reaching top management.

At Corning, two mandatory courses for managers address gender and racial issues. Two other new courses are being offered to black employees and supervisors of black employees. All salaried workers attend seminars to promote sensitivity and support for women and blacks. And the company has developed a network of mentors for women and blacks.

The benefits of the work in cultural diversity have reached beyond women and minorities. For example, the company's career planning programs began when the drive for diversity led managers to ask why women and blacks weren't making it to the top. Part of the answer was a lack of career planning. The result was career planning opportunities for everyone in the company.

"We have never had a formal career planning process here in Corning," Cross said, "and that played an additional hardship on blacks and women." Both the women and the black quality improvement teams identified the lack of career planning as a problem and began to initiate career planning programs for women and blacks.

"Hence, we now have a career planning system for the entire corporation, and we have career planning training sessions for managers and employees," Cross said. "We have one for the employees so that they understand what's required for them to take charge of their career, and we have another course specifically for supervisors to help them understand what they must do to help their employees be successful."

Progress on the diversity front is measured and the results are made public. Cross explained the process:

"We put together a quarterly report on how we are doing on all initiatives, and we send it out to managers in the company. We provide the analysis. If we are doing great, we say that. If we're not doing well, we also say that. We don't pull our punches.

"Our objective is to get the facts out to the organization. It is a way of demystifying what we are doing and providing people with information for their education.

"White males are concerned that they are getting the shaft and that things are now unfair. So we send the promotion data out. We send the division cash awards out. We send information on merit increases out. We break it down and say, `Look, you may think you are not being treated fairly, but here is the information.' If people want to look at the information and they want to learn from it, they can. If it's strictly emotional and they have no intentions of doing anything with the information, it doesn't help at all."

In the courses on gender and race, women and blacks take on the role of teachers, sharing their experiences and observations. It can be an intense, emotionally exhausting encounter.

"For women and black employees, my sense is that before you go to those courses, you do some assessing to determine how far you want to push the issue in the course, be it racial or gender," Cross said. "What risks do you want to take? How uncomfortable are you willing to make yourself in order to push an issue, in order to help these guys understand what the issues are? Because there are some risks in raising issues these guys don't necessarily want to hear. Maybe they are ready to hear it, and maybe they aren't."

In these courses, women and blacks assume the role of teacher. But by teaching, they also learn.

"They spend a lot of time disclosing, and a lot of time sharing in order to enhance or further the learning of the participants," Cross said. "In the women's course, the learning I think they take away is about how men see them in general. For blacks, it's how whites view the issues. So I think they come away with greater clarity about how others view their issues and a better sense of how to effectively communicate those issues."

For the white men attending the courses with women and minorities, the experience can be just as intense. Cross explained:

"My sense is that white men going through the gender course or the racial course come away with information that has been presented to them before, but for some reason, it didn't take. So they come away with more information about women, about blacks, about the issues they face in the corporation, about the barriers that they have to encounter in the corporation.

"Additionally, they have to do some self-assessment so they come away with a better sense of some of their own biases and stereotypes and myths that they carry with them. I think they also come away with a better sense of what their behavior should be, and if we get those three things, I'm really happy. That means we have been very successful."

Learning to Listen

To ensure that CEO Jamie Houghton keeps informed about diversity efforts, he meets with a group of four women and another group of four blacks once a quarter just to hear what is going on in the organization.

"They speak very frankly," Cross said. "For example, we had a reorganization not long ago, and we did not see women or blacks represented in some of those higher-level moves, and that's a pretty sensitive thing. We raised it with him, and we talked about it. He was delighted that we raised it, and we had a wonderful discussion around it."

After seeing the benefits of Houghton's meetings with the two groups, some of Houghton's direct reports have begun similar meetings of their own.

"What I try to encourage them to do is to sit back and listen," Cross said. "Do not challenge. Sit back and listen. It's not a problem-solving session, so don't feel like every time an issue or problem gets raised that you have to solve it. But understand what they are saying and ask questions to probe. Once you start challenging employees about what they are saying, it shuts the conversation right down because they think you just don't want to hear."

9

Eastman Kodak Company

Learn or Lose

In this computer age of rapid technological shifts and swings, strategic decisions aren't easy to make. The product that provided yesterday's home run may be obsolete tomorrow, and persisting with the strategy that made a company king of the competition could ultimately lead to its economic demise. Today's technological darling could be a passing fad.

The path is perilous, the answers evasive. But one thing is apparent. For technology-based companies, yesterday's knowledge is as valuable as yesterday's newspaper.

Eastman Kodak has latched onto learning as a navigating tool in this new era. The 110-year-old company—for decades the uncontested leader in film—now faces tough competition on every side. Interviews with company executives give insight into how they are using intentional learning to carry the company forward in a variety of ways. Their experience exemplifies how a large, dominant company moves from self-satisfaction to aggressively seeking self-improvement. Below are comments from two managers who are on the front lines of learning, and additional remarks from CEO Kay Whitmore.

Establishing a Vision

Kodak's Bob LaPerle is busy trying to harness a wave of new technology. With the entry of electronic cameras into the business picture,

Kodak must decide how to maintain and advance its core product—photographic film—yet not get left behind in digital technology.

In the late 1980s, LaPerle, director of business planning for the photographic products group, and his organization faced some major challenges. Worldwide demand for photographic film, paper, and chemistry was growing but not as fast as it did in the 1960s and the 1970s. And some external observers were beginning to call photography a "mature market." LaPerle stated:

"In addition, the bulk of our management experience and culture was based on little significant competition. Through the early 1970s, we were virtually uncontested. Then Fuji came at us in the early 80s. We've been doing a very good job of fighting Fuji off, but they haven't let up on the accelerator pedal at all, and now we find companies like Sony and Cannon right around the corner.

"With Fuji confronting Kodak in the core business, Sony and Cannon coming at us in a traditional Japanese fashion from the extremities, we have to think and act differently.

"The other thing that was really hurting us, and the thing that I decided we had to tackle first, was a lack of strategic alignment among the imaging business units."

LaPerle decided to use quality leadership principles to actually build a strategy for the group. As his first step, he wrote down five or six questions concerning what the group's future vision should be relative to the issues he had identified. The responses from the key managers in his strategic planning units "were all over the map. There was no common vision, no alignment around the issues."

LaPerle created a team of key people representing research and development, manufacturing, and the business units, that, for 9 months, spent at least 15 to 25 percent of their time hammering out a vision.

He brought in consultant Joel Barker to help the group explore the paradigms that could be holding back their vision, and he took 30 team members on a retreat. LaPerle brought a list of the last significant products and systems the photographic products group had introduced in the 10 previous years. They sorted the list into two piles: those that had been successful and those that weren't. They discussed what they did right, what they did wrong, and what the paradigms were that led to their actions. LaPerle told what occurred:

"What we found was that we could wallpaper a room with about 150 paradigms. Of the 150, ten rose to the top of the list. The value of this was that, for the next 9 months, whenever the team had a meeting and we were working on future strategy, these paradigms were up on the wall in large letters. Whenever anyone felt that we weren't moving forward because we were trapped in one of these, they could point and say, `I challenge you on paradigm number 4.'

"They were the traditional paradigms you would see in a 110-year-old company, such as `We need home runs to be successful.' That's the way we played the game.

"But some of our hits were falling well short of the outfield fence and that had real impact on the confidence level in the whole company because here is a game that, whenever we stepped up to the plate, we brought our biggest bat and we took the biggest swing we could. Whether it was Brownie Starflash cameras, the 126 System, the 110 System, you name it, we expected to hit a home run every time.

"Well, the game doesn't work that way anymore. Many of the people in the room felt that these major discontinuities, such as analog technology shifting into digital technology, posed only threats, not opportunities.

"However, whenever there is a discontinuity there is an opportunity for any player. If we seize the opportunity, we will benefit. If we don't seize the opportunity, someone else will benefit. Turning that thinking around is taking a long time. We still haven't turned it around completely, but we are making progress.

"Another paradigm is that `Kodak is big enough and strong enough to go it alone.' As we develop new systems that marry the advantages of film and the appeal of electronics, we are finding that, in order to move fast enough or deliver the full system our customers need, we've got to work closely with external partners…people like Sun and others."

After team members understood their own paradigms and what they thought the vision for Kodak should be, they invited in a number of experts in the areas that would have a direct impact on Kodak's future.

LaPerle said: "We identified the top four or five fundamental trends and discontinuities that were going to impact our future. We then brought in functional experts in each of these areas." Included were experts on innovation, high definition television, digital telecommunications, imaging software, and personal computers. "We also brought in a person who was more of a science fiction writer than anything else," LaPerle said. "He was the wild card."

"Once we understood our paradigms," LaPerle said, "we brought in people who were on the fringe and we asked them to tell us, in their own words, their own vision, where they thought the world of photography and imaging would be in the year 2000 and beyond, and we used them to help build some multiple future scenarios."

In addition to hearing those visions, the team took a hard look at the visions of Kodak's competitors to try and determine their long-term strategies.

At the same time, the team did a functional analysis of electronic versus silver halide photography. They broke both processes into a chain of functional elements. Then they presented the strengths and weaknesses of each for customer evaluation.

"What we discovered," said LaPerle, "was that the best strategy for us would be to build hybrid systems which, for at least the next 10 or 15 years, would combine the best of both worlds."

After pooling what they had learned, the team worked with a consultant to write a long-term strategic intent that they could convincingly present to management. LaPerle said that the toughest task his team faced was to recommend a longer-term vision and strategy to deal with the issue of full digital imaging. He explained:

"What my team did was this: We said we must be prepared for a transition in technology. It's the ultimate execution of the vision George Eastman had 100 years ago. Unless we become the world leader in imaging—which is much broader than photography—we would be threatened with decline. We would be giving up our heritage. How do we get from where we are today to a time in the future when we clearly are a world-class player in digital imaging systems?"

Promoting Inventiveness

While stressing real-life application, Kodak is careful not to overlook the importance of pure innovation. At Kodak's Center for Creative Imaging, the future is now. Located in a restored, turn-of-the-century forge and machine shop in Camden, Maine, this international learning center brings together imaginative visual thinkers to promote mastery of computer technologies. Supported by Kodak, Apple Computer, Inc., Adobe Systems, Inc., and other leaders in electronic imaging, it's goal is to empower creativity and extend imagination. The center invites original thinkers, from photographers to graphic designers, editors to art teachers, from film makers to desktop publishers, architects to computer musicians.

"The intention of the center is to bring together leading-edge practitioners and thinkers in areas like graphic arts; pure artists; people who are working in the area of desktop color imaging; people who are working in the area of printing and publishing; all the fringe application areas; and then the more creative areas that are bumping into imaging in a digital sense," LaPerle said.

Joel Barker, the consultant working with LaPerle, points out that paradigm shifts are led by people who operate on the fringes.

LaPerle asked, "How well are we capturing the learnings and translating those into our product development effort?" "I really can't answer that question. I hope it's good because that's a significant investment. There is a lot of learning going on there. How much of that learning is captured, analyzed, and syphoned back to Kodak I really can't answer. But it was set up with the absolute intention of learning."

How to Survive Getting Run Over by a Japanese Truck

Kodak's Dick Bourns, the senior vice president responsible for manufacturing, is very aware of the tough competition Kodak faces. As a former CEO of Verbatim Corporation, a small floppy disc company that Kodak acquired, he knows firsthand the tough Japanese competitors in the digital world. Bourns said of the Japanese:

"They have a totally different set of standards. And it makes no difference whether the product performs any better. I have a disc example where the magnetic layer had a very soft gloss difference on the surface.

"It had no recording difference at all. The disc was inserted inside a black envelope so you couldn't even see it. Japanese salesmen ripped the envelope apart and looked for any visible defect and would not accept the product. It didn't make any difference if it worked. They wanted perfection. We need to be driving for that perfection."

From his current position, Bourns is an advocate of benchmarking and performance gap analysis to identify how current capabilities stack up against the best in the world. He explained:

"I describe the learning process as having been run over by a Japanese truck and surviving. In doing external benchmarking we try to learn from other companies ways to help Kodak through the transition of being an industry leader without any serious challenges to operating in a world of tough competition. We benchmarked a series of companies, and the criteria for choosing them was, 'Had they been run over by a Japanese truck and survived?' And you've got companies like Motorola, Caterpillar Tractor, General Electric, companies that adjusted to the tough competitive world after having their leadership positions challenged by international competition. And they were challenged mainly from the Far East.

"There is a small subset of companies that survive, and when you take a look at that subset, there are some common characteristics. I think the ability to learn is clearly one."

Identifying the Performance Gap

Bourns explained the learning process at Kodak: "The learning process that we use is a very simple one. It is a gap analysis. Human nature is such that, if you find yourself behind, that's very difficult to accept. If you can create a vision of a gap, and you have good people and a well-run organization, you can create motivation. Now if that gap threatens extinction, then you get even more motivation. As I've looked within the company as well as externally, the threat of extinction appears to be one of the very important learning tools because it provides a motivation.

"The two things that I see as necessary are (1) to define gaps and then get people all the way through your organization to see that gap; and (2) having seen that gap, to create the motivation to close it. It will vary by individuals. Some individuals with a competitive spirit will go to close the gap without much push, but collectively an organization seems to come to the fore when there is really a threat. I found at Kodak there was not a collective belief within the organization that we had a negative gap. We were as we have always been, pretty self-satisfied with our position. I think that's typical of U.S. industry. One of the things that we came up with as kind of a parody on world class was Kodak Class (for a detailed description see Chapter 4).

"The interesting thing we discovered having a worldwide manufacturing network was that we made similar products in more than one plant. We set in motion an internal benchmarking process and a set of internal gaps. We had people who would reject external gaps, making comments such as `Are you sure Fuji is really doing that?' You could get in the classic steps: first you get denial, then you get anger, then you get action.

"In the internal process we had full access to each other's information, and then we broke that down by elements. What we found is that somewhere in the Kodak organization we had the elements to be significantly better than we were and, in fact, significantly better than any external gap that we could define. But we had not gotten that learning from one plant to the other.

"Then we set in motion a formalization of the internal benchmarking. We've had significant learning. Maybe the motivation is embarrassment. Maybe it isn't. Somehow you get over that hurdle of `not invented here' or the denial that I'm second or third to someone internally or externally."

In order to be the best, Bourns said that a company must look for the world's most demanding customers and try to meet their needs. Bourns explained:

"The learning that I see you get globally is by trying to find the area of the world with the most demanding customers and then trying to learn how their needs are fulfilled. Then you must make the assumption that their high standard eventually will cascade throughout the world.

"Unfortunately we're playing a bit of catch-up. We were such a quality leader and so good for 110 years that we got pretty self-satisfied. But clearly, we've got some areas where we are catching up. We weren't the best in the world at the last attention to detail."

In fact, Bourns said, Kodak sent some manufacturing people to Japan to visit Japanese customers, and the customers handed back some of the products. Bourns described what happened:

"Some manufacturing people were actually humbled by having the customer give them back their defective product and tell them what a sloppy job they were doing. That's helpful, and you try to convey it with your communications and with various benchmarking. We've done some buybacks of products and analyzed the products and displayed the information. Again it's the idea of trying to create a gap, and if you can create a gap then you can close a gap."

Once you see and can recognize a quality product, it affects your whole notion of what is satisfactory.

"I was in a hotel in Japan, and the thing that struck me was the little cotton swabs on the bathroom vanity," Bourns said. "Every last cotton fiber was wrapped to a constant level of tightness, not shaggy like the Q-Tip packs you might buy in the U.S."

Bourns said international competition has forced Kodak to change its business strategy. Bourns explained:

"As with most U.S. companies, in the past we sold off market share, as they teach in U.S. business schools. Keep raising prices and segment the market. Japanese markets love that, because they go to heaven when they get market share. And eventually, they kill companies who sell off market share. Fugi was building plants in Europe and starting to look at the U.S. while we were looking at which plants to close. The least efficient plant was Australia. We said, `Let's close Australia.' This threat of extinction caused our people to go to their government and ask for a subsidy for 2 years to give them a chance to become the best. They were able to get a subsidy, and we gave them 2 years to prove themselves.

"In the turnaround that followed, they behaved just like a company that was run over by a Japanese truck. This happened to be an internally generated rationalization but they did very well. They were small, with not too much economy of scale and not the newest capital equipment. But they moved to the head of the class in several areas. One was higher-class business on the 135 film. The real shining example was the day when the mighty giant, Kodak Park, that has massive economy of scale and all the newest manufacturing technology, the best of everything, sent a team to Australia to learn how to make 135 film with world-class efficiency. That would never have happened without having the Kodak Class process.

"It was a chain event because you identified a gap. The one company that was under threat did some breakthrough thinking, and moved to a new position. You got that learning to cascade through the company by the internal process.

"Now the dilemma that you have is that if you don't change your business strategy and you keep selling off market share in order to make the next quarter's earnings look good because you raised price and gave away share, if you don't stop that, eventually you break trust because you're going to have to close down plants anyway. Then people don't want to cooperate. So you have to break the basic mindset. That's where Kay, with his strategic intent effort, is really driving the vision of growth. You can't shrink your way to success in the competitive world that we live in. You must have growth and you can't let your competitor have a differential growth rate. If you have growth, you don't have to worry about which plant you're closing. You can worry about where to expand, and then you have a better learning environment. It can be absolutely cannibalistic if you're a traditional U.S. company that spends its time figuring which plant to close.

"Under Kay's leadership, we are now breaking that mold and saying we have a vision. We are going to grow, we are going to go through the broadening of the imaging world to include both electronics as well as chemistry."

When a Company Isn't Learning

There are telltale signs when a company isn't in a learning mode. Bourns cited some of the characteristics he looks for:

"First thing I would do is look and see if they are selling off market share. The first evidence of a sick company is one that allows their competitors to grow faster than they do. I think a similar one, harder to identify but highly related, is a company that allows itself to have a high cost of producing products and somehow finds a way to explain that away. I believe that you need low-cost *and* premium products. That's contrary to what they teach in school, that you can either have a differentiation strategy or you can have a cost strategy. What you learn in the competitive world is whatever featured product you have, you've got to be able to produce that product at least as well as your competitors do or you're eventually going to die."

Keeping Everyone Informed

With close to 40,000 people in his worldwide organization, Bourns said that he has had to find a way to consistently and coherently communicate the company's expectations. Every quarter he holds interactive sessions with over 1000 senior staff members. Bourns explained:

"First of all, we're trying to get a shared vision by showing benchmark data and so forth. But as you get that shared vision, you also try to get input on the barriers a group of leaders faces when they try to close the performance gaps and move in the direction of the shared vision. I found that quite effective.

"You need a shared vision, result areas, and metrics, and you need to display those metrics so people can see their piece of the action. Then you can hold people accountable for their commitments."

Extraordinary Work from Ordinary Managers

Every company has the basic ingredients it needs to improve and become more of a learning organization. What's often lacking, said Kodak CEO Kay Whitmore, is the motivation to change.

"What you want to do is get fairly ordinary people who are reasonably skilled and give them extraordinary motivation," Whitmore said. "The key issue is the principles that come out of quality, that is, determining what you should measure and being rigorous about what you measure. Over time, people will motivate themselves. Nobody wants to be at the tail end of the train. Not everybody is a go-for-the-jugular killer who wants to beat everybody, but most people want to do well and want to feel like they are contributing."

Success depends primarily on "getting the right framework, giving the right data, giving the right tools, and saying, 'Go for it,'" said Whitmore. "You do have to have the right management environment. You have to have a management that feels this is something that they need to do. I guess you end up selecting people who value learning."

In trying to build a learning organization, companies shouldn't look for an immediate payoff. Whitmore said Kodak is grappling with how to make sure learning doesn't get shuffled out the door in the rush to get today's work done. Promoting learning's often-delayed benefits isn't an easy sell in the business world, he said, where the short-term concerns are all-consuming. Whitmore explained:

"Right now we are struggling with the basic incentive systems we use. One of the incentives, of course, is pay, and we have various kinds of performance awards, but in many cases, we don't understand what we are motivating. The result is our incentive systems sometimes motivate the wrong things. Most companies, including this one, still motivate people around accounting earnings as opposed to long-term value creation.

"We clearly have a system in this company that motivates the short-term as opposed to the long-term. Everything is driven by `What are you going to do for me right now?' Not `What are you going to do 5 years from now?' So there are some pretty deep disincentives to learning built into the structure."

Tapping the World's Learning Centers

Organizations must stay abreast of worldwide learning, not just what is happening in their own company or their field. Whitmore said:

"I think you've got to recognize that learning occurs in lots of places, and you've got to go where the learning is. Some of that has a lot of us doing international travel, wanting to ensure that in the world we see coming, we have active people in locations where they can understand, learn, and keep track of things going on in North America, Europe, Japan, and the Pacific rim. They are the thought markets of the world today.

"A company that says it's going to be a worldwide player has to have a significant presence in the major thought markets of the world. It isn't going to happen any other way. You've got to be in the places where thought leadership is happening."

Learning for the Future

Whitmore emphasized the importance of intentional learning. He said: "Kodak is in a really challenging time. We are in the middle of a major technological transformation. We are a company that has built its strength, its reputation, and its current status on mastery of silver halide photography. There are other methods of making images these days. Some of them are electronically based. Others are based on alternate technology. Those newer methods are breaking into the game, and changing the ground rules which apply to our business.

"So virtually every manager here is in a changing environment. We are asking ourselves very actively whether we have the best skill-set as we go into this technological transformation. It puts a premium on learning because you've got to learn a whole new set of skills, and success in this other world is measured in very different terms.

"You've got to go from your basic paradigm of learnings to a whole new paradigm of learnings. That's proved to be very challenging."

10
Rosenbluth Travel

The Benefits of
Outrageous Learning

If you have a tendency toward cynicism, you may find yourself rolling your eyes when you read about Philadelphia-based Rosenbluth Travel. Conversations with their executives are peppered with words like *fun*, *happy*, and *positive impact*. They talk about cattle drives, and coloring with crayons, and playing basketball with candidates for executive positions. They go beyond the standard management buzzwords about "valuing employees." Instead, they talk about helping their people make dreams come true.

That may come across as hokey and sentimental. But the bottom line isn't. In the past 12 years annual sales at Rosenbluth Travel soared from $120 million to $1.3 billion. At the same time the staff grew from 600 to 2800, making the company one of North America's largest independent travel firms.

Critical to Rosenbluth's success has been the company's addition of proprietary software that helps corporate clients track and manage their costs. But when one talks to CEO Hal Rosenbluth, he always stresses the people side of the business and how their personal growth leads to company growth.

In Exhibit 7-3 in Chapter 7, Hal Rosenbluth tells how his commitment to learning flows from his vision for the company, which he describes as people, service, profits. He says, "We focus on our people, our people focus on service, and profits result." Here we talk to Rosenbluth and two of his managers, the director of corporate development and the director of training, about the role learning plays in the company's success.

Importance of First Impressions

At their very first day of work at Rosenbluth, new associates get a taste of the company's attitude toward learning. Instead of spending their first hours of employment filling out forms, everyone, regardless of position, comes to the Philadelphia headquarters for a 2-day orientation.

"We focus totally on the values of the organization," said Frank Hoffmann, director of training. "We don't have them fill out forms. We don't get into the insurance benefits at that point. We don't talk about the job skills. We do nothing but try to let them know what Rosenbluth is like as an organization. It's very clearly an attempt to let them know what the company expects of them and what they, in turn, can expect from the company. We spend the first day really talking about those things. The second day we focus on our product, which is service."

Much of the orientation involves skits and role playing, and the 2 days end with an unusual twist: Rosenbluth and other top executives serve high tea to the new hires. Hoffmann said the benefits of that gesture are multiple.

"The purpose of it is, first, we want the associates to meet Hal," Hoffmann explained. "But secondly, we've been teaching them that the organization believes in a supportive style of management, the inverted pyramid. What better way to demonstrate it than to have the CEO serve them. They absolutely remember that for years later."

Rosenbluth said another reason he serves the new associates (Rosenbluth has tossed out the word employee) is because he wants them to know he's happy they joined the company. He wants them to remain enthusiastic about their jobs.

"No one's ever joined a company with a bad attitude," Rosenbluth said. "Companies create those things. I know when I had my first job I got dressed 3 days ahead of time. I was going to go right in and set the world on fire. Companies have to capture that moment and keep it forever. Then you have productive companies with happy people, and they are having fun. Then that company has a positive impact on the people's lives. What better thing for a company?"

Vision Reinforcement

Rosenbluth Travel offers a wide assortment of training courses, ranging from basic reservation agent training to a leadership development program. The common denominator for all classes is that they reflect the company's vision. Hoffmann said the purpose of his department has changed dramatically in the past 10 years, expanding from job skill training to include all levels of learning.

"What we do is take the company's vision and try to determine what kinds of learning experiences are needed by every level and department within the company if we are to achieve that vision," Hoffmann said. "Our other function is to make sure we have the right people in training and that they continue to grow. In fact, I spend most of my time focusing not on the training itself but trying to maximize the abilities of the trainers. That's really one of my biases. I believe the impact of a learning experience is determined by the talents of the person facilitating the experience and the way it's put together."

Interactive Learning

Hoffmann is a great believer in interactive learning. It's a style of learning that defines all of the company's training and education programs. Hoffmann explained:

"People learn best when they are relaxed, when it can be interactive, when they see what's in it for them, and when they can enjoy themselves. I think that's a lasting kind of learning. Not only that, but I think it absolutely increases their motivation for being alert.

"In order to be cost effective we need to do a lot of our training in rather large chunks of time, like a full day. It's tough to sit in a classroom for a full day. Part of our challenge as trainers is to make it interesting."

One way to achieve that, Hoffmann said, was to use different teaching techniques involving as many of the five senses as possible. Hoffmann explained how this is done:

"What we try to do is present the same material in a variety of ways so that we meet diverse learning styles. That lends to a lot of interesting ways to train. Probably one of the training techniques that I can't stand personally, because I'm bored by it, is somebody standing up and talking at the group. After a while, I don't care how fascinating they are, my mind is going to start to drift. Not only that but I don't care who it is, whether it's Hal up in front or me or anybody, I think people are going to learn more from each other in that group than they will from the person standing up.

"My personal belief about education is that people should leave a training session not thinking, `Wow, did that woman or man who taught us know a lot! Boy, are they interesting!' I don't want the focus to be on the person who led it. I want people to leave thinking what an interesting topic that was or, `Boy, did I learn a lot.'

"I want them to focus on the learning itself and how they grew from it and the ideas that they came out of it with. If the trainer is invisible but was successful in doing that, then the trainer is a tremendous success. We try to really keep the focus off the person running it as much as we can."

The Rivery

One site where the learning experience always has center stage is The Rivery, a $1.5 million ranch-style conference center overlooking the Missouri River in North Dakota. Located 56 miles south of Bismarck and 23 miles west of Linton, it's close to nothing but open sky and mountains. It was one of Hal Rosenbluth's wild ideas that became a reality. The Rivery can trace its beginnings to the summer of 1988 when the Midwest was suffering a serious drought.

In an attempt to help some of the hardest hit farmers, Rosenbluth opened a temporary office in Linton, N.D., and offered 40 part-time data entry jobs. What he found was a group of hard-working, dedicated employees with low absenteeism and high productivity. Teaming up corporate and rural America had financial benefits for both Linton and Rosenbluth Travel, which now employs more than one hundred and sixty full-time employees in the North Dakota office.

That's how Hal Rosenbluth first was introduced to North Dakota. In 1989 he held a strategic planning session in Linton. The group stayed in a roadside motel and, instead of the usual recreational activities of golf or skiing, rode horses and did farm chores. He said it was the best meeting they ever had. Out of that experience he decided to build The Rivery, a 16-room ranch where companies can hold small meetings, one group at a time.

The Rivery was designed to provide a high-impact, unique learning environment for businesses. It also provided a high-impact, unique learning opportunity for Diane Peters, Rosenbluth's director of corporate development. When Rosenbluth decided to build this conference center, he handed Peters the deed to nearly 1000 acres of land and said, "Do it."

And she did. It was built and opened in just over 7 months. Hotels usually take years. Peters told how she accomplished her assignment:

"The first thing I did was to facilitate and oversee the construction, the design, and the building. I wrote the brochures and handled sales and marketing, hired staff, and trained them. That's kind of the way Hal does things. Nobody here had experience building a retreat. Nobody here knew how to do it or what direction to turn in, so when he gave me the job, it was with the understanding that if anything needed to be done surrounding this project, I would be doing it.

"I certainly called upon a lot of talents in the company and met with a lot of people, but I knew that the entire project would be mine and there is no better way to learn than that. Now I know how to build a hotel, and I would have never known. A lot of the learning is just baptism by fire. I don't think there is a better way to learn. Also, there is almost a mental safety net. I knew everyone understood that this project was a first for me, and I was going to do my best. That was an excellent learning experience."

Standard training, Peters said, could not have prepared her for the job. She explained:

"Most of our training is philosophical. According to the Rosenbluth way of thinking, what I didn't need was a hotel management seminar or a `Construct your hotel in 91 days with 100 percent success' seminar. What I needed were the kinds of programs that I get here, which are general topics like time management and negotiating skills, or a seminar on innovation that teaches you the development stages of an idea and how to bring it to fruition and test it.

"I think training can put you in the right frame of mind, but people shouldn't use training to tell them the actual steps. If I had gone to some hotel building seminar, I would have gotten caught up in the wrong things, and it would have felt like a hotel. But what we wanted, and what we got, is something that feels like the heart and soul of our company.

"It's done in a unique way and I think that's the only way you get something different. It's a good thing that I didn't know too much about hotels."

For instance, Peters said, at The Rivery they don't put mints and a card on the pillow at night. They provide freshly baked chocolate chip cookies and ice cold milk "because that's the way the farmers would do it." Also, there's no room service.

Peters said: "At first I thought, `Oh, hotels have room service. We'd better do that.' Then we asked `Who wants to sit by themselves in their room and eat? Let's have a big country style buffet breakfast where they can all eat together.'"

At the suggestion of one of the farmer's wives, they clang a big dinner bell when it's time to eat.

"People like—and come back for—all the things we do that are non-hotel," Peters said. "I didn't need hotel training. I just needed enough training to give me the confidence and the process to be able to think things through. The rest you learn on-the-job or on-the-go and by being hungry for information. There is specific and technical training, and then there is the nontechnical. Learning on-the-job is always going to be the key."

In building The Rivery, Peters was adept at gathering extensive outside information, a critical element in the learning formula described in Chapter 6. She met with a number of hotel executives to learn the operations side; she visited similar facilities; she polled clients; and every time she visited a hotel, she wrote down everything she did or saw.

She didn't want to waste time recreating knowledge she could quickly gather from other sources. Peters said:

"We have philosophical training, and we have a service orientation, but we don't have the training on the physical aspects of the hotel, so I went to the Ritz-Carlton organization and asked them to teach us. How do you make a hospital corner? How do you turn down the bed at night? How do you make a bed so elegantly? A lot of people don't know those things, and that was something that I didn't think we needed to recreate.

"They put together a weeklong training program, and we met at the Ritz in Philadelphia. We flew all of our people in from North Dakota in cowboy hats and they learned how to make hospital corners and serve tea elegantly.

"Those were things that, until I checked outside first, and then internally to see where we stood, I wouldn't have known how to do. I decided in some cases we were in over our heads and needed help."

Leadership Development

Rosenbluth runs a variety of leadership training programs. One operates like an internship program and is custom-designed, both in content and length, for each participant. Leadership development interns are given a mentor within the company who works with them throughout the entire program. Hoffmann explained how the programs work:

"We don't focus on their strengths. We focus on the things that we think would make them stronger. The purpose is to give them as many varied experiences with different parts of the organization as we possibly can, but it's not just them sitting there observing. These people roll up their sleeves and they are given real projects to do.

"For instance, one woman was given the responsibility to do every single thing attached to opening a new vacation and cruise headquarters here in Philadelphia. From working with the architects on the design of the building to picking out furniture, handling the grand opening, and putting in computers. I mean everything. She had done few, if any, of those things before that. That was part of our leadership training program."

Another part of the company's leadership development involves taking groups of executives to The Rivery, an exercise in which Rosenbluth clearly takes delight. Rosenbluth said:

"I took the vice presidents on a cattle drive because I wanted them to all see that they aren't great in everything and that when placed in a situation that none of us had ever faced before, we all exposed certain shortcomings. Then, as a team, we overcome that shortcoming. Cattle driving is one way I do it. Building a fence is another way.

"Three years ago I took those same vice presidents out to a farm in North Dakota and had a whole bunch of barbed wire, a whole bunch of tools that they had never seen before, and a bunch of posts and a tractor. I said `Ok, Let's put up a mile's worth of fence.' So everybody took charge. The company made them take charge. They were leaders. Fences need to be straight for the cattle because if there is a storm, the last thing you want is for the cattle to run into a barbed wire fence and get cut up.

"Well, that fence went all over the damn place and it was going nowhere fast because everybody wanted to take charge and no one knew what the hell they were doing because they had never done it before," Rosenbluth said. "That didn't slow them down until eventually somebody said, `Hey, this is crazy. It's a mess.' Then someone turned to the farmer and said, `Ok, how do we do it?' and that was the key. From that point on, we created a process and got the fence up real quick. That's typical of the kinds of things that we'll do to expose shortcomings."

Stretching Your Employees

Peters, who coauthored Rosenbluth's book entitled *The Customer Comes Second*, said that as a boss, Hal Rosenbluth always looks for ways to challenge his employees. His eagerness to provide stretch assignments has been a key to Peters' continuous learning. Peters explained:

"He has had more confidence in me than I had in myself. He has given me projects that I never would have envisioned that I could handle, and I found a way to do it. He always knew that I could.

"He entrusted me to build a hotel and write a book. If you had asked me 2 years ago if I could do either one, I would have laughed hysterically and said `No way.' But the fact is that he just gave me a deed to the land in one case and said `Go write this' in another. Every time I thought I couldn't do it, I would think `Hal thinks I can do it. I *have* to do it.' I surprised myself.

"He is not afraid to take risks, and he trusts people. These two projects taught me more than anything I've ever done in my life, and I would never have given myself that opportunity. I would never have said `Yes, I can do that.' If they called for volunteers, I never would have raised my hand."

Letting People Learn from Mistakes

People are only willing to take risks if they are sure they won't be crucified for a misjudgment or misstep. Mistakes are important learning tools. In developing leaders, Hoffmann said it is a tool he constantly emphasizes. Leaders, he said, must recognize that mistakes can provide the most dramatic lessons. Hoffmann explained how this happens:

"If people really learn by doing, by being challenged and being allowed to do new things, then the right atmosphere has to be set by the leader. There has to be an environment that permits that to happen instead of `No, your job is to take that little widget and stick it on this particular thing and then you take the next one and do it again and again. Don't vary outside of that. Don't think; just do it.'

"The environment that is created within this company by the owners and the executive board is that learning and constant growth are very important. So the atmosphere is there to support learning on the job."

To make sure that atmosphere is maintained, leader development seminars are not taught by outside consultants but by company executives who believe in the importance of allowing people to learn.

"We try to teach them ways for motivating and developing people," Hoffmann said. "We try to teach them that it's OK to allow people to try something new. Don't chop off their heads if they make a mistake. That's how you learn. You don't learn by having 100 percent success all the time. If you do that, you're probably inching your way along and that's not going to cut it here."

Live the Spirit

Learning takes place under a variety of names at Rosenbluth Travel. Hoffmann admits that outside of Rosenbluth, "Live the Spirit" is one that sounds pretty corny, but it's the title of an extremely successful monthly seminar program designed to encourage learning in the employees' personal and professional lives. The seminars are for the entire staff and are offered each month at all offices across the country. Typical topics are stress management, personal money management, recycling, and food and fitness.

"We feel that if it has something to do with the person's life, it is important to us here because it translates over into the workplace," Hoffmann said.

One of the most popular sessions is Perception versus Reality. The class divides into pairs and one person is blindfolded; the other is not. In front of them are placed plastic containers filled with different substances, such as powdered sugar, flour, cereal, candy red hots, and dish washing detergent. The blindfolded person can only touch the substance. Their partner can only look at it.

Then the seminar leader makes a list of what people thought was in the containers. The point is made that two people can have quite different perspectives of reality and that other viewpoints should be noted and respected.

"It's fascinating because a lot of time people visually make assumptions," Hoffmann said. "Sometimes the person who can feel but cannot see is more accurate. Each person can have the same reality but see it in a different way. We tie that [learning] in with our phone voice. We are our attitude that we have over the phone or face-to-face. It goes back to the idea that the very first impression is so critical. We need to control it as much as we possibly can."

Live the Spirit seminars are a way to bring together people from different segments of the company and offer interesting and fun learning opportunities. It's also a way for people to come together and get things off their chests.

"We wanted it to be a forum for bringing out any frustrations or concerns that people have about what was going on in the company," Hoffmann said. "Sometimes it is quite clear that they want to deal with something, and then we'll scrap the seminar and deal with that. If there is negativism, you can't stifle it. You can't tell them `I don't want to hear that.' You've got to let it out in the proper forum. You don't want them sitting around on-the-job complaining."

Putting Your People First

You also don't want them sitting around worrying whether their job will be there tomorrow, Rosenbluth said, or dreading another workday.

"We as companies have an absolute obligation to the people we employ to be the best we can possibly be," Rosenbluth said. "Most of their waking hours are at work, and I think that if you look at the root of a lot of family problems, they go right back to work. Whether it's a divorce, stress, whatever, it tends to have it's genesis at work. I don't want our company's epitaph to be that it ruined 20,000 lives on earth."

Rosenbluth said that as chief executive officer, his primary concern is providing job security for every staff member. He explained how he felt:

"We're lucky. We're not publicly held, so we can do basically anything. I can see us going into a shareholders meeting and saying, `We positively impacted 2600 lives this year, but earnings were down.' Last year we should have laid 289 people off. We didn't lay off anybody. We believe emotion plays a part in every business decision. It's not supposed to, but it does. And it should.

"Our people chose us as a company that they wanted to work for and work at. At that point begins our obligation to create a lifelong learning environment for them. Our learning has to be both personal and business oriented. It has to be both."

Rosenbluth repeatedly stresses his belief that when morale is good and his people are happy, the customers are well served.

"Each individual has a different dream, and we want dreams to become realities," he said. "That's the kind of company we look to be for our people. As a result of that environment, we are able to provide unbelievable levels of service."

The ultimate payoff for creating a learning environment, Rosenbluth said, is "having a positive effect on someone's life. If we can just add to the knowledge someone has, that's where it's at. They are going to be better for their family. They are going to be better for their friends. They are going to be better for the clients. They are going to be better for each other."

11

J. P. Morgan & Co. Inc.

Learning for an Uncertain Future

In its 1991 annual report, J. P. Morgan offers an explanation for its success: "Our combination of character and capabilities—the logic of J. P. Morgan—defines our competitive advantage in a complex world."

You can't argue with their achievements. In 1991 the firm had a net income of $1.146 billion and earnings 44 percent above the previous year. It is the only U.S. money center bank with a AAA credit rating and is one of only a few U.S. commercial banks that the Federal Reserve Board allows to underwrite corporate securities.

In the past decade, New York–based J. P. Morgan has transformed itself from a traditional bank to a multiproduct, multimarket, financial services institution. With major subsidiaries that include Morgan Guaranty Trust Company of New York, J. P. Morgan Securities Inc., J. P. Morgan Investment Management Inc., and J. P. Morgan Futures Inc., J. P. Morgan provides a wide range of financial services to governments, central banks, financial institutions, and major corporations worldwide.

What separates J. P. Morgan from the crowd? What do they do differently from other businesses? From studying the company and interviewing executives there, it's clear that the way they develop their people and encourage continual learning is a major part of the answer.

Building a Flexible Work Force

Given the volatility of the financial world, long-term planning is a luxury that banks can't afford. Instead, Morgan relies on a large pool of talented managers with wide-ranging capabilities. While business needs are immediate, developing talented, well-rounded employees is a gradual, long-term process. Morgan could go out and buy the expertise they need, but instead, they mostly develop their own. That way the firm always has capable employees waiting in the wings.

"We don't have a plant or physical products, so in the financial industry we can have tremendous volatility in the product range," said Anthony Beale, who is in charge of the "people side" of corporate personnel. "Our planning range, or planning window, is very short, and the cycle for creating resources is relatively long. From recruitment through training through experience is a cycle far longer than our planning window."

Due to the short time available for planning and the long time needed to develop resources, Beale said a company such as his has two options:

"You can say, 'Well, it's impossible to plan.' Or I think you can say 'I can't plan specifically, but what I can do is create pools of talent that give me the flexibility to absorb the volatility, hopefully at any pace and of any magnitude.'

"I think that is the huge return you eventually get in putting time and money into creating breadth of knowledge and flexibility in leaders. It gives you pools of talent that you can draw on for basic knowledge and basic product skills. You can very rapidly add whatever extra piece of technical knowledge is required in order for your employees to be productive in a reasonably short space of time. That offsets what might, in the short term, be the gain from just exploiting an individual's talent in a specific area. We need specialists, but specialists with breadth and ability to do other things gives us another dimension."

Making Every Assignment a Stretch

At J. P. Morgan, there is no easy assignment. If you are fully and absolutely capable of doing a job, don't expect to get it. Executives there believe individual growth is critical for every employee and the company as well. Mirroring what Beale said, Marion Gislason, head of Morgan's corporate training unit, explained that it is company doctrine that people should work with an eye toward maximizing learning and development to achieve organizational and personal goals. The result, she said, is the best service possible for their clients. Gislason explained:

"We are dealing with an employee population that, at its best, has clearly articulated, values-based, long-term personal life and career objectives. If we're doing our job right, then the job that each person is in today is the best possible job for the first step on that lifelong journey. People understand that the reason to take the next job is to develop skills that can't be developed in this job, skills that are a value to the firm and of meaning to the individual's long-term career objectives.

"So the notion of staffing a position with someone who is fully capable of executing that role is an anathema. You would never do it. Even if you have people in place who are 100 percent capable of taking that role. You would never staff a position with someone who from day one is fully capable of executing the job. You want fear of a good kind. You want `Oh my god, I'm not sure I can really do this' kind of feelings.

"By stretching and challenging people, a company maximizes their confidence and learning. If the company runs out of `big jobs' or if the person feels there is nothing else to learn, it's time to find a position outside the organization."

J. P. Morgan is still sorting out how to encourage and equip employees to exert more control over their own learning. Having employees who rely on the company for their career growth is dangerous, Gislason said, because "what you may end up with is people who don't have the skills and don't understand why they don't have them because they thought the firm was taking care of that for them. That is ultimately very unhealthy because the firm can only be a partner; the firm is best served by employees who have a strong sense of their own self and their life and work objectives." Gislason said that at a recent career development day, the message was "It's your life. It's your career. Here are skills to function and plan and manage your own career."

Gislason describes the best employee for Morgan as the one who has the guts to say: "This is not the right assignment for me. The firm benefits the most when I'm well matched to my work because I'm growing and thinking and getting ideas in the shower."

Reflecting on Mistakes and Successes

As with all of the learning organizations we have observed, J. P. Morgan tries to learn from mistakes as well as success.

Gislason said that at Morgan, they make an effort to reflect on their actions:

"Every experience is a learning experience. We never want to do the same thing twice unless it is by choice. After we have concluded anything, whether it is a meeting or a transaction or a project or a year's worth of work, we individually and collectively sit down and ask ourselves, `What were the choices we made? What were we right about?

Where would we try something else the next time around?' We treat mistakes as learning opportunities not as failures. It goes back to learning from each other and getting feedback.

"It's about giving and extracting from each other information about ourselves, about our performance, about what we have done. It's about asking our clients `How are we doing? Are you happy? Do you have any ideas that could be helpful to us?' It's like putting tent cards on the tables in the cafeteria, asking `Do you like the food?' We try to take advantage of opportunities to build feedback into our work and lives."

Heightening the Motivation to Learn

A company can't create the desire to learn, but it can build upon it. At Morgan, executives try to magnify and commend that desire by matching employees with work that is personally fulfilling. Gislason explained:

"The foundation of learning is really wanting to become something that you are not yet. It is moving towards something. If there is nothing that you want to try to be, or become capable of, or do, or accomplish, there is no motivation to learn anything.

"People can only be well matched to their jobs if both the firm and the individual acknowledge the personal meaning that is found in work. If they are well matched, there will very high motivation to learn. If they are poorly matched, there will be all kinds of conflicts and very low energy. Personal meaning in work gives access to a whole new energy pool— one would think we would have figured that out by now. But generally speaking, I think American companies have not figured that out."

Senior Leaders as Role Models

At Morgan, one of the primary responsibilities of senior managers is to act as role models. By showing an eagerness to learn, by admitting mistakes, by asking questions, they set an example of learning. Gislason explained:

"What's the role of the senior leader in any organization? Role modeling. It's very important for the senior managers to behave in a way that conveys the message, `There is a lot that I don't know. There is a lot that I can learn from the kids who just graduated from school and joined us because they are the ones closest to the academic world where research is being done. So I'm a learner, and you can watch me act and see how I learn.'

"There is just a tremendous amount that senior people can do to shape and influence people down the line. It's not even a matter of influencing. It's a matter of freeing people below them in the organization to act in ways that are very natural. People want to be able to express their own confusion about something, or to be open about mistakes that they made, or open about uncertainty that they feel. They want to be free to ask for help. The only reason that people don't do it is that they are afraid of consequences. They are afraid that if they show vulnerability or lack of perfection that they will pay a price for it. Senior managers, by behaving in a way that signals acceptance of normal behavior, free people up to be their natural learning selves."

The J. P. Morgan Culture

When J. P. Morgan executives are asked what puts their organization at the forefront of financial institutions, their answers vary to some extent. But ultimately all responses come back to the "Morgan culture." What is the Morgan culture? The shortest answer comes from the annual report mentioned earlier: it's the company's unique "combination of character and capabilities." They view themselves as different. They view themselves as better than most. They view themselves as having a unique society that should be protected and promoted.

That culture is reflected in the company's aggressive recruiting, in the sense of partnership between employees and the organization, and in the expectation that everyone will always act on behalf of the collective good. Beale said new employees go through a 3-month training program that familiarizes them with the entire J. P. Morgan operation.

The training program provides a broad base of knowledge that, as career directions change, employees can call on again as they move into other specializations. It also provides employees with a network of colleagues throughout the organization, which helps to keep them from becoming isolated in their own fields or specialties. Additionally, the initial, intensive training gives employees a sense of investment in the company, Beale said.

Developing a Breadth of Knowledge

Tying in with the company's culture is Morgan's effort to give people a breadth of experience and knowledge. The company tries to move managers across specializations and between different segments of the organization, which is another way of providing stretch assignments. "We do it consciously and we build from that a very broad base of skills," Beale said. Sometimes that results in sacrificing depth of knowledge for breadth of knowledge.

"There is a trade-off, of course. When you go for breadth you are possibly limiting the return on any particular specialization," he said. "If you are particularly good at something, then presumably you are going to get better at it at least for some time. By moving people across specialties you may cut those peaks off, but I think eventually that is outweighed by having the flexibility that comes from having the breadth of experience. Practice, I think, proves it to be true."

What was the origin of the company's strategy to consistently expand an individual's capabilities? Beale listed four contributing factors:

"Morgan was a partnership, and I don't think it ever lost the partnership mentality," he said. "Certainly when I joined the institution people always talked with pride about how small we were. Actually it wasn't that small. We have about 13,000 people, but I think people truly believe it is about a fifth of that size. That's because they feel they know everybody, partly because of the initial training program."

The second factor is an internal belief that J. P. Morgan employees are exceptional. "It's a mentality of the old sort, of J. P. Morgan doing first-class business in a first-class way," Beale said. "If you employ first-class people, they presumably can do anything, and there really is a belief here that people can do anything. They have the basic talents. You just need to give them the technical knowledge or product knowledge or whatever it is they need for the task at hand, but they have the basic skills to be successful."

"The third factor, I think," said Beale, "is that for a very prudent institution Morgan has always been quite willing to take risks to give people opportunities. I think there's a mindset that the talent is there, so give them a chance. Create the right environment and people will perform."

Lastly, Beale said Morgan's dedication to promoting employees' continual growth is built into the company's reward system. In stark contrast to most companies, managers are expected to move valued employees through their department, even when it means giving up talent and resources. No human resource embezzlement is allowed.

"There must be a willingness on the part of management to give up talent and resources to make these transfers possible," Beale said. "In the short term, that may have an adverse affect on the managers, but if you are going to stretch people, you have to be willing to take a chance on somebody else. Human resources are regarded as a corporate asset, not as a sort of private fiefdom."

It's back to the J. P. Morgan culture of team effort, collective good. It's valuing people enough to let them go, said Jean-Louis Bravard, managing director in technology.

In his department, he said, "I'm taking the best people, and I make an obligation to myself to offer them new challenges outside the department. My turnover in this job so far is above 40 percent in 7 months. I took the best players, moved them out and I replaced them with the best people I could find, and in 7 months I probably have one of the best departments in the bank. It's very flat and very dynamic."

Bravard said that the ability to give up good people is best demonstrated by Peter Woicke, managing director of technology and operations.

"I think his strength is that he values people," Bravard said of Woicke. "He values them to the point of placing them away from him in good jobs. It's hard. It's very hard to build good war machines and then give them out. He's one of the few managers in that position doing this."

Increasing Importance of Specialization

Woicke said experiencing a wide range of jobs and living in a variety of locations remains an important element for most successful J. P. Morgan senior managers, but a new career path has emerged.

"For quite a long time the firm had only one real career path, which was that you had to be in different jobs," Woicke said. "In fact, if you really wanted to make it to the top, you had to be in different locations. That, interestingly, is changing. We have discovered that we also needed to create career path specialists. If you are really good in your area, you can make it today in terms of compensation as well as titles and levels. That's a more recent phenomenon of the firm. As I said, the traditional one is that you had to sort of move around locations and ideally jobs as well."

The development of a specialist career path was in response to the marketplace, Woicke said.

"We underwent a transition from a commercial bank with basically very few products—lending and some operational services—to the securities business where international expertise was important. I think we recognized that we needed specialists, such as product specialists, traders, and analysts, who would not benefit the firm by having to move around. So we had to respond to the market. We have had to respond to the fact that we needed these people as specialists in the firm."

Sharing Responsibility, Sharing Information

As part of the transition from a traditional bank to a multifaceted financial institution, the company's ability to communicate rapidly became crucial. Global clients needed immediate, accurate information. It was another marketplace demand. Sharing responsibility and information at Morgan is not only expected, but "we go to great lengths to make sure that people understand that it is not appreciated and not rewarded to hoard either one," Beale said. He explained:

"When I came here I found that you did not have to work through a hierarchical structure. You go directly to the individual from whom you wish to get information in order to achieve something. That also comes back to what we talked about in terms of the culture. There is an absence of the need for self. It means that people are willing to share information and resources and actually willing to pool time and effort for somebody else's benefit.

"You can't actually divorce any of these things. Collectively they form the basis of the way we work and enable very open and swift communication. Because of the nature of our business, there is a sophisticated communication network anyway. Even if the news in and of itself is not always important, the intrinsic value of that flow of information is enormous. The institution is extremely flat in it's organization. There is little correlation between title, level, remuneration, responsibility for decision making, or access. It truly is more on an expert basis."

Learning for Future Success

Sometimes future success ties in directly with something learned long ago. That which appeared to be useless knowledge can become quite valuable. Bravard gave an example:

"I stopped worrying about computers in 1974. It was pretty irrelevant to me until 9 months ago. Then some of this early learning about how to write a computer program became very useful as background knowledge in this job. You have reinforcing learning loops all along, and something that looks like it is irrelevant might be the most relevant thing 10–15 years down the road.

"I think the challenge is to have a narrow and a wide learning focus at the same time, because you do not really know what is going to be crucial in the future."

Beale said Morgan's future depends on keeping a vision of what it wants to become, coupled with flexibility and the ability to learn:

"I think the key thing as we go forward is the ability to learn. You cannot arrest the pace of development in the marketplace, in the world, socially, and technologically. It is coming at an increasing rate. You've got to be able to learn and adapt and use. That's terribly important in the selection of the people that you hire. It is equally important to make sure that you keep their minds open once they are here. I think it is essential that you try and create a culture within which people do not feel overly threatened by change, which is clearly difficult to do. Different people learn or adapt at different rates. It creates tensions within an institution, and you have to be conscious of those. That's part of the cost of doing business. You've got to spend time and money on making sure it works."

12

Motorola, Inc.

A New Model for Executive Development

Based in Schaumburg, Illinois, Motorola is an excellent example of a company that aggressively anticipates the future and positions itself accordingly. It acts on the belief that the company's current strengths *won't* be the areas that make it successful in the future. Since it was founded more than 60 years ago, it has successfully undergone a complete transformation from producing consumer products, such as car radios and televisions, to being a world leader in high-technology industrial electronics. With annual sales of more than $10 billion, the company's products now include two-way radios, pagers, cellular telephones and systems, semiconductors, defense and aerospace electronics, computers, and data communications and information processing.

Motorola continues to redefine itself. Its stated goal is to provide customers with "what they want, when they want it, with Six Sigma quality and best-in-class cycle time." Six Sigma is a statistician's way of saying 3.4 defects per million. Learning has been a cornerstone in Motorola's push for total quality, a quest that in 1988 earned the company a Malcolm Baldrige National Quality Award.

As part of helping its 100,000 employees upgrade their skills and learn new ways of working, the company spends more than $100 million a year on education and training.

Here we take a look at the company's new model for senior executive development. It involves solving real-life, critical problems benefit the company and teach its top executives how to learn on-the-job.

Perhaps more than any other company we observed, Motorola is pursuing the kind of intentional learning at work that this book advocates. By growing smart managers, they are building a smart organization.

Creating a New Paradigm

In 1991, Motorola's senior executive training program came out of the classroom and went into the workplace. It began as an experiment that remains in progress. Deborah King, director of executive and management education, worked closely with CEO George Fisher to develop the format.

The company's old model of executive education was considered successful in terms of what it was intended to accomplish. It involved a yearly conference or symposium on one topic chosen by former CEO Bob Galvin. It was primarily a forum for discussion where world-class experts would speak and raise issues that Motorola should be considering. Topics included the Japanese threat, customer satisfaction, and cycle time. All the vice presidents participated in the program, which was held several times a year for groups of about 25.

In 1990, King moved into executive education and asked Fisher, the new CEO, what topic he wanted to address that year. He selected leadership, and with that, Fisher and King started down the road that led to the new model for executive development, one that has executives examine a problem and actually implement the solution. The two spent hours upon hours discussing what Fisher wanted from the program, trying to pinpoint what the company wanted out of its leaders that it wasn't getting, trying to determine what could be taught and what could be learned. King and Fisher were still thinking in terms of the old model of executive development, which was a 3- to 5-day program. They couldn't identify common traits that they wanted to teach everybody, and there was no common style of leadership that they wanted to promote. King told the story:

"Finally, in one of our discussions I said, `George, just what is it about our leaders that you want improved?' He said `They can't get things implemented on time.' From that we were able to say that the aspect of leadership that Motorola could improve on was not visioning. We do a really good job of that. It wasn't necessarily motivating people. We seem to do okay in that. The aspect we could improve on really was implementing change. Once you get an idea, how do you make it happen? Given that, I went to work on another proposal for a program.

"The more I pondered it and tried to come up with the traditional senior executive program design, the more I was aware that it wouldn't work. I called George and said to him, `If I do one of those programs for you, what I can guarantee to you at the end of the 3 to 5 days is that all of your officers will be able to describe change models for you. They will be able to describe roles that should be played. They will be able to tell you lists of common pitfalls and barriers. They will be able to describe for you the emotional impact that change has on people. They will be able to do all those things. But I won't be able to tell you that they can, in fact, manage change.' He said, `What does it take for you to do that because that's what I want.' For them to learn to manage change, they have to manage change.

"With that statement it really took the senior executive program out of the classroom and put it into the workplace. George wasn't convinced that that was the model we should do. I wasn't either. I'd never done it before. So again through a series of meetings and discussions, we agreed that we would experiment. So this new senior executive program (SEP) model is George's and my grand experiment with executive education. We knew once we decided to do that that we had to have a topic for them to manage change around."

Real Problems, Real Solutions

To choose the topic they asked the top 15 executives to identify the most critical issues Motorola faced. Part of the criteria for selecting a topic was that it had to be a corporatewide issue with the potential for a corporatewide solution. And it had to be one that participating executives were empowered to solve because they actually had to implement whatever they thought needed to be done. It also had to be a problem with a high interest level so people would feel compelled to solve it despite other pressing business issues.

Two issues were chosen: (1) to value and promote software initiatives and employees; and (2) to accelerate Motorola's entry into new markets, using Eastern Europe for the prototype. Two teams were formed, each composed of about 24 company vice presidents.

"The first topic we chose to deal with in this format was working with the software engineering culture within Motorola," King said. "Motorola is a hardware engineering company. It's run by hardware engineers. It's staffed by hardware engineers. Its accounting systems reflect hardware engineering. As we look at our products, the functionality of our products is very quickly becoming software-based. That means the company is going to be shifting more to software, and it should put its resources and talents into software engineering in addition to hardware engineering.

Motorola, Inc.

"That's a hard shift for a company to take," King said. "The software is invisible. It's hard to learn if you weren't in it. I think one of the other major changes is all of a sudden we are dealing now in technologies that we didn't create. Before, it was easy to be a learner because we were the ones creating it. So we grew up with it. Now we are working with an engineering discipline that we didn't create."

King said team members were selected based on three criteria: (1) their business dealt directly with software; or (2) they were creative thinkers who would benefit the team; or (3) working with more senior vice presidents would be a good developmental activity for them because they could see how decisions are made within the company.

While developing the executive education model, King said she and the CEO realized the importance of the vice presidents learning how to learn.

"We talked about the fact that what we really wanted them to do was to learn how to manage change, but from that we wanted them to learn how to learn," King said. "If we only accomplished two things—for them to learn to manage change and for them to accomplish whatever business issue was chartered to them—then we would have to continue to do these kinds of programs over and over again. Quite honestly, I don't look forward to a career of doing that. So what we wanted them to do was reap from this experience the ability to learn from processes that they were going through. So the learning to learn became a very big part of the program."

King said her two pivotal points in selling Fisher on the new program were: (1) whereas the old method of executive development produced incremental increases in learning, the new model could produce quantum leaps; and (2) the new model would be an advanced learning lab where experimentation is valued and people learn from mistakes.

"The way you really get good at things is to reduce the learning curve," she said. "So I drew a graph that had time against learning. It was the traditional, very slow start kind of a curve that went up. What I said was that when we do other kinds of developmental activities, we expect them to have some kind of impact, but it's an incremental impact. So by giving them repeated SEPs or by doing job rotations or whatever we are doing, we are getting incremental improvement. By really focusing on the learning to learn piece, I thought we could get a quantum leap jump. Because what we would be doing throughout the process, is trying to take incidental learning and have it become conscious learning. One of the questions that we had posed to us continually is, `Why do some people go on a rotation and come back and have learned so much that they are not the same person while other people go on the rotation and come back having learned nothing?' Part of it is because some people incidentally pick up a lot of stuff but turn it into conscious reflection, and that's what we want them to do with this model. That became part of the turning point for George, that it looked like we could get some quantum benefit from this model."

Initially, Motorola planned to have multiple teams participating in the new SEP model so all 315 vice presidents would participate concurrently, but Fisher decided not to.

"My question was 'Why not?'" King said, "and his response was that too many vibrations inside the company at one time would tear it apart, which I thought was very insightful. I do think a lot of the learning from the two teams that we do have are permeating into the organization."

Going into Eastern Europe

After the software team was off the ground a second team formed, focusing on acceleration into new regions. Its first meeting was held in Budapest in October of 1991.

"We decided that if we are going to be learning about new regions, we needed to hold the meetings in the new regions," King said. "That was a learning experience for me. How do you organize an event for 25 vice presidents in a country you've never been to and a country that is not yet used to doing business with westerners? A country where they speak a different language and whose fax machines' tone that says 'hang up' is the same tone that on our fax machine says 'send?'"

Gary Tooker, president and chief operating officer, gave the group a three-part charter. One directive was to develop a model for Motorola's acceleration into a region. The second was to try it out in eastern Europe. And the third was to learn how to manage change.

The group organized itself as a business, appointed a board of directors, and divided into teams to develop a manual, or 'cookbook' as they called it, for entering a new market. The board of directors met in January in Schaumburg, shared the information they had developed, and put together a plan for the next 6 months. In February, the group sent a six-member SWAT team into Prague, armed with the cookbook. Despite the amount of time and energy invested in developing the manual, they found it wasn't the right way to approach a new market. Instead, they developed a new set of brief guidelines.

"They had an opportunity in our next meeting in Prague, in February of 1992, to actually try out pieces of it," King said. "We had set up visits for each of the team members, working in pairs or triads, to go into different businesses and organizations within Prague and actually do some field trips. The field trips were extremely meaningful. I would recommend them for any of the programs that we do in the future."

"They came back together," King continued, "and I think all of them were somewhat startled by the fact that although we'd only been in the country 3 or 4 months, we already had some pretty confused customers out there because we were in there trying to sell competing technologies.

The Sum of Our Parts Is Less Than the Whole

"The real breakthrough," King said, "came from Merle Gilmore, senior vice president and general manager of the radio products group. Gilmore had just returned from visiting a potential customer in Prague." King explained:

"In some pretty poetic ways he described for us his visit. When he sat down in front of the customer, the customer opened his desk drawer and pulled out five or six different business cards from Motorola. Each one had a different company name on it in terms of the business within Motorola, and they had different cities, and in most cases different countries, listed on the business card. Merle pulled his business card out, as did the other two people visiting with him, to add to the man's collection. Merle said at that point the man's facial expression was of utter confusion. He posed the question to Merle, `If I wanted to buy something from you, who would I call?'

"So Merle and Eike Baer, our country manager in Germany, tried to begin explaining Motorola's configuration: businesses within sectors, groups within sectors. We also have country managers. The man's question after that was still, `Who do we call?'

Back at the meeting with fellow senior vice presidents, Gilmore said the look on the man's face was an indictment against Motorola. And Gilmore told them that "the sum of our parts is less than the whole."

"That was the real turning point," King said, "because we realized that at worst, you want the sum of your parts to be equal to your whole, and certainly you would hope for more than that, but for the sum to be less than the parts is just not acceptable and Merle said we have to change." King recalled what happened:

"There was a look of disbelief on a lot of people's faces when Merle said that. That just gave a whole different turn to the direction of where the team was going. Before, they had really been spending their energies sort of thinking about how do we look like we are doing something as a company but not really. So it was more of a marketing idea than it was a `doing business' idea. It was really more a matter of how do we keep each other informed but certainly not anything more than information sharing. Now all of a sudden we realized we were going to share customers and we have to look like Motorola, Inc. This is a tremendous culture change for this company. This team, if it really pulls it off, will have accomplished something that in the past, not only did nobody think would ever happen, but nobody wanted to happen.

"I think we are realizing now, maybe not worldwide, but in certain regions, that this is an appropriate approach."

Reflective Learning

King said that although team members may not have realized it, a lot of reflective learning had taken place. She explained:

"I think the energy level around the work that they do is extremely high. They've shown a lot of willingness to look at what they are doing and how they are doing it. They are really going back in their own history and saying, `We tried something like this. It didn't work before, but here's why I think it didn't work. What are we going to do to avoid that kind of a pitfall this time around?' So it's not that `We tried it before, it didn't work, and it's not going to work this time,' which is a real positive find for me. They use lots of phrases like `I wonder if this is going to work?' Particularly around the cookbook, they said things like `Boy, I really thought that was it but it wasn't, was it? What do you think we need to do?'

"I think it is still pretty unconscious to them that they are doing reflective learning, but they are doing a lot of reflection on their processes.

"They don't have to really understand reflective learning to do it, and they really don't have to use the same terminology and jargon. It's okay if they don't talk about doing double loop learning."

She said that it often is difficult to explain reflective learning. "The people who understand reflective learning are the people who do it intuitively," King said, "so they haven't a clue why you are talking about it. They just assume everybody does that. But people who don't do it intuitively don't understand it when you try to explain it intellectually, so they haven't a clue why you're talking about it. So both sets of people are looking at you like `What are you talking about?' So talking about it doesn't work. You just have to do it. That's one reason I think you need a good facilitator who can lead them into that learning process."

No Team Training in Advance

In its new executive training program, Motorola intentionally avoids using the "outward bound" approach to team building. Instead, teams build naturally during the process. King said of the software and Eastern Europe acceleration groups:

"They didn't do team training. We didn't take them out for 3 weeks in the wilderness beforehand. As they are going through the process, they are beginning to gauge how much they can say to whom and when and how. We see people adjusting their styles in order to be heard. They adjust to each other and gauge how long they are willing to go down a road that they think is the wrong road. Then, rather than just saying, `That is the stupidest idea I've ever heard in my life,' which would have happened in the past, they are finding ways to try to find something good in an idea and use it as a bridge to a new way of thinking.

"A lot of people ask me, `If you had it to do over again, wouldn't you do some teaming stuff up front so that they would work as teams?' My answer is no, I would not. Part of that is a personal bias. Part of it is, to me, teamwork is a lot of the learning. Let them learn it in a natural way. They are going to have to be in new environments in this company with different people in the room all the time. Every time they go in to make a presentation there is probably somebody in the room they haven't worked with before.

"I don't want them to think that the way you get to work together as a team is to go climb a mountain. I want them to figure out the way you work together as a team is to figure out how do you work together as a team on-line and do it on-line. If we want them to learn to solve the problems on-line, and we want them to learn how to manage change on-line, and we want them to learn how to influence each other on-line, why would we take them off-line to have them learn how to be a team? That, to me, is a carry over from the traditional model.

"It's hard to think of white water rafting as traditional executive education, but in my mind it is because it's an artificial environment. That is one of the primary things I think is wrong with traditional executive education. The transfer of learning doesn't happen. Quite honestly, I don't think the learning from white water rafting or rappelling down mountains transfers either. It does with the people you went through it with. If I take an intact team out there and let them do something, they are going to learn things about each other, some good and some bad. That part may come back and transfer with them when they sit down at a conference table. But again, if I look at the learning-to-learn piece, and I want to get that quantum leap and application skill, I don't know how that happens if we learned it on a river."

When You Have a Nonparticipant on Your Team

One problem, King said, has been deciding how to handle team members who don't fully participate. She said that for the SEP, the company tries to select vice presidents who will contribute and benefit, but it doesn't always work. As King explained:

"You're not going to have 24 totally active participants. You need to know up-front what you are going to do about that. Are you going to let people drop off the team? Is that okay and if so, you make that clear that it's okay for you to leave. If you do, what kind of message does that send? I don't know the answer to that. If it's not going to be okay to drop off the team, what do you do with the member who doesn't support anything and who doesn't spend any energy or any time or resources towards this? Do you just tell the other members, `Well that's the way life is?' If so, what kind of message does that send?

"That's the message that really scares me, that it's okay to sign up but not do anything," King said. "Is that what we really want leadership within our company to have as its model? It's a real issue. What do you do with a member whose name's on the list but he's not there? I don't know the answer to that one, but I know it's not working well in a few cases and I need to resolve that."

Executive Education as a Catalyst for Growth

King said that she believes that the "success of the company honestly belongs to the managers and to the people. So I see my responsibility as getting those people prepared to do that part of their role. Not doing it for them." King explained how her personal experience has taught her the importance of empowering others:

"My oldest brother was profoundly mentally retarded. He was supposed to die when he was 2; he died when he was 28. They didn't think he would ever sit up. They didn't think he would ever roll over or anything like that. Mother had him scooting, which was his primary mode of transportation, when he was about 4 or 5. She finally had him walking when he was about 10. He never learned to talk but he vocalized. He made up his own sign language and communicated beautifully. He learned to dress himself. He learned to feed himself. She got him toilet trained when he was about 16.

"It would have been so much easier for her to do those things for him because having him put on his shirt took him 45 minutes on a fast day.

There were several kids in our family, and we were always on time, everywhere we went. Mother didn't believe in being late, but she also didn't believe in putting his shirt on for him.

"It is, for me, a real parallel to executive education. It would be easier for me just to do the executive education. It would take less time. It would take less energy. I would be a little more assured of the results. Yes, my brother often got buttoned up the wrong way, and occasionally we were allowed to straighten it out for him, but generally just the first button, and he had to fix the rest of them.

"For me, the analogy is there. As he got older, Mom didn't have to do it. If she'd always done it, she would always have to do it. I don't want to always have to do it. I want the managers whose responsibility it is anyway to do the learning."

Tips for Developing a Senior Executive Education Program

Pat Canavan, vice president of corporate human resources for Motorola, identified several factors that helped make the new education program successful:

- The programs are directly linked to critical business concerns.
- Those concerns are identified by the chief executive office and the policy committee, which creates ownership from the very top.
- Each senior executive program has a sponsor from the CEO's office.
- Programs are given internal consultation, facilitation, and support.

"I feel confident in saying that by some minimal criteria of success, we are hitting our targets as expressed by the group and agreed by the CEO," Canavan said. "We are not overspending budgets where budgets exist. We are focusing on the right issues with the right people who are stimulated and who say, `If we work in these new and unusual ways, reflect on it, and get better at it, we are actually going to make a difference in the way Motorola performs and succeeds.'"

That's a notable difference from the old model of executive education, Canavan said, where the vice presidents "would have sat politely through 2 days of world-class speakers and left saying, `That's a big issue. I ought to go back and do something about it.' And they forgot about it immediately."

Parviz Mokhtari, a corporate vice president and director of Central and Eastern Europe, echoed Canavan's assessment, saying that to him, the big difference in the new executive education program is that the CEO has clearly identified it as "a process, not an event."

"It's a 2- or 3-year involvement, and we are expected at the end of 2 or 3 years to show that something has changed, that we've made a difference," Mokhtari said. "It is viewed very differently in my mind and everybody else's mind. For example, this has a 90 percent attendance in any of these meetings. Considering the seniority and the level of these people and considering the travel involved to Prague and to Budapest—considering that it blows 1 week out of people's calendars, it is a major, major commitment on everybody's part."

Not Just Another Task Force

The SEP program operates very differently from a task force that is simply charged with studying an issue. Canavan explained:

"At Motorola, task forces are a horizontal slice of folks who get together at some senior executive's request to look at an issue, develop alternatives, spend some money by benchmarking or hiring consultants, and then come up with a written recommendation, which may include numerous alternatives or just one. They then take responsibility for lobbying that conclusion or set of solutions to the decision makers inside the corporation and finally presenting it at one of our formal corporate bodies. `Here is what our task force discovered, the process we used, our conclusions and our recommendations. Thank you very much.'"

That's not what happens with the new SEP. "You don't get to hand in the paper and walk away," Canavan said. "You have to implement it and live with it."

Mokhtari said that the trouble with task forces is that they usually have no way to implement their suggestions. "They have to come up with the recommendation and go sell it to somebody," Mokhtari said. "Oftentimes everybody says `That's a great report.' Wonderful, but there is no easy transition from recommendation to actual action. Whereas with this group, they do have the power among them. They control much of the relevant resources of the corporation for addressing the particular issue. The transition is much easier from recommendation to action. If, in the course of discussion, we come up with something that we think is a damn good idea, we never say `Let's put this in the final report.' We say `Let's just go do it,' and everybody says that's great and immediately goes off and does it. I've been on many task forces that started with a lot of enthusiasm and ended with excellent reports but never really got action from it."

Canavan said that at Motorola, the new SEP has been strikingly different from anything they've ever done because "we don't do across-the-board projects, and this is an across-the-board project, across the world, across all business units project, and we don't have the experience of doing those."

Other differences between a group brought together for a particular project and the new SEP model is that in a project "they might have zero facilitation, human resources, and organizational consultation support," Canavan said. "They'd just be the best and the brightest, banging around trying to make something different because somebody at the top has said `I'm not happy with this' or has said `There is an opportunity out there that we're not actualizing, and you seven or eight folks are going to make that happen for me. You've only got 6 months.' The SEP has facilitation and has a learning component by being part of this SEP history, which is now 7 or 8 years old in the company. It has a self-improvement and organizational-improvement task to it. So we didn't just add on the organizational-learning. If there wasn't the organizational learning component, it would have no business being the senior executive program."

Burning Platforms

Canavan, who is the facilitator for the Eastern Europe group, said that from the beginning, it was made clear to the group that they would be part of a change process:

"We said that as you start working with each other and coming up with a new methodology for Motorola to enter new markets, you'll be changing the rules of the game about how things get done around here. You're facing an enormous adversary, which is the history of the company that says worldwide product groups should have complete autonomy and do what they want to do.

"We were somewhat anticipating that if we were going to enter these new geographies, we were going to have to do it more as a concerted team of Motorolans than as representatives of a particular business group.

"Daryl Connor, an outside consultant who led discussions on organizational change and theory, told one analogy that really struck a note with the group.

"He's a good pragmatic consultant and he reminded people that lining up sponsors was part of what got them there, and if they wanted to make changes, they'd have to line up sponsors for what they wanted to accomplish. He also introduced some phrases like a `burning platform.'

His story was about a North Sea oil drilling platform a couple of years ago. A guy jumped off the platform into the North Sea. He went through burning debris and was picked up by the rescue boat within 10 minutes. So he survives and is interviewed live on TV. When asked by the reporter, `Did you know that you were 70 feet up in the air and you were jumping into burning water with big chunks of debris and that you would freeze to death in 10 minutes?' The guy replied, `Yes.'

"The reporter asked, `Well, why did you jump?' And the guy replied, `Sir, when standing on a burning platform, one is certain death and the other is probable death. I jumped.'

"If you're trying to make major change in an organization, assure yourself you are on a burning platform," Canavan said. "If you don't, you won't have around you the forces for change that will get people through the pain. Because change will cause pain. If you're not on a burning platform, somebody in power will turn around and say `Why the hell are we doing this?' If there is not a reasonable answer, it grinds to a halt.

"Sponsorship and burning platforms. Well, that sunk in with the group. These people started saying burning platforms are related to geographies. Who are the sponsors and the targets and the change agents? So Connor gave them some political models for managing themselves, which were absolutely superb, and he gave them some language that they could use amongst themselves to say, `Why are we doing what we are doing? And how should we go about doing it differently?'"

Measuring Success

While the final results of the programs are not in, King said that the new model clearly has had tremendous benefits: "We are getting growth at an individual level. We are getting growth at a team level, and we're getting growth at a company level, at an organizational level. Is it without fault? No. Is it perfect? Absolutely not. But we are a lot closer to what we want."

King said both the software and Eastern Europe teams had made "quantum leaps" in their targeted areas: "In both cases, absolutely. And I think both of them would attest to this. If we didn't have the senior executive program going in central Europe right now, every single business would be in there instead of having a coordinated approach. Several years down the road we would be coming to the realizations that we're coming to right now."

Harry Mankodi, a corporate vice president, said the new model for executive education far surpasses the old one. Mankodi explained:

"We had SEPs where all the senior executives went through a single, objective-oriented SEP in a year. All 200 of us went through it. We went to the class, we went out, and it was over. The new approach is to follow-through as a team. It also is oriented toward a major company objective, so we stay together for 3 to 4 years. We are addressing a very large issue rather than some micro issue.

"The SEP environment makes you learn together, talk together, and go and implement together. And when you do those three things together, there is no choice. You learn. It's funny. SEP provides a forum to be different, but in the end, we have some very strong common ground. That's almost like a laser beam theory. Focus and get the power of laser to a solution, and I think that's what SEP does. The new system does that better than the old one."

Parviz Mokhtari, who is responsible for marketing and maximizing Motorola's opportunities in Central and Eastern Europe, said that for him, the most impressive result of the new SEP, so far, has been its ability to change people's thinking:

"The biggest satisfaction I get is out of the mind change of people. When we started the process here in Budapest back in October 1991, there were several very talented people who were very much focused on the U.S. domestic situation. They were saying `What are we doing here? Why is it so important?' By the time we got to the second meeting in Prague, those same people were really vocal in their urgency and the need of doing it differently. To me, that transition was just absolutely fantastic. Nobody could have transformed a group like that through a classroom-type setting. It's just being there, talking to customers, talking to people who tell us repeatedly, `You could be so much better, so much bigger if you did things differently.' So in my mind, that transformation and transition of people has been the biggest positive effect and the one that will probably last the longest."

The next phase is for the insights gained from the SEP to permeate the entire organization.

"That's the real test," Mokhtari said. "We are going to take specific countries in each region and apply the model. Through that application, by the end of the year we would be reaching more like 3000 people rather than 30 people. To me, the power of the learning is when you get to the 3000 and more people. So we are going to have a marketing plan on how to actually present these concepts to various layers of the organization in varying degrees of depth."

Mankodi said that a key learning out of the Eastern Europe group has been that "fragmentation never helped us," which gets back to Gilmore's observation that customers viewed the sum of the company as less than its parts.

"Motorola did not go in as a singular entity that had a solution for a customer," Mankodi said. "We went as five, six, seven different companies that sold products, rather than as a single company that sold communication component solutions. And the customer doesn't like that. I think the entire SEP, if we are successful, will come up with a platform to do that."

Epilogue

By being an enthusiastic learner you not only prepare yourself for the inevitable changes in your daily work, but you position yourself and your company to take advantage of them. In this book you've journeyed from individual learning to organizational learning. In the final five chapters we chose five organizations whose learning is in high gear. They represent a broad spectrum of industries and situations. Their insights are offered for stimulation, imitation, and adaptation. Finally, reflecting on these companies and managers, we close with 10 learning lessons.

1. *Recognize a performance gap between where you are now and where you want to be.* "We want to be the best" won't work. Be specific. If it takes you a week to manufacture and deliver your product, and it takes your competitor 2 days, then that becomes the new standard. Survival issues work best. When it's "do or die," the only answer is to learn to "do."

2. *Create a plan to close the performance gap.* That is, the gap between your current performance and how you want to perform in the future. Decide where to begin, set measurable goals, and then get started.

3. *Try to get the top tier of management interested in learning.* If you're the boss, that's you. Otherwise, engage the most senior leader you can and present learning as the solution to the learning gap you have identified. Then take a small action that provides some early success.

4. *Measure your organization against the formula: A Learning Organization 5 A Leader with Vision 3 (Plan/Metrics) 3 Information 3 Inventiveness 3 Implementation.* Be truthful and don't mask any shortcomings. To make progress you must correctly identify where you are.

5. *Gain an outside perspective to break through the isolation that stifles so many organizations.* Take advantage of free ideas and advice by seeking out best practices, whether they involve managing or manufacturing. Get senior leaders out of the company to talk to customers and bring customers in to share ideas so their needs can be heard loud and clear.

6. *Harness the work environment to energize learning.*   Use stretch assignments to motivate and educate. Use work to propel learning and learning to propel work. As a result, people will feel valued, proud, and empowered.

7. *If you provide formal training, make sure it has strategic impact.*   To create lasting value, ideas presented in the training course should be reinforced on the job.

8. *Speed the flow of information.*   Share information across department lines. Operate as one company, not as separate, competing factions. Your ultimate competitor shouldn't be found across the hall but outside your organization's door.

9. *Hold people accountable for learning at work.*   Give praise for successes and recognize mistakes as an opportunity to learn.

10. *Maintain a constancy of purpose.*   Repeated, half-hearted attempts at new initiatives lead to skepticism and distrust. Persevere in your learning initiative.

Our hope is that you will take charge of your own learning, energize others to learn, and be the catalyst for your entire organization to learn. You can get smart by focusing on your own learning and striving to fashion your company into a learning organization. You will then move forward with a sense of urgency, exhilaration, and inspiration. The time to begin is now.

Notes

1. Arie P. De Geus, "Planning as Learning," *Harvard Business Review,* March–April 1988, p. 74.

2. Russell Baker, *The New York Times,* March 19, 1991. Copyright © 1991 by The New York Times Company. Reprinted by permission.

3. John A. Byrne, "Headhunter to the Stars," *Forbes,* June 20, 1983, p. 107.

4. Peter Senge, *The Fifth Discipline: The Art and Practice of the Learning Organization,* Doubleday/Currency, New York, 1990, p.14.

5. Sally Jenkins, "Racket Science," *Sports Illustrated,* April 29, 1991, p. 72. This excerpt is reprinted courtesy of *Sports Illustrated,* Time Inc. Copyright © 1991 Time Inc. All rights reserved.

6. Peter F. Drucker, *Management,* Harper and Row, New York, 1974.

7. Ibid., pp. 427–428.

8. "What Leaders of Tomorrow See," *Fortune,* July 3, 1989, p. 48. Copyright © 1989 The Time Inc. Magazine Company. All rights reserved.

9. Peter Senge, *The Fifth Discipline: The Art and Practice of the Learning Organization,* Doubleday/Currency, New York, 1990, p. 340.

10. Calhoun W. Wick, "Why People Develop: An In-Depth Look," Copyright © 1989 Buraff Publications, Washington, D.C.

11. Peter Senge, *The Fifth Discipline: The Art and Practice of the Learning Organization,* Doubleday/Currency, New York, 1990, p. 174.

12. Joel A. Barker, *Discovering the Future: The Business of Paradigms* (video), Infinity Unlimited, St. Paul, Minn.

13. Morgan W. McCall, Jr., Michael M. Lombardo, Ann M. Morrison, *The Lessons of Experience: How Successful Executives Develop on the Job,* Lexington Books, an imprint of Macmillan, Inc., New York, 1988. p. 5.

14. David L. Bradford and Allan R. Cohen, *Managing for Excellence,* Copyright © 1984. Reprinted by permission of John Wiley & Sons, Inc., New York, p. 78.

15. Ray Stata, "Organizational Learning—The Key to Management Innovation," *Sloan Management Review,* Spring 1989, p. 64.

16. David L. Bradford and Allan R. Cohen, *Managing for Excellence,* Copyright © 1984. Reprinted by permission of John Wiley & Sons, Inc., New York, p. 162.

17. Morgan W. McCall, Jr., Michael M. Lombardo, and Ann M. Morrison, *The Lessons of Experience: How Successful Executives Develop on the Job,* Lexington Books, an imprint of Macmillan, Inc., New York, 1988, p. 147.

18. John W. Gardner, *On Leadership,* Copyright © 1990 by John W. Gardner. Reprinted by permission of The Free Press, a Division of Macmillan, Inc., New York, p. 173.

19. Robert C. Camp, *Benchmarking,* ASQC Quality Press, Milwaukee, 1989, p. 12.

20. Alexandra Biesada, "Benchmarking," September 17, 1991, p. 28. *Financial World Magazine,* September 17, 1991, p. 28.

21. Robert C. Camp, *Benchmarking,* ASQC Quality Press, Milwaukee, 1989, p. 8.

22. Alexandra Biesada, "Benchmarking," *Financial World Magazine,* September 17, 1991, p. 35.

23. John Markoff, "An Aging Dancer Fights to Keep Up," *The New York Times,* February 10, 1991. Copyright © by The New York Times Company. Reprinted by permission.

24. Peter H. Lewis, "The Executive Computer,"*The New York Times,* November 17, 1991. Copyright © by The New York Times Company. Reprinted by permission.

25. Robert C. Camp, *Benchmarking,* ASQC Quality Press, Milwaukee, 1989, p. 16.

26. Ibid., p. 100.

27. Stephen R. Covey, *The Seven Habits of Highly Effective People,* Covey Leadership Center, Provo, Utah, p. 278.

28. Ray Stata, "Organizational Learning—The Key to Management Innovation," *Sloan Management Review,* Spring 1989, p. 64.

29. Peter Senge, "The Leader's New Work: Building Learning Organizations," *Sloan Management Review,* Fall 1990, p. 8.

30. John P. Kotter, "What Leaders Really Do," *Harvard Business Review,* May–June 1990, p. 105.

31. Charles Handy, *The Age of Unreason,* Harvard Business School Press, Boston, 1989, p. 229.

32. Peter F. Drucker, "Japan: New Strategies for a New Reality," *The Wall Street Journal,* October 2, 1991.

33. Peter Senge, "The Leader's New Work: Building Learning Organizations," *Sloan Management Review,* Fall 1990, p. 21.

34. "The U.S. Must Do As GM Has Done," *Fortune,* February 13, 1989, p. 70.

35. Peter Senge, "The Leader's New Work: Building Learning Organizations," *Sloan Management Review,* Fall 1990, p. 9.

36. Hal Rosenbluth, "Tales From a Nonconformist Company," *Harvard Business Review,* July–August 1991, p. 28.

Index

About the Authors

CALHOUN W. WICK is president and founder of Wick and Co., a Wilmington, Delaware–based research and consulting firm specializing in executive and leadership development for both established and emerging firms. He has devoted the past 12 years to the study of how people learn and grow through work experience, and has compiled one of the country's largest databases of key work experiences that directly result in career development. He was an Alfred P. Sloan Fellow with MIT's Sloan School of Management, and graduated from Trinity College in Hartford as a Rockefeller Fellow.

LU STANTON LEÓN is a business writer, editor, and journalist with 13 years' experience at major metropolitan newspapers.